A volume in the series
Cornell Studies in Money
edited by Eric Helleiner and Jonathan Kirshner

A list of titles in this series is available at
www.cornellpress.cornell.edu.

FROM CONVERGENCE TO CRISIS

Labor Markets and the Instability
of the Euro

Alison Johnston

CORNELL UNIVERSITY PRESS **ITHACA AND LONDON**

First published 2016 by Cornell University Press

Printed in the United States of America

Library of Congress Cataloging-in-Publication Data

Names: Johnston, Alison, 1982– author.
Title: From convergence to crisis : labor markets and the instability of the euro / Alison Johnston.
Description: Ithaca : Cornell University Press, 2016. | Includes bibliographical references and index.
Identifiers: LCCN 2015038093 | ISBN 9781501702655 (cloth : alk. paper)
Subjects: LCSH: Economic and Monetary Union. | Monetary policy—European Union countries. | Labor market—European Union countries. | Financial crises—European Union countries. | Euro.
Classification: LCC HG3942 .J64 2016 | DDC 331.1094—dc23
LC record available at http://lccn.loc.gov/2015038093

Cloth printing   10 9 8 7 6 5 4 3 2 1

For Angie

Contents

List of Illustrations   viii

Preface   xi

List of Abbreviations   xv

1. Incomplete Monetary Union and Europe's
Current Crisis   1

2. From Order to Disorder: How Monetary Union
Changed National Labor Markets   26

3. Monetary Regimes, Wage Bargaining, and the
Current Account Crisis in the EMU South:
Empirical Evidence   54

4. National Central Banks and Inflation Convergence:
Danish and Dutch Corporatism Inside and Outside
of Monetary Union   78

5. Strength in Rigidity: Public Sector Employment
Reform and Wage Suppression in Germany, the
Netherlands, and Italy   110

6. Sheltered Sector Dominance under a Common
Currency: Irrational Exuberance in Ireland and
Fragmentation in Spain   137

7. EMU, the Politics of Wage Inflation, and Crisis:
Implications for Current Debates and Policy   163

Appendix I. Exposed and Sheltered Sectors and the
Meaning of Wage Moderation   183

Appendix II. Variable Measurement and Data Sources   187

Notes   191

References   201

Index   217

Illustrations

Tables

Table 2.1. Timeline of public sector disciplinary policies under the EMS (early 1980s)   37

Table 2.2. Annual growth in real compensation of government employees for the EMS's original participants (period averages)   38

Table 2.3. Wage moderation by bargaining regime and country (1999–2007)   52

Table 3.1. Differences in sheltered sector and manufacturing sector annual wage growth by bargaining regime (1979–2007 average)   65

Table 3.2. The influence of EMU and central banks' monetary threat on sectoral wage differences   68

Table 3.3. The influence of sheltered sector wage suppression on export growth   74

Table 3.4. The influence of export-favoring wage governance institutions on export growth   75

Table 7.1. Inflation and exchange rate (real and nominal) movements (1980s decade average)   171

Figures

Figure 1.1. External imbalances between the EMU core and peripheral economies (1980–2010)   4

Figure 1.2. Wage moderation by sector for the EMU10, three-year moving averages (1979–2007)   8

Figure 1.3. Annual differences in manufacturing and sheltered sector hourly wage growth for the EMU10 (period averages)   9

Figure 1.4. Pre-crisis current account balances (1999–2007 average)   17

Figure 2.1. Sequential bargaining game between unions and employers   30

Figure 3.1. Differences in sheltered and exposed sector wage growth for the EMU10 (1979–2007)   57

Figure 3.2. Central bank non-accommodation toward inflation (weighted by the size of the sheltered sector)   61

Figure 4.1. National wages in efficiency units (real hourly wage growth minus labor productivity growth), three-year moving averages (1979–2007)   82

Figure 4.2. Sectoral wages in efficiency units (real hourly wage growth minus labor productivity growth), three-year moving averages (1980–2007)   83

Figure 5.1. Current account balances, as a percentage of GDP, for Germany, Italy, and the Netherlands (1992–2007)   114

Figure 5.2. Annual differences in sheltered sector and manufacturing real wage growth (1992–2007)   117

Figure 6.1. Spanish nominal wage increases, by sector, in relation to nationally agreed pay targets (1998–2007)   140

Figure 6.2. Irish nominal wage increases by sector (1998–2007)   157

Figure 6.3. Nominal wage restraint, by sector, for Ireland and Spain, three-year moving averages (1990–2007)   157

Figure 7.1. Current account balances for the EMU11 (1990s and 2000s decade averages)   168

Figure 7.2. Extra-EU exports as a proportion of total exports (1990–2014)   178

Preface

On July 12, 2015, following intense negotiations for the third Greek bailout, a draft document was circulated to the Eurogroup, the committee of finance ministers for the Eurozone's nineteen economies. Outlining actions that Greece had to fulfill in order to receive further bailout funds, the document concluded with a recommendation that had previously been perceived as politically unthinkable—the (temporary) expulsion of a member-state from the Eurozone. For the first time in the European Union's history, breakup was on the table. Led by German Finance Minister Wolfgang Schäuble, a cluster of Eurozone finance ministers from northwest Europe and the Baltic states viewed Greece as a lost cause. Despite enduring GDP output declines and increases in unemployment in excess of those witnessed in the Great Depression and being on the verge of financial collapse, Greece had not done "enough" to put its fiscal house in order. Rather than pour more money into Greece, Germany and its northern satellites appeared ready to hedge their bets and let Greece go.

Schäuble and his allies' perceptions were a culmination of an established story. In northern European political circles, the narrative of the Greek tragedy, and the European debt crisis more generally, is a simple one. Greece overspent before the 2008 financial crisis, found itself in deeper fiscal crisis with the bailing out of its banks, and unleashed a contagion effect of debt crisis to the rest of peripheral Europe. The Eurozone's creditor states, led by Germany, came to the rescue of Greece and other peripheral states with loans conditional on fiscal consolidation and structural reform; the latter, it was hoped, would clean up Greece's public sector. However, Greece, unlike other Eurozone bailout recipients, did not undertake the fiscal measures required for economic recovery, according to this narrative. With the election of the left-wing Syriza government in January 2015, Greece abandoned what little progress had been made in fiscal consolidation and pressed for debt relief from its creditors. Greece, the profligate fiscal villain, was not playing by the Eurozone's (fiscal) rules, and the poor German taxpayer would have to foot the bill as a result.

This book provides a counter-narrative to the European debt crisis. Shifting away from the crisis as a fiscal problem—a stance already refuted with ample empirical evidence—I explain that labor market politics before the 2008 global financial crisis distinguish the debt crisis's winners from its losers. I argue that the European Economic and Monetary Union (EMU) established a playing field that economically advantaged her low-inflation northwest European economies, with their corporatist labor markets, over her high-inflation peripheral economies, with their noncorporatist labor markets. This unbalanced playing field meant not only that EMU's corporatist north could run persistent trade surpluses with its noncorporatist southern neighbors, forcing the periphery to externally borrow in order to finance them, but more important, that such imbalances would grow to unsustainable levels, which would require abrupt changes in economic and financial activity—the only kind that crisis can produce—to correct. Germany and her corporatist allies were not the victims of further monetary integration, which the conventional fiscal narrative suggests. Rather, they and their export sectors were possibly its greatest benefactors and equally responsible for the borrowing and consumption "binges" that arose in the periphery before the walls came crashing down.

E(M)U's corporatist labor markets always had a comparative low-inflation advantage over the more disorganized labor markets in their southern neighbors. Such an advantage is delivered through centralized and highly coordinated wage-setting institutions, which were largely a product of the political power of their export sectors in economic policymaking. However, monetary union made these comparative advantages toxic for the North's noncorporatist trading partners. Before monetary union, two adjustment mechanisms limited inflation's direct effect on trade and external borrowing, ensuring that the southern periphery's relatively higher inflation would not destine these countries to significant trade and external lending imbalances vis-à-vis their northern trading partners. The first, which had important implications for external adjustment in the 1980s, was strictly economic in nature. Under the early years of the European Monetary System (EMS), *nominal exchange rates* promoted automatic or managed adjustment between the current EMU North and South, ensuring that imbalances in trade and external lending remained contained.

The second adjustment mechanism that monetary union eliminated was national-level central banks promoting *low-inflation mandates*. This institutional mechanism led to unprecedented nominal convergence among EMU candidate countries in the 1990s. To qualify for monetary union, EMU's noncorporatist states had to mimic the inflation performance of their corporatist neighbors. The desires of the national central banks and policymakers to join EMU forced organization onto labor markets in peripheral economies, which caused wage-setters to deliver the levels of aggregate wage moderation and, in turn, low inflation previously witnessed only in the corporatist North. Convergence in income growth, inflation, and (real and nominal) exchange rates further promoted containment in external trade and lending/borrowing balances between EMU's candidate countries.

European policymakers hoped that this belle époque of macroeconomic performance would be sustained with the launch of the single currency. Yet in rendering obsolete the national central banks that promoted convergence between countries, removing adjustment capacity via the nominal exchange rate, and failing to provide any form of cross-border fiscal adjustment between member-states, EMU placed the burden of economic (inflation) adjustment on labor markets in general and on wage determination in particular. The EMU North, thanks to its corporatist labor markets, was well equipped to produce external trade and lending surpluses. Given their capacity to deliver nationwide wage restraint, these economies could consistently undercut the price and real exchange rate competitiveness of their trading partners, which enabled them to impose persistent trade deficits onto the EMU periphery. Such trade deficits required banks in the EMU North to provide ever-increasing flows of credit to the EMU South so that they could finance them. Throughout Europe's ongoing debt crisis, German policymakers continually chastised the European periphery for overspending. However, they failed to acknowledge that these consumption booms fueled, and were partially fueled by, Germany's export miracle and were made possible because German banks willingly financed them.

Northern Europe's false fiscal narrative has had devastating effects on economic growth and political unity within the EU. The labor market approach I advance in this book suggests that the euro-crisis is a more holistic problem that is dependent on how the pre-crisis economic performance of the North, underpinned by its suppressive wage-setting institutions, shaped that in the South. EMU does not have to be destined to perpetual crisis and stagnation. In addition to taking its foot off the austerity accelerator, the EMU North has a very important role to play in crisis recovery. A pro-growth strategy of demand expansion via wage inflation in Germany and her northern satellites would not only temporarily reverse the beggar-thy-neighbor economic policy that gave rise to the gaping external imbalances underpinning the South's untenable macroeconomic position; it would also provide a solidaristic approach to recovery at a time when economic and political divisions threaten to unravel the fabric of the European project.

Work on this book began back in 2007 at the London School of Economics (LSE). This manuscript would not have been possible without the help and guidance I have received over the past nine years. First and foremost, I must thank Richard Jackman, Waltraud Schelkle, and Bob Hancké, whose consistent feedback and critique during the early days of my intellectual journey on EMU and wage-setting politics was a crucial foundation for this book. Bob deserves special praise and appreciation as he was my intellectual partner-in-crime on this project from the start and provided encouragement and moral support until its finish.

I was very fortunate to work with great minds while I was at the LSE. Discussions with Nick Barr, Zsofi Barta, Willem Buiter, Katjana Gatterman, Simon Glendening, Andrews Kornelakis, Niclas Meyer, Vassilis Monastiriotis, Jim Mosher, Marco Simoni, David Soskice, Tim Vlandas, Christa Van Wijnbergen, Helen Wallace, and Andrew Watt provided invaluable feedback and food for thought. Since leaving the LSE, my colleagues at Oregon State University—Amy Below, Sarah Henderson, and Rorie Solberg, most notably—have added further insights for the development and direction of this book in general and the progression of getting it published in particular. As an institution, Oregon State University has provided me with ample time and resources to write this manuscript, which has speeded the process considerably. In addition to my two academic homes, I have been privileged to interact and engage with a network of scholars who provided excellent suggestions for chapters in this book. Kerstin Hamann, Niamh Hardiman, Aidan Regan (whose coauthored work inspired the direction of the book's conclusion), and especially Costanza Rodriguez D'Acri deserve special praise for their insights into the six case studies I document in this book.

I have also been incredibly privileged to work with a stellar editorial team at Cornell University Press. During the process of soliciting interest from presses for this manuscript, one of my colleagues at Oregon State mentioned that writing my first book would be the most arduous, frustrating, and taxing undertaking of my academic career. I can safely attest to the fact that Roger Malcolm Haydon and the editors of the Cornell Studies in Money series have made this process one of the most painless and seamless endeavors that I have embarked on so far. Together with two anonymous reviewers, they provided exceptional and very speedy feedback and straightforward guidance on how to complete the book and make it more accessible to a general audience.

My most significant debt of gratitude goes to my family. My parents, Gary and Shirley, and brother Gary provided me with unconditional love and advice since the start of this nine-year project, which helped me get through some of its roughest patches. Finally, I am most indebted to Angie and her endless love and support. Without her patience with my lows, good kicks in the pants during my deepest episodes of self-doubt, and encouragement during the final stretches, I would not have been able to complete this manuscript. In an attempt to convey my deepest gratitude, I dedicate this book to her.

Abbreviations

AICV	(Spanish) Interconfederal Agreement on Bargaining Coverage Gaps
AINC	(Spanish) Interconfederal Agreement on Collective Bargaining
AMECO	European Commission's Annual Macroeconomic Database
ARAN	(Italian) Agency for the Representation of Public Administrations in Collective Bargaining
ARF	Danish Federation of County Councils
BDA	German Employers Association
BDI	Confederation of German Industries
CCOO	(Spanish) Workers' Commissions
CDA	(Dutch) Christian Democratic Party
CES	(Spanish) Economic and Social Council
CFO	(Dutch) Public and Health Sector Workers' Union
CGIL	Italian General Confederation of Labour
CGTP	General Confederation of Portuguese Workers
CNV	(Dutch) National Confederation of Christian Trade Unions
CO II	(Danish) State Public Servants' Trade Union
DA	Confederation of Danish Employers
DBB	Deutscher Beamtenbund, German Civil Services Union Confederation
DGB	Deutscher Gewerkschaftsbund, German Trade Union Confederation
DI	Confederation of Danish Industries
DLF	Danish Union of Teachers
DSR	Danish Nurses Association
ECB	European Central Bank
ECU	European Currency Unit
EDP	Excessive Deficit Procedure
EFSF	European Financial Stability Facility
EIP	Excessive Imbalance Procedure
EIRO	European Industrial Relations Observatory
EIRR	European Industrial Relations Review
EMF	European Metalworkers' Federation
EMS	European Monetary System

EMU	European Economic and Monetary Union
ERM	European Exchange Rate Mechanism
ESM	European Stability Mechanism
ETUC	European Trade Union Confederation
EU	European Union
EU ECOFIN	European Union Directorate General of Economic and Financial Affairs
FDI	Foreign and Direct Investment
FE	Fixed effects
FNV	Dutch Trade Union Federation
GDP	Gross domestic product
HK	(Danish) Union of Commercial and Clerical Employees
HTS	(Danish) Cartel of Employees in Trade, Transport, and Services
IB	(Dutch) Industries' Union
IBEC	Irish Business and Economic Confederation
ICTU	Irish Congress of Trade Unions
ILO	International Labour Organization
IMF	International Monetary Fund
IMPACT	Irish Municipal, Public and Civil Trade Union
ISIC	International Standard Industrial Classification
KL	(Danish) National Association of Local Government Employees' Organizations
KTO	(Danish) Association of Local Government Employees
LO	Danish Confederation of Trade Unions
LR	Likelihood-ratio
MFP	Multifactor productivity
MHP	(Dutch) Federation of Managerial and Professional Staff Unions
MiP	Macroeconomic Imbalance Procedure
MNC	Multinational corporation
NPM	New Public Management
OECD	Organization for Economic Cooperation and Development
OLS	Ordinary least squares
P2000	(Ireland's) Partnership 2000
PCSE	Panel corrected standard errors
PNR	(Ireland's) Programme for National Recovery
PP	Spanish People's Party
PPF	(Ireland's) Programme for Participation and Fairness
PSOE	Spanish Socialist Workers' Party
RE	Random effects
RER	Real exchange rate

SER	(Dutch) Social Economic Council
SGP	Stability and Growth Pact
SiD	(Danish) General Workers' Union
SIPTU	(Irish) Services Industrial Professional and Technical Union
StK	Association of Danish State Employees
TdL	Employers' Association of German Länder
TFEW	Treaty on the Functioning of the European Union
TFP	Total factor productivity
TVöD	Tarifvertrag öffentlicher Dienst, (German) General Framework Collective Agreement
UGT	(Spanish) General Union of Workers
VKA	(German) Local Government Employers' Association
VNO(-NCW)	Confederation of Dutch Industry and Employers
VVD	(Dutch) People's Party for Freedom and Democracy
WEU	Wages in efficiency units

FROM CONVERGENCE
TO CRISIS

INCOMPLETE MONETARY UNION AND EUROPE'S CURRENT CRISIS

In the wake of the 2008 global financial crisis, countries of the European Union (EU) faced economic calamities of a level not witnessed since the Great Depression. Gross domestic product (GDP) plummeted in some countries by over 25 percent of pre-crisis levels, unemployment rose sharply, and for the EU's peripheral economies[1] (Greece, Ireland, Italy, Portugal, and Spain), interest rates on government bonds increased substantially as markets doubted the capacity of these sovereigns to repay public debts. Politically, between 2008 and 2012 alone, eight EU governments (Slovenia, Slovakia, Greece, Italy, Portugal, Romania, Ireland, and the Netherlands) collapsed between elections; two EU countries (Greece and Italy) introduced unelected, technocratic governments to manage their economies; and countries in the EMU North and South witnessed the decay of traditional party alignments as new extreme right and left parties arose to exploit popular frustration.

The EU also faced a pivotal legitimacy juncture as member-states that previously were supportive of the supranational polity are now questioning its value. Voters in southern economies have turned their backs on an EU associated with harsh austerity measures that have caused significant reductions in living standards (Matthijs 2014). Anti-EU parties have benefited significantly from this crisis, not only in national elections but also European Parliamentary elections, as far-right and far-left parties urge either the exit of the euro (Marine Le Pen's National Front in France) or a "different Europe" (Beppe Grillo's Five Star Movement in Italy) (Kundani 2014). While the EU's political modus operandi as an elite-driven regulatory state (Majone 1994) may have survived during good economic times, its lack of democratic accountability, coupled with its imposition of devastating redistributionary policies on some member-states (most potently in the terms of Greece's July 2015 bailout and Cyprus's bank levy), is proving difficult to manage as a great number of EU citizens question the economic and political benefits of further integration.

European Economic and Monetary Union (EMU), perceived as one of the boldest steps forward in European integration, has also come under heavy scrutiny. Many of the EU's fledging economies lie within EMU's boundaries and lack important economic instruments to adjust to the crisis. EMU was a major political project, driven by neoliberal and monetarist ideals of delivering low inflation in Europe (Streeck 2014). It was also an incomplete project. Of the three macroeconomic conditions required for a complete and functional currency union (centralized monetary policy, centralized fiscal policy, and labor market flexibility), EMU possessed only the first. Due to the unlikelihood of European fiscal union, labor market flexibility was perceived by many as the only feasible means of economic adjustment for countries facing asymmetric economic shocks in a currency union with a one-size-fits-all monetary policy (Eichengreen 1993). Yet even here, EMU did not possess the degree of labor market flexibility required for economic adjustment in the event of an asymmetric crisis (Sibert and Sutherland 2000; Puhani 2001). While European leaders hoped for the best at the start of the monetary union, the current debt crisis delivered the worst to Europe's single currency, which, thus far, has witnessed little economic adjustment within its peripheral economies. Eight years after the global financial crisis, the South remains unable to reverse its economic misfortune.

How did EMU succumb to the serious economic crisis that it finds itself in currently? The U.S. subprime mortgage crisis and the 2008 global financial crisis have been acknowledged as critical catalysts of Europe's crisis (Hellwig 2009; Martin 2011; Mishkin 2011). Expanding from this trigger event, however, public and academic debate has searched for factors before the 2008 financial crisis that may have contributed to crisis exposure in the periphery. The exponential rise of international capital flows and the failure of banks to properly assess default risks, coupled with lax regulation of lending practices, have been identified as one source of the crisis on the credit supply-side (E. Jones 2014 and 2015). Others have attempted to explain differences in the demand for lending and the accumulation of debt. One argument that gained traction early in public debates, especially among Europe's policy elites and the "troika" (the EU Commission, European Central Bank, and the International Monetary Fund), is that the accumulation of pre-crisis *public* debt is to blame. Peripherial economies are exposed to crisis because of their reckless fiscal records before 2008, while EMU's northern economies (Austria, Belgium, Finland, France, Germany, and the

Netherlands, also referred to as the EMU core) were more fiscally responsible and therefore have been largely immune to speculative attack.

A second line of thought on the crisis's origins connects divergence in speculative pressures in EMU's North and South to persistent current and capital account imbalances (or differences in the accumulation of both public *and* private external debt). Advocates of this competitiveness hypothesis argue that the current crisis stems from the failure of EMU's peripheral economies to control unit labor costs after the launch of the euro, which led to a rise in inflation, appreciating real exchange rates and persistent trade/current account deficits vis-à-vis EMU's northern economies that successfully moderated national wage growth. This was not due to the significant rise in wage inflation in the periphery per se; the severe wage moderation that was produced by EMU's northern export-led economies was also a major component of current account divergence within the Eurozone (Wyplosz 2013). To finance their current account deficits, peripheral economies borrowed externally (not just publicly, but also privately) from northern economies, incurring capital account surpluses.

Such imbalances would not have been a persistent problem before monetary union, as *nominal* exchange rate movements could assist high-inflation economies with competitive readjustment. With relative rising unit labor costs and inflation, the nominal value of the national currency would decrease, improving exports and hindering imports. Such nominal exchange rate movements would also facilitate adjustment in a country's demand for foreign capital, as more volatile exchange rates imposed higher interest rate premia on debt instruments, decreasing demand for external borrowing. Upon entering the monetary union, EMU's member-states lost their national exchange rates as adjustment mechanisms for current and capital account imbalances, and these deficits grew persistently over time (see figure 1.1). Once the global financial crisis hit, markets perceived these current account deficits and capital account surpluses as unsustainable, prompting an exodus of capital from the South as investors became worried about possible default.

The substantial worsening in external lending and trade imbalances between EMU's northern and southern economies have been cited by economists and policymakers as crucial determinants that separated EMU's strongest from its weakest links (Bernanke 2009; Obstfeld and Rogoff 2009). Countries that were overexposed in external borrowing and consumption were those that were picked off by markets first in the flight to quality. However, what is more conspicious about these growing and gaping external imbalances between EMU's member-states is that they were largely limited to the years of the single currency (see figure 1.1). Historically, EMU's northern economies produced healthier current account and net external borrowing balances than their southern neighbors,

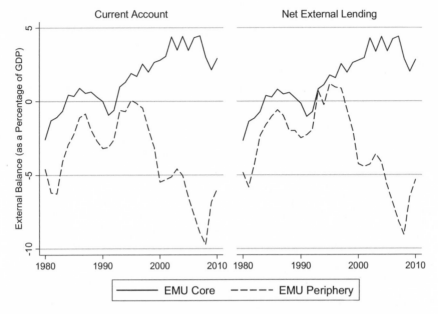

FIGURE 1.1. External imbalances between the EMU core and peripheral economies (1980–2010)

Note: EMU core includes Austria, Belgium, Finland, France, Germany, and the Netherlands. EMU periphery includes Greece, Ireland, Italy, Portugal, and Spain. Net external lending data prior to 1995 excludes Greece (for which data was unavailable until 1995).
Source: EU Commission AMECO Database (2014).

but differences in external macroeconomic performance between the two regions only became egregious once monetary union came into play.

In this book, I argue that this recent rise in the external imbalances of EMU's member-states under monetary union is not coincidental. The general argument I propose is that EMU's current crisis, and the growing external imbalances between its member-states that helped produce it, is a direct consequence of structural flaws in the governance of labor markets that are present in EMU's institutional design. In examining the impact of supranational institutional shift on national governance and economic outcomes, I dissect two empirical puzzles that are present within Europe's current sovereign debt crisis: 1) why EMU's core economies have emerged from the crisis with little speculative pressure, despite the fact that some of these economies had poor pre-crisis fiscal records, while EMU's peripheral economies have encountered heavy speculation, despite the fact that some produced consistent budgetary surpluses in EMU's pre-crisis years, and 2) why the persistent growth in current and capital account imbalances between

EMU's core and periphery was a phenomenon that was largely restricted to the EMU period.

I argue here that Europe's monetary union, in line with its neoliberal and monetarist origins, was structured in such a way that advantaged its low-inflation performers. The common currency's new real exchange rate calculus, which, with the disappearance of nominal exchange rates between member-states, became solely a function of relative inflation, provided countries that could consistently produce low inflation with a *persistently* competitive real exchange rate and, in turn, growing current account surpluses. However, EMU's low-inflation bias was not solely present in the construction of the real exchange rate for its member-states. EMU also removed two pivotal institutions that were responsible for increasing inflation-aversion in the domestic labor markets of its peripheral economies: *national level* inflation-averse central banks and fiscal rules with significant compliance penalties (the exclusionary nature of the Maastricht deficit criteria).

Though labor markets were acknowledged as perhaps the only realm of economic adjustment under Europe's single currency, member-states' diverse wage-setting institutions were neglected during European monetary integration, which had serious consequences for the stability of the euro. Monetary union's contribution to the current crisis can be partially explained by how it altered inflation dynamics in its member-states through the altercation of sectoral wage-setting politics within nation states. Before monetary union, wage-setters in both sectors exposed to trade, where incentives for wage moderation are high, and in sectors sheltered from trade, where wage moderation incentives are not as prominent, were disciplined in their wage-setting strategies by national central banks that upheld either formal or informal low-inflation mandates. The ultimate result of this institutional movement toward the mass adoption of inflation-averse central banks, which was heavily reinforced by the Maastricht nominal criteria, was an unprecedented level of inflation and real exchange rate convergence among EMU candidate countries. As a consequence of inflation and real exchange rate convergence, external imbalances between current EMU member-states were contained before 1999.

Under EMU, wage-setters within national economies did not encounter similar wage discpline by inflation-averse monetary authorities. National central banks were more easily able to target sectoral wage-setters if they produced inflationary wage settlements, as these actors constituted a significant share of these banks' inflation target. The same could not be said of the European Central Bank (ECB), whose mandate applied to the Euro-area as a whole rather than individual nation-states.[2] What emerged in the new politics of national wage setting across EMU's member-states was a collective action problem in the exertion of wage moderation—because monetary authorities could no longer penalize sectoral or national wage-setters if they produced wage inflation, incentives to pursue inflationary settlements increased. Yet wage inflation did not emerge en masse across and even within EMU member-states. Wage-setters in tradable goods and services sectors continued to exert wage moderation because of the output and employment consequences of wage inflation in the presence of high market competition.

Wage inflation in nontradable sectors, on the other hand, exhibited wide heterogeneity across EMU member-states. In EMU's peripheral economies, wage increases in nontradable sectors outpaced those in the tradable sector, placing upward pressures on inflation. In EMU's core economies, heavy wage moderation in nontradable sectors was maintained because these economies possessed coordinated corporatist institutions that limited nominal labor cost growth. Domestic politics in EMU's export-oriented core economies have historically been aligned toward inflation-aversion, and wage-moderating labor market institutions reflect this. EMU's core economies entered the single currency with their long-established national collective-bargaining institutions, which granted agenda-setting and veto powers to wage-setters in their export sectors. These institutions enabled the EMU core to moderate national, and sheltered sector, wage growth in order to promote their trade-surplus-prone export growth models. In contrast, labor market politics in the EMU's southern economies, given their more confrontational and fragmented nature, traditionally have not been conducive toward wage moderation and low inflation, particularly within nontradable sectors. However, EMU's institutional predecessors—the European Monetary System (EMS) and the Maastricht criteria—promoted converging inflation trajectories between these diverse labor markets by standardizing the monetary and EMU-conditionality penalities associated with high (sheltered sector) wage inflation.

EMU was a distinct break from this regime. Once common monetary and fiscal constraints were removed in 1999, the true "inflationary" nature of the periphery's labor market institutions was allowed to organically unfold. These economies did not witness a significant resurgence in *absolute* wage inflation. EMU's peripheral economies witnessed lower inflation rates under EMU than they did in the 1980s and 1990s. Rather, *relative* inflation divergence was largely facilitated by severe wage moderation in the EMU core, promoted by its export sector favoring labor market institutions (Wyplosz 2013). With *comparatively* higher inflation rates, southern economies quickly lost competitiveness in their real exchange rates, leading to the persistent, and ultimately unsustainable, accrual of current account deficits vis-à-vis the North and the need for international borrowing to finance these deficits. The rising imbalances between EMU's northern and southern economies that helped precipitate crisis exposure within the latter can therefore be understood by how EMU created an unbalanced playing field between countries with wage-setting institutions prone to low inflation and countries lacking these institutions.

Calm before the Storm: Inflation and Wage Growth Convergence before Monetary Union

In political economy debates about inflation, many acknowledge that some industrial sectors are more prone to low inflation than others. Within national labor markets, the delivery of low national inflation through moderated wage growth is dependent on power dynamics between conflicting sectoral interests. Several have outlined how the dualistic nature of wage setting in sectors exposed to and sheltered from trade[3] influences national price developments (Crouch 1990; Iversen 1999a; Garrett and Way 1999; Franzese 2001; Traxler and Brandl 2010). These national price developments, in turn, influence exchange rate patterns and the trade competitiveness and external borrowing balances of countries.

Employers (and unions) in the exposed sector (i.e., manufacturing) are more likely to establish low wage settlements than their sheltered counterparts, as their output and employment are more sensitive to cost-induced price changes given the presence of multiple competitors in international markets. Unions in sectors sheltered from trade (e.g., the public sector, most services sectors, and construction) bargain with employers who face more lax competitiveness constraints and, in the case of public employers, softer budget constraints in their capacity to run deficits. Consequently, sheltered sector unions have greater political capacity to push for higher wages than their exposed sector counterparts. Because these sheltered sectors constitute a significant proportion of the national labor force, their inflated wage settlements influence aggregate wage growth and ultimately prices. This implies that the sheltered sector's incapacity to deliver wage moderation has important implications for inflation and, through the real exchange rate, international price competitiveness.

Despite these theoretical predictions, however, current EMU countries witnessed a surprising reduction in real wage growth in the sheltered sector during the 1980s (for most of EMU's northern economies) and the 1990s (for EMU's southern economies), as sheltered sector employers and governments succeeded in imposing a prolonged series of wage freezes and wage cuts on their workers. Figure 1.2 presents three-year moving averages in wage moderation (the difference in sectoral real hourly wage growth and productivity growth), for the exposed manufacturing sector and the sheltered services sector of countries in EMU's first entry wave, the EMU10 (appendix I provides formal details on how wage moderation is measured, as well as details on the sectoral proxies).[4] Contrary to EMU, where the manufacturing sector witnessed significant wage moderation while the sheltered sector experienced wage inflation, under the European Monetary System (1979–1998) and Maastricht period (1992–1998), differences in wage moderation exerted in both sectors were largely contained.

A similar story emerges when comparing sectoral wage developments between the EMS/Maastricht and EMU periods, in absence of productivity developments. Figure 1.3 presents differences in annual wage growth between the exposed manufacturing sector and the sheltered services sector for three periods: the pre-Maastricht EMS period (1979–1981), the Maastricht period (1992–1998), and the pre-crisis EMU period (1999–2007). Positive/negative values indicate that wage growth in the manufacturing sector was consistently above/below that of wage growth in the sheltered sector, on average, for each year in that period. Most of EMU's core economies and two of its peripheral economies (Ireland and

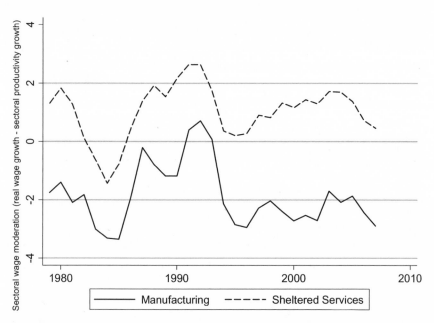

FIGURE 1.2. Wage moderation by sector for the EMU10, three-year moving averages (1979–2007)

Note: Sheltered services is an employment weighted composite of public administration and defense (ISIC category L), education (ISIC category M), and healthcare and social work (ISIC category N).
Source: EU KLEMS Database (2010).

Spain) witnessed the suppression of wage growth in the sheltered sector, relative to the manufacturing sector, in the pre-Maastricht EMS period. Providing a frame of reference from figure 1.3, annual manufacturing wage growth in Belgium exceeded that in sheltered services by more than 2 percent each year during the 1980s, translating into the emergence of a more than *20 percent wage gap* between manufacturing and sheltered services over the decade. Under the Maastricht period, similar wage suppression emerged in sheltered sectors relative to manufacturing, even in Italy, where sheltered sector wage growth was kept below that in manufacturing by 0.5 percent per year. However, under EMU, these trends reversed themselves. With the exception of Austria and Germany, all countries experienced reductions in sectoral wage differentials in favor of the sheltered sector between the Maastricht and EMU periods. Wage growth in the sheltered sector, relative to that of manufacturing, was particularly prominent in EMU's peripheral economies after 1999, with both Ireland and Portugal recording 1 percent per year wage gaps in favor of the sheltered sector (translating into a 10 percent wage gap between the sheltered and manufacturing sector over a decade), and Italy and Spain experiencing wage gaps of 0.5 percent per year.

Though the deliverance of sheltered sector wage moderation under the EMS and Maastricht regimes has not been thoroughly examined, scholars have attempted to understand how both northern and southern European countries were able to deliver such impressive degrees of *aggregate* wage moderation, which led to convergence in inflation rates, in the run up to EMU. Two crucial factors identified as instigators of this deflationary shift were the rise of inflation-averse

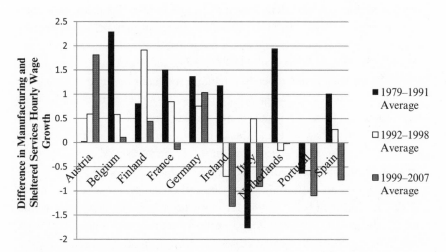

FIGURE 1.3. Annual differences in manufacturing and sheltered sector hourly wage growth for the EMU10 (period averages)

central banks under the European Monetary System (EMU's institutional predecessor) and the strong conditionality associated with the Maastricht inflation
and deficit criteria (Scharpf 1991; Hall 1994; Iversen 1998 and 1999b; Johnston
2012). Inflation-averse central banks increased the economic penalties associated with generous wage settlements in sheltered sectors. Unlike monetary regimes that accommodate inflation, the passage of inflated wages onto prices
must be counteracted by central banks via monetary tightening in order to moderate inflation developments. This had adverse implications for domestic demand
and sheltered sector employment as higher interest rates reduced the demand for
borrowing and domestic consumption. Because sheltered sectors were large
enough to influence national inflation, central banks whose main objective was
to reduce inflation could respond to high wage settlements with higher interest
rates, depressing domestic demand.

As central banks participating in the EMS increased their credible commitment
to low-inflation policies, sheltered sector employers, including governments in
their roles as public employers, used these institutions in the 1980s to make significant downward adjustments in wages. In 1992, sheltered sector employers and
governments encountered further pressures from the Maastricht inflation and
deficit criteria to enforce low wage settlements, as EMU membership was jeopar-
dized if inflation and deficits were too high. The Maastricht criteria proved to be
pivotal catalysts for sheltered sector wage and national inflation adjustment in
Italy, Spain, Portugal, and Greece, as governments resorted to national social pacts
to manage the economy throughout the 1990s (Fajertag and Pochet 2000; Hassel 2003; Hancké and Rhodes 2005). Partially the result of this renaissance of cooperative corporatism in both the North and South in the 1990s, EMU candidate
countries witnessed historically unseen convergence in national inflation rates
between 1992 and 1999, as candidate countries made difficult wage and price adjustments for the sake of belonging to EMU's first entering class (Johnston and
Hancké 2009). Such convergence in inflation rates had important implications
for convergence in real exchange rates, which led to a narrowing of current account balances in EMU candidate countries during the 1990s.

How and why did EMU change this impressive trajectory of nominal convergence, facilitated by wage adjustments in its member-states' sheltered sectors?
Surprisingly little has been addressed in regard to this question, despite its important implications for national inflation and real exchange rate developments in
EMU's core and peripheral economies. Most projections on how EMU would
alter this dynamic focused on the aggregate economy. It was argued that once
Maastricht conditionality was removed, and once inflation-targeting central
banks were moved to the EU level whose supranational central bank had little
capacity to enforce moderated wage and inflation growth in national economies,

inflation would rise (Cukierman and Lippi 2001; Hancké and Soskice 2003). However, though there was a slight divergence in inflation rates between EMU's core and peripheral economies after 1999, inflation itself proved relatively moderate compared to the early 1990s (EU Commission AMECO Database 2014). Rather, a sharp bifurcation in sectoral wages occurred within EMU member-states (see figures 1.2 and 1.3) that was most prominent in peripheral economies, where sheltered sector wage growth outpaced that in exposed sectors. In EMU's peripheral economies, the inflation rates and real exchange rates, which became purely a function of relative inflation for countries sharing the same currency, increased relative to the EMU core, leading to a prolonged worsening of current account balances. These worsening current account balances required surpluses (or net external borrowing) in the capital account to support their financing, leading to an increase in external borrowing, both in the public and private sector.

Such bifurcation was not so prominent in EMU's core economies. These countries possessed corporatist institutions that gave wage-setters in the export sector, or the state, veto powers over nationwide collective bargaining, thereby empowering employers to continue producing wage moderation under the new regime. This led to low inflation and persistently competitive real exchange rates, improving current accounts in these countries and hence capital account deficits (or net external lending). Because of a strong home bias in European investment (Gros 2012), current account deficits in the South during EMU's first decade were largely financed through lending from the North. Therefore, taking the competitiveness argument full circle, I argue that countries *without* export-sector favoring corporatist institutions suffered three distinct insults under monetary union: they lost competitiveness vis-à-vis their corporatist neighbors; they incurred persistently rising trade/current account deficits; and in turn, they relied more heavily on international borrowing, once EMU removed previous constraints that allowed sheltered employers to deliver wage moderation. In failing to integrate sectoral and national labor markets alongside monetary policy, the EMU project created an asymmetric union between a supranational monetary policy and national labor markets that has forced countries to rely on national corporatist institutions to adjust.

The remainder of this chapter addresses the two primary debates—the fiscal hypothesis and competitiveness hypothesis—that have, thus far, made the most significant inroads in the public domain in explaining the roots of speculative divergence between EMU's core and peripheral economies. Despite the fact that the competitive hypothesis is more empirically robust to the fiscal account of euro crisis, gaps within this argument remain unaddressed in the current literature and policy debates. Various proponents of the competitiveness hypothesis attribute differences in nominal unit labor cost growth/wage moderation as a principal driver of current account imbalances between EMU's core and periphery. However, this argument fails to explain *why* the core was more effective than the periphery in delivering wage moderation, especially in nontradable sectors, and why this divergence in wage moderation between the North and South was largely limited to the pre-crisis EMU period. The theory presented in chapter 2 reconciles both of these gaps and provides an encompassing argument for how EMU's institutional change created a dichotomy in wage and inflation outcomes between the North and South that set the stage for EMU's present economic crisis.

Explaining the Origins of the European Crisis: Fiscal and Competitive Positions

Within the young debate about the origins of the European debt crisis, two camps have emerged to explain the divergence in market speculation exposure across E(M)U sovereigns. The fiscal position (Buiter and Rahbari 2010; Lane 2012) or the "fundamental interpretation" (Burda 2013, 5) has identified the euro crisis as a consequence of fiscal excesses prior to the 2008 financial crisis. While Buiter and Rahbari argue that the current crisis resulted from a perfect storm of macroeconomic problems, including lax banking regulation and the end of asset booms and bubbles, they also state that one primary contributing factor to the crisis in southern Europe, and other economies, was the pursuit of "strongly pro-cyclical behaviour by the fiscal authorities during the boom period" (Buiter and Rahbari 2010, 1). These countries should have pursued fiscal surpluses and structural reforms in EMU's early years, but instead amassed public debts. These public debts increased further as these sovereigns were forced to respond to the 2008 financial crisis, and the resulting financial contagion, by offering financial assistance to failing banks (Burda 2013, 3).

The fiscal argument gained traction quickly among European decision-making circles because it provided an accurate assessment of Greece, the epicenter of the crisis. Given the steady deterioration of its fiscal indicators during EMU's early years, Greece was a perfect example of how poor macroeconomic mismanagement, coupled with corrupt and dyfunctional political institutions, made an untenable fiscal position worse once the global financial crisis was in full swing (Kouretas and Vlamis 2010; Arghyrou and Tsoukalas 2011; Featherstone 2011). However, as contagion spread, this fiscal explanation transplanted itself on other EMU southern economies through political and medial discourse that (falsely) chastized them for their high fiscal spending, generous pension systems, and fewer working hours (Weeks 2011; Petry 2013).

Once the debt crisis embedded itself more fully across EMU's southern economies, European elites, notably German policymakers, flocked to the fiscal view. Unsurprisingly, because these elites perceived the problem as fiscal, the remedies they provided were also fiscal and delivered devastating effects for EMU's southern rim. Harsh austerity measures produced a vicious cycle of low growth/employment and high deficits. The troika and political leaders in the North not only called for harsh austerity measures for EMU's peripheral economies, but also for themselves. German Chancellor Angela Merkel made public assurances before the 2013 election that she would continue to extract austerity concessions from peripheral economies if she was re-elected, while the troika remained steadfast in demanding cuts from Greece despite its rapidly deteriorating economic condition, threatening to withhold funding if its austerity demands were not met (Petrakis 2013). Jyrki Katainen's conservative coalition government in Finland also stood firmly with austerity hawks during the crisis, imposing fiscal tightening on its own economy despite the fact that Finland had one of the Eurozone's best fiscal balances in 2012 and was the only Eurozone country with a stable AAA debt rating (Matlack 2014).

Others highlighting the fiscal interpretation have attributed peripheral governments' binge borrowing to two design flaws of monetary union. Through its one-size-fits-all monetary policy, EMU provided low nominal interest rates to its members, offering cheap credit to sovereigns in peripheral economies that did not have access to such low rates in the early and mid-1990s (Lane 2012; Burda 2013). Between 1990 and 1998, average long-term nominal interest rates in EMU's five peripheral economies were 11 percent, compared to 7.4 percent in EMU's core economies. Under the EMU's pre-crisis years (1999–2007), average long-term nominal interest rates dropped to 4.6 percent for EMU's peripheral economies and 4.4 percent for its core economies (EU Commission AMECO Database 2014). Theoretically, variation in nominal interest rates within Europe's currency union should have been more pronounced to reflect premia for default risk. However, markets and then-ECB president Jean-Claude Trichet discounted for the best-case scenario for nominal convergence even when some nations were showing signs of fiscal deterioration (Baskaran and Hessami 2012; Burda 2013). The result was that EMU's peripheral economies continued to take advantage of cheap credit, further worsening their fiscal balances as the global financial meltdown grew near.

A second fundamental flaw in EMU's design that further exacerbated fiscal borrowing in the South was the poor enforcement of EMU's Stability and Growth Pact (SGP) (Hodson 2011; Baskaran and Hessami 2012). Under the SGP, which stipulated strict budgetary rules over the short- and medium-term, the European Commission was endowed with the legal capacity to monitor fiscal performances of member-states and to punish them with nominal fines if they failed to address deficits in excess of 3 percent of GDP. Yet though the Commission and ECB were granted authority in the EU Treaty to monitor and penalize fiscal spending within member-states, they proved ineffective at its enforcement. The reluctance of EU finance ministers to consider the use of financial penalties on the SGP's large member-state transgressors, France and Germany, ultimately spelled the end of the SGP's credibility (Hodson 2011, 58). Once France and Germany succeeded in relaxing the SGP's preventative and corrective arms in 2005, there was little confidence in the EU's enforcement of fiscal responsibility, sending further signals to high deficit nations that excessive fiscal spending could be tolerated under monetary union.

Though the fiscal hypothesis clearly outlines why EMU's poor design may have contributed to overborrowing in countries where market premiums for government debt would otherwise be much higher outside of a currency union, a second origins argument for the European debt crisis—the competitiveness hypothesis—doubts that overborrowing problems rested solely in the public sector. Indeed, several within the competitiveness camp question whether some governments that are current targets of heavy market speculation, such as Spain and Ireland, could be defined as "fiscally reckless," given their consistent budget surpluses and low public debts before the crash. Though pre-crisis government debts in Greece and Italy were high, they were also high in Belgium, which was largely spared from severe debt downgrades by rating agencies after 2008: in November 2011, Standard & Poor's downgraded Belgium's credit rating not because of its 100 percent debt-to-GDP ratio before the crisis, but because it had not formed a coalition government in over 500 days since the 2010 general election (Martens and Costelloe 2011). Likewise, Ireland and Spain exhibited some of the healthiest public debt balances in the pre-crisis EMU years and, along with Portugal, even outperformed Germany in maintaining low public debt before 2008 (EU Commission AMECO Database 2014).

A similar empirical contradiction to the fiscal hypothesis emerges when comparing annual net government lending, or fiscal deficits/surpluses. Though Greece, Italy, and Portugal conform to the fiscal argument, Spain and Ireland ran consistent budgetary surpluses in EMU's pre-crisis years (EU Commission AMECO Database 2014). Germany, whose politicians are quick to highlight the nation as the poster child of pre-crisis fiscal conservatism, had average public deficit levels not significantly different from Italy between 1999 and 2007. While the pre-crisis experiences of Greece and Italy, as well as Finland and the Netherlands, may conform well to the fiscal view, this hypothesis fails to provide a systematic explanation for why EMU's peripheral economies en masse became subject to market speculative attack while EMU's core economies did not.

The competitiveness position provides a more encompassing explanation for the tragedy of EMU, focusing on the rise of persistent imbalances among the current accounts of the Eurozone's member-states. Current account and trade deficits of a country are symmetrically mirrored by the *total* external borrowing (both public *and private*) in the capital account by the balance of payment identity (Obstfeld and Rogoff 2009; Wihlborg, Willett, and Zhang 2010; Belke and Dreger 2011; Bibow 2012; Shambaugh, Reis, and Rey 2012). Various European and American economists, including Paul Krugman who has been a vocal opponent of the fiscal thesis, as well as several influential American and European policymakers, including the IMF's Christine Lagarde, claim that the encompassing competitiveness argument is far more convincing (Young and Semmler 2011). In his 2009 address to the Council on Foreign Relations in Washington, D.C., Federal Reserve Chairman Ben Bernanke claimed that "it is impossible to understand the crisis without reference to the global imbalances in trade and capital flows that began in the latter half of the 1990s" (Bernanke 2009). More recently, the U.S. Treasury rebuked Germany that its excessive current account surpluses and dependence on exports "have hampered rebalancing at a time when many other Euro-area countries have been under severe pressure to curb demand and compress imports in order to promote adjustment" (U.S. Treasury Office of International Affairs 2013).

According to the competitiveness argument, divergence in speculation by financial markets was tied to a country's total, not fiscal, solvency, as reflected in the size and persistence of a country's current account deficit during EMU's first decade (Giavazzi and Spaventa 2011). Current account deficits can be sustainable if external borrowing is used to enhance productivity in the export sector. If a country is able to transform enhanced productivity into export growth in future periods, future current account surpluses imply that the intertemporal solvency constraint will hold (i.e., external borrowing under current account deficits are repaid once current account surpluses emerge). However, if foreign borrowing primarily goes into nontradable sectors, which are not capable of producing future export surpluses necessary to correct current account deficits, in times of crisis, markets will view these persistent imbalances as unsustainable and a signal of possible solvency problems. In considering both public and private elements of borrowing, this argument highlights why the fiscal camp offers neither a necessary nor a sufficient condition for speculative attacks. Countries with high public debt can avoid speculative attack if they produce significant private savings (e.g., Germany) in the capital account, while countries with public savings can be subject to aggressive speculation if they produce significant (external) private dissavings (e.g., Ireland and Spain).

Divergences in current accounts in the Euro-area between the North and South, which grew persistently since EMU's introduction in 1999, can be explained by divergent trade balances and national competitiveness. Because monetary union removes nominal exchange rates between Eurozone member-states, real exchange rate (RER) competitiveness is determined by relative inflation: countries with lower inflation hold more advantagous real exchange rates, and hence greater propensities for trade surpluses, than those with higher inflation. Wage moderation, the supression of real wage growth below productivity growth, is an important determinant of national inflation due to the heavy influence of wage growth on prices. If countries are able to exercise wage moderation, they will have a lower inflation rate and therefore, under monetary union, a persisent, more competitive real exchange rate vis-à-vis their trading partners. Under a fixed monetary system, where the majority of trade is intraregional,[5] wage moderation pursued by one group of countries (the EMU core) to enhance their relative price competitiveness position serves as a "beggar thy neighbor" policy vis-à-vis those countries (the EMU periphery) that are unable to deliver wage moderation (Caldentey and Vernengo 2012; Bibow 2012). In other words, since the majority of trade occurs within EMU itself,[6] current account/trade surpluses in EMU's northern economies were symmetrically reflected by current account/trade deficits in EMU's southern economies (see figure 1.1).

For nations to hold a trade surplus vis-à-vis deficit nations, the former must lend money to the latter via the capital account. Under EMU, savings in the countries with trade surpluses were invested in capital and consumption projects (mostly in real estate, which further fueled wage spirals) in countries with trade deficits (Gros 2012; Giavazzi and Spaventa 2011; Holinski, Kool, and Muysken 2012). Because banking systems within Europe possessed a heavy home bias, the excess savings in EMU's northern economies was predominantly invested in the Eurozone itself. As peripheral countries witnessed consumption (and real estate) booms, their competitiveness further deteriorated relative to the core where wage moderation was strictly enforced. Though such imbalances could easily be recitifed outside of monetary union via a depreciation of the nominal exchange rate, a common currency removed this option, pushing the burden of adjustment onto labor costs. The South's failure to adjust labor costs and hence external public *and* private borrowing imbalances, relative to the North preceding the crisis, prompted markets to doubt its solvency, attaching higher interest rate premiums to its sovereign bonds once the crisis was in full swing.

Unlike the fiscal thesis, empirics measuring pre-crisis current account balances better separate the EMU's core economies from its struggling peripheral

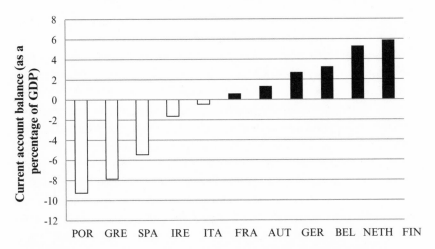

FIGURE 1.4. Pre-crisis current account balances (1999–2007 average)

neighbors. Figure 1.4 presents average current account balances between 1999 and 2007. While EMU's northern economies ran current account surpluses in the run-up to the crisis, its southern economies ran current account deficits. Rather than merely explaining Greece and Italy, the competitive argument also helps generalize the experiences of Ireland, Spain, and Portugal, which witnessed stagnant export growth, larger current account deficits under the pre-crisis EMU period, and speculative attack in the late 2000s, as well as Germany and Belgium, countries that witnessed current account surpluses in the pre-crisis EMU period, despite their poor fiscal performances. Moreover, current account performances dramatically reversed themselves for some EMU countries between 1999 and 2007. Germany entered EMU with a 1.3 percent (of GDP) current account deficit, yet it entered the 2008 global financial crisis with a 7.4 percent current account surplus. In contrast, Ireland, a quintessential small trading nation, entered EMU with a healthy 1 percent current account surplus, yet by 2007, Ireland had amassed a 5.4 percent current account deficit and a capital account surplus (or net external borrowing) of 5.5 percent of GDP to finance it (Eurostat 2014; EU Commission AMECO Database 2014).

Though the robustness of descriptive statistics in explaining crisis exposure is not proof of causality, the competitiveness position does a better job at drawing a hard line in the sand between EMU's creditor and debtor countries than the fiscal hypothesis. More recently, however, the competitiveness position has been contested by scholars who doubt whether EMU's debtor countries can be classified as "uncompetitive." Several of them highlight that the inflation and real unit labor cost growth of the EMU periphery after 1999 was quite mitigated, particularly compared to these countries' pre-1999 performances (Bentolila 2008; E. Jones 2014), that export performance and trade balances for the EMU South did not change after 1999 (Gros 2012, 8), or that "push" export growth in the periphery was either on par with or stronger than individual core economies (Gaulier, Taglioni, and Vicard 2012). While these assessments of the EMU periphery are accruate, they suffer from three problems. First, they select an improper temporal benchmark period in assessing the periphery's EMU performance (E. Jones 2014 and Gros 2012). Second, they combine peripheral countries' EMU data with that from the latter half of the Maastricht period, when extreme wage adjustments took place (Bentolila 2008). Third, they disaggregate competitiveness in examining only countries' export sectors, neglecting the important impact of nontradable sector price inflation on *aggregate* competitiveness (Gaulier, Taglioni, and Vicard 2012).

Studies that compare the periphery's pre- to post-1999 performance, instead of benchmarking the periphery's EMU performance to the core's EMU trajectory, miss the important distinction that the South's relative EMU performance is where its external divergence problem lies (see figure 1.1). *All* EMU countries witnessed improvements in their inflation rates and unit labor costs since the early 1990s—indeed, the height of the 1992 Exchange Rate Mechanism (ERM) crisis is not a tough bar to clear. Because southern economies started from a high-inflation equilibrium in the early 1990s, their inflation and unit labor cost improvements were notable compared to the North. Despite these temporal improvements, what was most problematic for peripheral economies after 1999 was that their inflation rates were significantly undercut by extensive beggar-thy-neighbor wage moderation in EMU's core (Wyplosz 2013). Between 1990 and 1998, real unit labor costs in the EMU core outpaced that in the periphery by 0.15 percent per annum. In the pre-crisis EMU years, real unit labor costs in the core undercut those in peripery by 0.25 percent per annum, and Germany alone undercut periphery unit labor costs by almost 0.6 percent yearly (EU Commission AMECO Database 2014).

The same benchmarking problem also exists in the use of trade statistics against the competitiveness hypothesis. While the periphery's 2007 export share increased by 2.5 percent of its 1999 value, the core's 2007 export share increased by 28 percent. Regarding the periphery's losses in the EU's total export share—that is, the proportion of an EU27 member's exports to the EU27's total exports—Gros (2012, 8) highlights that the EU27 export share of Greece, Ireland, Spain, and Portugal remained unchanged between 2000 and 2010. However, examining the trade shares in the total EU27, and the multiple currencies and exchange rates that exist within it, dilutes a direct analysis of how inflation developments within countries sharing *common currency* influence their relative trade dynamics. When aggregating EMU's peripheral countries' trade share for the *EMU's original twelve entrants (EMU12)* only, Greece, Ireland, Italy, Portugal, and Spain's collective share of EMU12 exports declined, albeit marginally, from 25 percent in 2000 to 23 percent in 2010, while Germany and its small-state satellites (Austria, Belgium, and the Netherlands) witnessed a more substantial increase their collective share of EMU12 exports from 55 percent in 2000 to over 61 percent in 2010 (EU Commission AMECO Database 2014).

The weakness in Bentolila's critique (2008) of Spain's "uncompetitive" wage performance lies in the fact that he merges the Maastricht and EMU periods when wage inflation performances were distinctly different. He argues that low productivity, rather than excessive wage growth, harmed Spain's capacity to deliver wage moderation under EMU: since *1995*, he argues, real wages have fallen by 0.5 percent per year. Yet this statistic ignores the fact that Spain made significant strides in cutting real wages in the final years of the Maastricht period to qualify for EMU. As further highlighted in chapter 6, the most emphatic wage adjustments in Spain occurred between 1994 and 1998; within these five years alone, Spanish labor productivity outstripped real wage growth by 15 percent. Spanish wages did *not* decline every year, on average, during the pre-crisis EMU period. Between 1999 and 2007, real hourly wage growth in Spain, while not significantly high, *grew* by 0.45 percent per annum (EU KLEMS 2010). Spanish real wage growth under EMU was an improvement since that seen in the 1980s and early 1990s. However, as Spain's real wages moderately but persistently increased under EMU, its wage trajectory was undercut by real wage declines in the core, making it uncompetitive in a relative sense.

Finally, Gaulier, Taglioni, and Vicard (2012) argue that the periphery's lack of competitiveness does not stem from export sectors. They highlight that, once geographical and sectoral effects are controlled for, the export "push" performance of Portugal, Italy, and Greece is similar to that of Germany between 1999 and 2007, while Spain, whose large firms did not suffer competitiveness losses under EMU, witnessed more considerable export "push" growth. In other words, the authors confirm that the *tradable goods sectors* in the EMU South were just as competitive, if not more so, than those in the EMU North. Their results do not fully refute the competitiveness hypothesis or the argument I develop in this book. In my two-sector theoretical approach, I fully agree with the authors that the tradable-goods sectors of EMU member-states produced similar levels of wage restraint, given the common price-competition constraints they faced in international markets. Rather, the basis of my argument (and more general arguments in the competitiveness literature) rests on how wage inflation in *nontradable sectors* placed upward pressures on inflation, making countries where sheltered sector wage moderation was prominent more competitive than countries where nontradable sector wage growth outpaced that in the manufacturing sector. In other words, I argue that the South's nontradable sectors, *not* their tradable sectors, ultimately led to their comparatively high inflation and worsened real exchange rates and competitive decline.[7]

Another critique against the competitiveness hypothesis is lodged against its identification of the causal mechanism (i.e., large current account deficits) behind the speculative crisis in the Eurozone's peripheral countries. Several scholars highlight that the trigger of the debt crisis was a financial one, reflective of the consequences of significant capital inflows into booming peripheral economies, not the growing current account imbalances between the North and South (Gros 2012; Diaz Sanchez and Varoudakis 2013; E. Jones 2015). According to these accounts, current account imbalances were not the *causal* mechanism behind the crisis but rather the *consequence* of the true cause of the crisis: heterogeneity in the demand for foreign capital inflows. The peripheral economies' exposure to debt speculation stems from their access to cheap and plentiful credit, which in turn fueled domestic demand booms, robust import demand, inflation, and real exchange rate decline.

The main challenge that this "global finance" hypothesis poses to the competitiveness hypothesis is a chicken-or-egg dispute about the original cause of the Eurocrisis. Yet while increasing foreign capital inflows were certainly important in the manifestion of Europe's current debt crisis, this hypothesis largely neglects the "original sin" of demand dynamics that made the peripheral countries net demanders of foreign credit and the core economies net suppliers. After all, financial liberalization, the removal of capital controls, and nominal interest rate reductions affected all E(M)U economies during the 1990s. Little consideration is given to the underlying dynamics behind the heterogeneous rise of domestic demand booms; financial accounts almost treat these booms as exogenous and fail to adequately unpack why they happen in some countries but not in others. This major shortcoming subjugates the global finance hypothesis to the same problem as the fiscal one, in that the "domestic demand boom" argument does not adequately travel across country cases. As I highlight in greater depth in chapters 4, 5, and 6 (the three case studies in this book), Italy's economy was stagnant throughout the pre-crisis EMU period and yet was still exposed to speculative crisis. The Netherlands and Denmark, on the other hand, had robust domestic demand booms in the early 2000s, due to their 1990s employment miracles, and yet they were largely spared from speculation. Admittedly, general arguments in the competitiveness camp do not provide a much better account of these different demand trajectories either, beyond a synthetic unit labor cost divergence explanation. However, the institutional account I provide here rectifies this problem by offering a more holistic explanation for why, in the process of monetary integration, trade deficits *and* domestic demand booms emerged in the EMU South rather than the North.

In understanding the current crisis in Europe from a competitiveness perspective, it becomes clear why the imposition of fiscal austerity on EMU's periphery is not a conducive policy solution. Under a fiscal view, countries run imbalances independently of their neighbors; national performance is conditional on national political and economic factors that create deficits. Under a competitiveness view, however, national imbalances are dependent on economic strategies pursued by other countries. Therefore, what matters is not how a country performs in isolation of its neighbors (in fact, Greece, Portugal, Spain and Italy had much better inflation and fiscal performances in the 2000s compared to the 1990s), but how a country performs relative to its neighbors. This implies that current account deficits amassed in southern economies, which have traditionally pursued domestic demand-led models of growth, were possible because northern economies pursued significant wage moderation in line with their export-growth models (E. Jones 2003a). Southern wage adjustment therefore relies on northern inflationary adjustment if the competitiveness imbalance problem is to be rectified. Yet though austerity measures have initiated a severe downward adjustment in wages and employment in the South, northern economies are not playing ball with inflationary adjustment, sticking to the fiscally prudent view of limiting wage growth and fiscal expansion. The core's failure to contribute to parallel inflationary adjustment has placed EMU in an adjustment deadlock, as both its northern and southern economies embark on stagnant/declining growth trajectories.

Gaps in the Competitiveness Hypothesis and the Outline of the Book

Simple descriptive statistics suggest that the competitiveness argument of the origins of the EMU crisis is more empirically sound and encompassing than the fiscal argument when examining the pre-crisis national experiences of all EMU member-states. Though this argument can extend to EMU's entire first wave, it suffers from two caveats. First, it fails to provide specific explanations as to what fostered internal adjustment, and hence current account surpluses, within the EMU core that were largely absent within the EMU periphery. Many within the competitiveness camp acknowledge the important role of nominal unit labor costs and wage moderation in driving competitive divergence between the North and South (Stockhammer 2011; Young and Semmler 2011; Holinski, Kool, and Muysken 2012). Between 1999 (the launch of the euro) and 2007, nominal unit labor cost growth in EMU's peripheral economies surpassed that of the core's by over 15 percent and Germany's in particular by over 27 percent (EU Commission AMECO Database 2014). With Hall (2012, 2014) and Johnston, Hancké, and Pant (2014) as notable exceptions, few have attempted to outline the institutional features of the core economies that enabled them to deliver such intensive wage moderation vis-à-vis their southern counterparts. Given the multitude of theoretical arguments that emphasize how corporatist institutions promote low inflation and trade competitiveness via wage restraint (Katzenstein 1984; Calmfors and Driffill 1988; Soskice 1990; Rhodes 2001), this lack of analysis into the institutional determinants of competitive divergence in the Euro-area is puzzling.

The second caveat with the competitive argument is that, though it works well in explaining how divergences in current and capital accounts contributed to significant overexposure to external borrowing, it is largely an EMU-centric story. As figure 1.1 demonstrates, current account imbalances between the EMU North and South were relatively contained in the 1980s and much of the 1990s; these imbalances only became significant under monetary union.

I address these two caveats by providing an institutional account for how the shift to the European Monetary Union created a governance vacuum in peripheral economies that prompted a steady rise in relative prices, notably in their nontradable sectors, vis-à-vis the core. Such increases in (nontradable sector) prices ultimately contributed to the deterioration of real exchange rates in the periphery and, consequently, their current account balances. My argument relies on the examination of how the EMU altered sectoral labor market governance within its member-states. One crucial determinant in the rise of significant current account imbalances between EMU's North and South was diverging performances in national inflation, which were strongly influenced by sectoral wage bifurcation within EMU's (southern) economies.

Within national economies, inflation and price competitiveness are largely determined by aggregate wage growth, which is a composite of wage growth in all national industries. Aggregate inflation, in turn, influences international price competitiveness through the real exchange rate. All else equal, if countries are able to undercut their trading partners' inflation rate, they will have a more competitive real exchange rate *if, and only if,* they share a common currency with their trading partners. Yet despite the fact that there is an empirical link between wage moderation, low inflation, and real exchange rate competitiveness, not all industrial economies are capable of producing aggregate wage moderation. One root of this incapacity lies in the sectoral politics of wage-setting between sectors exposed to and sheltered from trade. For the former, incentives for employers and unions to deliver wage moderation are clear. If wage growth remains restrained, goods become more price competitive and international demand for these goods, and consequently output and employment, increase. If wage growth is too high, however, goods become less price competitive, reducing international demand and ultimately output and employment. Because employment in the tradables sector is tied so closely to price competitiveness and wage moderation, unions in these sectors have the incentive to internalize the costs associated with high wage increases (Crouch 1990; Iversen 1999a; Franzese 2001; Traxler and Brandl 2010).

Despite such incentives, wage-setters in the exposed sector are not the sole determiners of aggregate wage moderation; their wage settlements are also paired with those in sectors sheltered from trade. Unlike unions in the tradables sector, sheltered sector unions do not possess similar competitiveness incentives to deliver wage moderation (Garrett and Way 1999). In the absence of international competitors, unions within sheltered sectors are able to push for higher wages because the price increases that result will not translate to substantial drops in demand and employment, given the relative lack of available substitutes. In the public sector, this effect is even more magnified because, for some public subsectors, the government acts as a monopoly provider of goods and services.

The divergence in wage-moderation incentives has important implications for sectoral cleavages within national economies and the level of wage moderation that is produced: while unions in the exposed sector have incentives to moderate wages to remain (price) competitive, sheltered sector unions do not, although they are able to influence the employment status in the former if they price wages high enough to influence national inflation. Given that exposed-sector wage-setters operate under similar incentive structures to produce wage moderation, economies with institutions that enable sheltered sector *employers* to deliver wage moderation will be best placed to deliver low inflation and competitive real exchange rates.

Institutions that increase the political or economic costs of inflation, or grant greater political power to exposed sector wage-setters, can play an important role in mitigating sheltered sector wage moderation. EMU's institutional predecessors, the European Monetary System and Maastricht regimes, imposed institutions that increased the costs of inflation—inflation-averse *national* central banks and EMU conditionality—on sheltered sector employers, enhancing their ability to deliver wage moderation and contribute to low national inflation. Inflation-averse *national* central banks, whose reaction function was influenced by national sectoral wage-setters, were not simultaneously adopted by current EMU member-states (Austria, Belgium, Germany, the Netherlands, and to a lesser extent France made the transition to inflation-averse central banks earlier than other current EMU member-states), whereas Maastricht conditionality was more homogenously imposed on candidate countries. Nevertheless, once countries made the credible commitment to these institutions, the political and economic costs of sheltered sector wage inflation rose, and (downward) sheltered sector wage adjustment and inflation convergence followed. Non-accommodating central banks and Maastricht's inflation and deficit rules increased the unemployment/ output costs of passing on inflationary wage settlements to higher prices, in the case of private employers, and to higher deficits, in the case of public employers. Subsequently, participation in these regimes prompted sheltered employers' to resist rent capture from sheltered sector unions, else they risk monetary tightening from the central bank or, in the case of the Maastricht criteria, exclusion from EMU.

Monetary union's alteration of these constraints weakened sheltered sector employers' and governments' abilities to deny inflationary settlements. Costs attached to inflated wage settlements under the EMS/Maastricht regime (increased interest rates and EMU exclusion) no longer existed once these countries gained access to the Eurozone. Though the European Central Bank, like its national central bank predecessors, was heavily inflation-averse, this supranational bank did not pose the same monetary threat to sheltered sector wage-setters because the influence of these actors, on their own, was nowhere near significant enough to alter inflation in the Euro-area, in contrast to their influence on national inflation. Likewise, EMU conditionality associated with the Maastricht inflation and deficit criteria was removed upon entry; countries could not be excluded from the common currency if they failed to comply with these rules or the deficit criteria's successor, the SGP. Monetary union promoted a shift from a symmetrical institutional arrangement, where wage-setters in all sectors were constrained either by competitiveness (exposed sector) or national central banks and EMU conditionality (sheltered sector), to an asymmetrical institutional arrangement where one segment of the labor market continued to be constrained in self-maximizing behavior by competitiveness while another segment was not.

However, sheltered sector wage inflation did not emerge uniformly in all EMU member-states. Sheltered sector employers in the North were largely able to carry on with enforcing wage moderation due to the presence of strong corporatist institutions that granted exposed sector employers and/or the state important agenda-setting and veto roles in national wage negotiations. Sheltered sector employers in the South did not possess these institutions, nor could they rely on the institutional constraints of the EMS and Maastricht to bind their hands in wage-setting. Sheltered employers in the South entered EMU's new bargaining environment with significantly less power and capacity to deliver wage moderation. Rising wage inflation in the South's sheltered sectors led to a rise in national inflation, leading to an uncompetitive real exchange rate and worsening trade balances vis-à-vis the North, which were financed by the North's external lending to the South.

In the following chapters, I present a formal theoretical argument for why EMU unleashed an important regime change that facilitated the persistent growth of trade and external borrowing imbalances between the North and South. Using a sequential bargaining game, I outline why the ERM and Maastricht criteria were conducive to limiting sheltered sector wage inflation before 1999; why monetary union contributed to sector wage inflation divergence afterward, especially in the EMU periphery; and how national corporatist institutions fueled the capacity of social partners in the North to significantly curtail sheltered sector wage inflation once monetary union removed important wage moderation commitment devices. In addition to demonstrating this argument empirically via comprehensive panel analyses, I compare the experiences of Denmark, Germany, Ireland, Italy, the Netherlands and Spain, focusing on how their delivery, or lack thereof, of public sector wage moderation influenced national inflation, international price competitiveness and ultimately external imbalances under the EMU era. I conclude with a discussion of how EMU created a regime with a low-inflation bias that advantaged its northern economies, and with suggestions for policy solutions that European leaders should undertake to correct this structural problem.

2

FROM ORDER TO DISORDER

How Monetary Union Changed National
Labor Markets

My account of the sectoral origins of competitiveness divergence between the EMU
core and periphery hinges on how institutions impacted the capacity of sheltered
sector employers to deliver wage moderation, and how such sheltered sector
wage moderation influenced national inflation and price competitiveness before and after 1999. Monetary union removed two institutional constraints
that enhanced employers' ability to uphold wage moderation, which in turn
facilitated low-inflation governance in national labor markets across Europe—
national-level, non-accommodating central banks[1] and the Maastricht criteria.
By removing these two constraints, monetary union eliminated two important
hand-tying mechanisms upon which sheltered sector employers previously relied. The absence of national-level, non-accommodating monetary authorities
and Maastricht's exclusionary penalties did not change much for employers in
the exposed sector, as competitiveness pressures continued to constrain their
price markups. Employers in sheltered sectors, on the other hand, entered a new
macro-bargaining environment, negotiating with unions that had little to gain
from wage moderation and were eager to compensate for wage increases that
were forgone before 1999.

Sheltered employers in EMU's core economies, however, continued to deliver
wage moderation under monetary union given the presence of national corporatist institutions that provided the export sector or the state with veto and/or
agenda-setting powers within national collective bargaining. These institutions
were a long-standing feature of the North's export-centered, low-inflation politics
and had been embedded into their labor markets far before 1992, when Maastricht

harmonized the prioritization of low inflation across all EMU candidate countries. The core's wage-setting institutions, which favored low inflation, and the significant degree of sheltered sector wage moderation that resulted, enhanced the real exchange rate competitiveness of these countries and improved their trade and current account balances, reducing the need for external borrowing. Peripheral economies, on the other hand, which lacked a historical tradition of wage-setting institutions favoring low inflation and the export sector, were unable to produce similar levels of (sheltered sector) wage moderation after 1999. Though the Maastricht criteria provided social partners in the EMU South with strong incentives to deliver wage moderation for the sake of fulfilling EMU's nominal entry criteria, causing wage-setting in peripheral economies to mirror that in the EMU core, such criteria could not be sustained indefinitely. Despite its impressive corporatist strides between 1992 and 1998, wage-setting in the EMU South reverted back to its traditional fragmented (Spain and Greece) and/or sheltered sector favoring (Greece, Ireland, Italy, and Portugal) nature once EMU membership was guaranteed. Sheltered sector wage growth placed upward pressures on inflation rates, which prompted the periphery to lose real exchange rate competitiveness vis-à-vis their corporatist neighbors. Consequently, countries in the EMU South incurred trade/current account deficits and hence had to rely more heavily on international borrowing, precipitating their heavy exposure to the crisis.

A Tale of Two Sectors: Assumptions and Theoretical Foundations

The discussion of the pre-EMU era as an institutional construct that facilitated first inflation convergence and then competitive crisis rests on the foundation of a dual-sector economy consisting of one sector that is exposed to trade (the exposed or tradables sector) and another sector that is relatively sheltered from trade (the sheltered or nontradables sector). Employers and unions in the exposed sector face more intense competition given the presence of multiple substitutes for their products in international markets. If labor costs increase, producers must either raise prices or shed labor. However, the first option is limited for firms exposed to international competition, as doing so prompts consumers to find substitutes for these firms' goods and move toward cheaper alternatives, reducing output and market share. Rather, these firms have the incentive to cut employment to preserve price competitiveness. Because high competition increases unemployment costs associated with wage increases, unions in the exposed sector have the incentive to exert wage moderation.

Employers and unions in the sheltered sector are confronted with less competition, given that they provide goods/services to domestic markets only. These wage actors face lower demand elasticity than the exposed sector; consequently, sheltered employers have greater leeway to increase market prices than their exposed sector counterparts and, given the limited availability of substitutes, consumers cannot so easily flock to cheaper alternatives if sheltered sector firms increase their prices. In a purer form of the sheltered sector, the public sector, employers and unions face negligible competition. In certain circumstances, they are monopoly suppliers and because public services are universally provided, it is difficult to suggest that these wage-setters are confronted with any type of price elasticity, though higher spending on such services should impose higher tax burdens in the medium/long run. Due to the state's capacity to tax and run deficits, public sector unions are confronted with a softer budget constraint than those in the private sector. These unions have the least to gain in restraining their wages, employment wise, as domestic demand for public services is relatively fixed (Iversen 1996; Franzese 2001).

These sectoral cleavages have important implications for aggregate inflation. If sheltered sector unions are effective at establishing the dominance of their inflationary wage preferences at the national level, they not only have the capacity to place upward pressures on national inflation independently but also, if they operate within a coordinated wage-setting system, to put upward pressures on wage settlements in other sectors. Economic studies have highlighted linkages between wage developments in the private and (sheltered) public sector. Afonso and Gomes (2014), Pérez and Sanchez Fuentes (2011), Lamo, Pérez, and Schuknecht (2008), and Holm-Hadulla et al. (2010) outline that there is robust contemporaneous correlation between public and private sector wages, with direct and indirect (via prices) feedback effects between the two over the course of the business cycle.

Yet though the primary findings of these studies empirically validate (unsurprising) sectoral wage linkages, they fail to adequately unpack why public and private sector wages move en tandem, beyond generic "signaling effects" either through public sector wage leadership (Pérez and Sanchez Fuentes 2011) or through the indirect effect of (expansionary) fiscal policy on private sector wage growth (Afonso and Gomes 2014). More important, they largely neglect study of how coordinated wage-setting mechanisms influence "signaling" behavior, completely ignore the relative political strength of private vs. public sector interests in (national) peak-level union and employment confederations, and, in the case of Holm-Hadulla et al. (2010), incorrectly assume that centralized bargaining structures in the public sector enable unions to inspire inflationary wage settlements within the private sector. (I will show in chapter 5 that Germany's highly centralized and rigid public sector collective-bargaining framework em-powered public sector employers to deliver comprehensive wage moderation in the 2000s, while the more decentralized public sector bargaining systems of Italy and the Netherlands produced wage inflation.) Linkages between public and private sector wages are important in understanding how sectoral dynamics impact aggregate inflation. However, to better understand *why* these linkages happen and which sector drives them, it is necessary to dissect these sectoral politics and coordination mechanisms that govern them within national labor markets.

A repeated sequential bargaining game between employers and unions, where the signaling of types (strong or weak negotiators) depends on the institutional context, can help explain the difference in wage equilibria in exposed and sheltered sectors. Beginning first with a simple sequential bargaining game, unions propose either a high wage or low wage settlement.[2] If a low wage settlement is proposed, the employer accepts. If a high wage settlement is proposed, employers can either challenge the union and impose a low wage increase, at the expense of industrial action, or they can accept the proposal either as a consequence of the union's success in an industrial dispute or in an attempt to preempt industrial action. Figure 2.1 provides a simple game tree with all possible equilibria: a low settlement proposed initially by unions (call this LOW); a low settlement imposed by employers but only after industrial action from unions, who originally proposed high (call this STRIKE LOW); and a high settlement proposed by unions and accepted by employers (call this HIGH). All employers, regardless of sector, have the same ranking of preferences: LOW is preferred over STRIKE LOW, which is preferred over HIGH. Unions also have similar preferences, regardless of sector: HIGH is preferred over LOW, which is preferred over STRIKE LOW. The probability of obtaining these payoffs, however, is determined by both the employer's and the union's type.

The strategy for proposing a high vs. a low wage settlement depends on whether the union is a strong/confrontational (probability of λ) or weak/consenting (probability of $1-\lambda$) type. Weak and/or consenting unions have less capacity to challenge employers and hence should propose lower wage settlements. Union weakness/consent is attributed to one of three factors. First, unions may lack comprehensive representation within a particular sector and hence do not have the capacity to mobilize against employers when they propose low wage settlements. Such an equilibrium is typical within sectors characterized by heavy incidence of part-time, atypical, and/or precarious employment (i.e., low-skilled services sectors, where contracts are less formal or nonexistent and where workers' representation is further complicated by the legality of their employment status). Second, unions' positions are weakened in the event of high unemployment, which offers employers a larger reserve pool of unutilized workers to replace

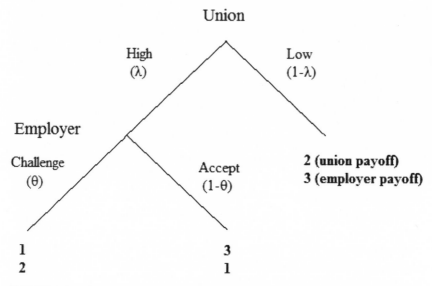

FIGURE 2.1.   Sequential bargaining game between unions and employers

employees who request generous wage increases. Third, unions may be more consenting toward low settlements if higher pay awards present employment penalties to their members. This outcome would be typical within sectors where demand for products is more elastic. In demand-elastic product (and services) markets, employers' price markups have greater output consequences, which may prompt employers, in the event of a high wage settlement, to do more with less (i.e., dismiss workers). Because these properties are more inherent in private, low-skilled services sectors and the exposed sector, as well as in stagnant economies, we should expect wage settlements within these sectors to congregate toward the LOW equilibrium, given unions' lower value of λ.

Strong and confrontational unions, on the other hand, can better challenge employers and hence propose higher wage settlements. Union strength, and the capacity to be confrontational toward employers within wage negotiations, is the result of factors that juxtapose characteristics of weak/consenting trade unions. First, unions are generally stronger in sectors where they either have greater representation (i.e., high union density) or more comprehensive influence over wage settlements (i.e., high bargaining coverage). Second, unions have greater bargaining leverage in overheating economies where labor shortages are widespread (in chapters 4 and 6, I highlight that labor shortages granted Dutch and Irish unions considerable political leverage in securing generous wage settlements during the 2000s). Third, unions are also likely to have greater bargaining power in sectors where goods/services are demand-inelastic. In these sectors, employers are penalized less, demand-wise, for additional markups on products and services. Rather than risking the costs of a strike, employers may prefer to pass these settlements on to prices because, comparatively, the demand penalties associated with price increases are not so high. These properties suggest that union strength should be most pronounced in the public sector, where union representation is highest for most developed economies and where demand is largely inelastic given the lack of available substitutes or, in extreme cases, the state's monopoly on production/provision. Due to their higher values of λ, strong unions should congregate toward a wage equilibrium on the left hand side of the game tree in figure 2.1. However, where they land—STRIKE LOW or HIGH—ultimately depends on the strength of the employers they bargain with.

Employers' capacity for challenging or accepting a high wage settlement also depends on whether they are a "strong" (probability of θ) or "weak" (probability of 1-θ) type. Strong employers, like strong unions, are better organized and have greater representation density within a given sector. Unlike union strength, however, employers' strength is enhanced in the event of high unemployment and low vacancy rates, as well as within demand-elastic sectors where they are able to credibly threaten unions with employment shedding in the event of an inflationary wage settlement. Exposure to trade enhances employers' bargaining strength by increasing the number of substitutes available. Greater market share decline associated with price markups provides employers with a greater incentive to hold out against strikes, because forcing low wage settlements on unions will offset these holdout costs. Weak employers, on the other hand, are more likely to congregate in sectors where demand elasticity is low and, consequently, where output repercussions of price increases are lower than the costs of strike holdout. In the public sector, the costs of wage absorption for employers is even lower than in private sheltered sectors because the state, in its capacity to run fiscal deficits, does not encounter as strict a budget constraint.

In the event that strong unions bargain with strong employers who are more effective at strike holdout, repeated interaction should prompt them to conform toward a more "consenting" stance, as the LOW wage equilibrium is always preferable for unions compared to an equilibrium where wages are low and strike funds are exhausted (STRIKE LOW). This ultimately means that employers will achieve wage moderation in labor markets with strong unions, *only* if they are able to convince strong unions of their holdout power and hence their capacity to force a STRIKE LOW outcome. Applying this to a national (inflation) context, the transition toward a low-inflation regime rests on *all* employers' capacity, particular of those in the sheltered (public) sector, to shift nationwide collective bargaining from a HIGH to STRIKE LOW equilibrium. Within current EMU member-states, this (historical) low-inflation transition depended on *institutional* factors that increased employer strength (θ) relative to union strength (λ). Many have dissected what types of institutions increase the bargaining strength of employers relative to unions they negotiate with (see Mishel 1986; Wallerstein 1989; Stephens and Wallerstein 1991; Kittel 2000; and Schnabel and Wagner 2007, among others, for structural determinants of union power; see Crouch 1993; Traxler 2000; Martin and Swank 2004; Martin and Swank 2008; and Kuo 2012, among others, for structural determinants of employer power). Here, the emphasis is placed on how *monetary policy commitments* and *(EMU) conditionality* enhanced the bargaining leverage of employers over unions, specifically for those in sheltered sectors.

In repeated bargaining games, actors have the ability to establish reputations that may alter perceived values of θ and λ and, consequently, resulting equilibria. In these types of games, a player maintains the assumption that another player will adhere to her optimal equilibrium strategy. Yet such assumptions can be challenged if one player entertains doubts about the intention of her opponents' ability to act according to their optimal strategy. If a weak employer wishes to establish a reputation for being strong, it can repeatedly aberrate from its rational strategy of consenting to high wage settlements and challenge the settlement instead. Such behavior yields lower payoffs in the short run, in the form of high industrial action, yet repeated aberration may fool unions that the employer is strong and hence able to withstand strike activity, convincing them to consent to moderation in the long run. In perturbed reputational games, players may find the short-term loss from imitating aberrant strategies are outweighed by long-term gains from spurring opponents' doubts about their motivations. If sheltered sector unions are unaware of their employer's (or the government's) true bargaining strength, an employer, in resisting the temptation to cater to generous wage settlements, can develop a reputation for being anti-inflationary (Kreps and Wilson 1982; Backus and Driffill 1985). Institutions play a crucial role here, if they introduce penalties for inflated wage settlements. Employers can use these institutions as signals to unions that their price strategies are limited, suggesting their resolve against generous wage settlements will increase as these institutional commitment devices become embedded. Over time, employers can defer to institutions that expand θ, increasing their probability of being a strong type.

The adoption of inflation-averse central banks and, for public employers, credible fiscal rules may allow (weak) sheltered employers to be *perceived* as strong. If such institutions introduce credible penalties for inflated wage settlements, they can also alter sheltered employers' *probabilities* of being a strong type. Put otherwise, over time, employers can defer to institutions that expand θ so that it becomes a function not only of organizational strength and competitiveness, but also (monetary and fiscal) institutional costs attached to inflated wage settlements. In the transition from a Keynesian regime, where central banks accommodate inflation, toward a monetarist one, where central banks do not, generous wage settlements from unions trigger central banks to raise interest rates that dampen aggregate demand and ultimately increase short-term unemployment (Weber 1991; Iversen 1998; Cukierman and Lippi 1999). Such induced monetary tightening increases the output costs for price increases made by sheltered employers within the short run, forcing employers in the sheltered sector to pursue similar bargaining strategies as their exposed sector counterparts.

These costs also arise for employers in the public sector. The responsibility that follows a low-inflation monetary policy is that a government's capacity to maintain it depends on its ability to avert inflationary pressures with fiscal policy (Fischer 1987). If there is doubt about a government's ability to deliver low inflation on grounds of prolonged deficit spending, then higher interest rates, stifling demand, and ultimately employment will result. Deficits do not have to result from excessive public sector pay settlements if governments are able to increase taxes or decrease other social transfers. Monetary non-accommodation, however, increases the political costs of such a move. In the event that the private sector is forced to moderate its wages to facilitate labor market adjustment to a monetarist regime, increasing taxes or reducing benefits to accommodate more generous public sector pay settlements would not bode well for a government's popularity.[3] Especially for (rightist) business-friendly governments, the imposition of wage moderation on the public sector provides a more convenient alternative in limiting reproach from the central bank. Furthermore, the imposition of public sector wage moderation to facilitate the transition to a low-inflation regime may also be easier for public employers in countries where a large, export-centered manufacturing sector dominates national economic activity. It should perhaps not be so surprising that EMU's export-oriented core economies made sheltered sector wage adjustments toward a low-inflation regime before their domestic-oriented peripheral counterparts, because the influence of their exposed manufacturing sectors in domestic politics was more considerable.

When central banks threaten rising interest rates in response to inflationary wage increases, sheltered sector employers are confronted with less maneuvering room to increase prices, or in the case of public employers run deficits, compared to a situation where monetary authorities accommodate inflation. Increased short-term unemployment and interest rates, which are a consequence of wage inflation in non-accommodating monetary regimes, force sheltered sector employers to impose wage settlements on services unions in line with their (lower) productivity developments.[4] While the strength probability of sheltered sector unions, λ, remains unchanged, an increase in θ will change employers' dominant strategy in the simple sequential bargaining game, incentivizing them to challenge high wage proposals and impose downward wage adjustment.

Convenient Institutional Constraints: The European Monetary System's Exchange Rate Mechanism

Prior to 1979, the majority of EU15 countries possessed central banks that were accommodating toward inflation.[5] The EMS system,[6] however, changed this dynamic by facilitating the transition toward a non-accommodating monetary regime within its participants. At first glance, it does not seem obvious that the EMS would enhance central bank conservatism toward inflation. With the exception of Germany, Austria, and the Netherlands, central banks in many EMU countries had low levels of legal independence throughout most of the 1980s (Cukierman 1992). However, central bank independence is not synonymous with monetary non-accommodation toward inflation. As Iversen (1999a) and Mares (2003) point out, dependent central banks can develop credible commitments to low inflation by adhering to fixed exchange rate arrangements where the anchor currency belongs to a monetary authority that is anti-inflationary. Even if inflation targeting is not a central mandate within its charter, central banks can import inflation aversion via the credible hard peg commitment to a currency whose national monetary authority is inflation-averse.

The key institution introduced by the EMS that enhanced the central banks' inflation aversion was the European Exchange Rate Mechanism (ERM). With the German mark as the unquestioned center of the ERM's fixed exchange rate regime because of its disproportionate weight in the European Currency Unit (ECU), national central banks were forced to shadow the Bundesbank's interest rate policy in order to avoid their currencies sliding outside of the established exchange rate bands. These fixed exchange rate arrangements implied that German monetary policy was de facto imposed on countries and the wage actors within them. Credible commitments to the EMS raised the unemployment and output costs of inflationary policy. The success of such credible commitments, however, depended on the cooperative behavior of trade unions and their pursuit of moderated wage settlements (Hassel 2003). Trade union cooperation could either be consensual or forced by employers. The "stickiness" of union adjustment in several EMU member-states, partially the result of employers' reluctance to impose moderation in the presence of union militancy and heavy strike action, resulted in wide variation toward the adoption of a credible commitment to the ERM.

Austria, Denmark, and the Netherlands adopted a credible commitment to a hard currency policy early in the ERM regime. The Netherlands initiated only one (2 percent) devaluation under the ERM prior to the 1992 ERM currency crisis in 1983 (Enderlein 2006, 122). Austria, likewise, made two devaluations in the late 1970s and early 1980s in its (separate) bilateral fixed exchange rate arrangement with the German mark. In September 1979, the schilling was re-valued against the mark by 1.5 percent, and between then and the end of 1981, the schilling gradually appreciated by 4.5 percent; after 1981, there was minimal fluctuation between the two currencies (Hochreiter and Winckler 1995, 93). Denmark intensified its commitment to a hard currency policy under the ERM after 1983. In the mid-1980s, Belgium and Ireland abandoned their soft currency stances for the Bundesbank's hard currency option, and France's last (major) devaluation with the German mark, around 6 percent, took place in 1986 (Iversen 1996; Enderlein 2006). The credible adoption of the ERM in Europe's southern economies (Greece, Portugal, Spain, and to a lesser extent, Italy) failed to materialize in the 1980s. The Spanish peseta did not enter the EMS until 1989, the Portuguese escudo formally entered in 1992, and Greece did not transition to a hard currency policy until 1994 (McNamara 2005; Tavlas and Papaspyrou n.d.). Nonetheless, with Maastricht's nominal exchange rate, inflation, and interest rate criteria, central banks within these countries quickly adopted a non-accommodating stance toward inflation, if they had not done so already.[7] The early years of the ERM, 1979–1983, were marked by multiple currency realignments, yet the frequency of these alignments slowed after 1984; between January 1987 and September 1992, realignments were few and minor (McNamara 1998, 159–160).

The pursuit of a credible hard currency stance required the imposition of pay restraint on not only sectors exposed to trade, which were already familiarized to wage moderation, but more importantly on sheltered sectors. Adjustment was particularly acute in Europe's heavily organized and sheltered public sectors. Because the public sector constituted a significant share of the national labor force in all countries participating in the ERM, inflationary wage settlements were likely to impact national inflation and consequently provoke monetary tightening from banks upholding the peg. This potential for aggregate demand repercussions prompted governments to change their bargaining stance.

Over the course of the 1980s, governments in countries that developed a credible hard currency peg with the German mark early within the EMS regime initiated significant spending cuts in public sector pay (a brief timeline of adjustment efforts is provided in table 2.1). In Belgium, the government introduced a number of special powers laws that enabled it to not only dismantle its wage indexation system for all employees, but also restrict the salary level of newly employed civil servants to 80 percent of their normal salary in their first year of employment.[8] In the Netherlands, wage indexation was also absolved for all employees.[9] During the early 1980s, the Dutch government undertook strict reductions in fiscal spending: in 1981, it increased social security contribution rates for employees and employers by 3.8 percent and 1.9 percent, respectively, and cut real wages by 2 percent.[10] In its 1983 budget, it implemented a public sector pay freeze and introduced nominal pay cuts to particular sectors (notably education).[11] In late 1983, it passed a further 3 percent nominal public pay decrease for its 1984 annual budget.[12] In Denmark, Poul Schülter's center-right coalition abandoned its goal of full employment after it fully committed Denmark to a peg with the ECU/mark and adopted a formidable bottom line: "any changes in wages and prices that were incompatible with the fixed exchange rate policy would be met by a tightening of monetary policies" (Iversen 1996, 419). In response to the failure of unions and employers to produce a new two-year pay agreement, government passed a law that imposed pay limits on private and public sector workers: private sector employees received a 2 percent/1.5 percent nominal wage increase in 1985/1986 while public employees received a 1.75 percent/1.25 percent nominal wage increase.[13]

As a consequence of these austerity efforts, growth in public sector wage bills was relatively stagnant in the original EMS participating economies during the 1980s and 1990s (see table 2.2). Countries that implemented the strictest pay moderation measures early in the regime witnessed the slowest growth in their real public sector pay bills during the 1980s. Between 1980 and 1989, Belgium and Germany had stagnant annual growth in the real public sector wage bill, while the Netherlands witnessed an average decline of 1.3 percent in the public sector wage bill each year throughout the *entire* decade. Only Italy witnessed substantial growth in real compensation toward government employees during the 1980s, given the country's late commitment to upholding a strict peg in the ERM (Weber 1991; Walsh 1999), but witnessed more considerable public sector wage suppression during the 1990s.

One can question the endogeneity of the influence of non-accommodating central banks on public sector wage adjustment. (Rightist) business-friendly governments are more likely to impose such institutions if they are predisposed to public sector austerity. Although conversion to a hard currency policy

TABLE 2.1. Timeline of public sector disciplinary policies under the EMS (early 1980s)

1979		
	Nov 30	**Denmark:** Short-term price and wage freeze.
1981		
	Mar 22	**Italy:** Government spending cut plans.
	Jul	**Italy:** Banca d'Italia freed from the obligation to purchase unsold public debt at the Treasury auctions, which gave the government preferential access to monetizing fiscal deficits.
	Jul	**Netherlands:** The Nederlandsche Bank abandons control of domestic liquidity and gears its monetary policy toward the external constraint (the DM exchange rate).
	Oct 5	**France:** Temporary price and profit freeze.
1982		
	Feb 22	**Belgium:** General price freeze until end of March; selective freeze thereafter; freeze of wage indexation (until May); also longer-run measures to impede complete wage indexation.
	Mar 25	**Ireland:** Austerity budget by Fianna Fail government; initiation of fiscal consolidation program.
	Jun 14	**France:** Temporary freeze of prices, wages, rents, and dividends until October; reduction in 1983 budget deficit plans.
	Jun 23	**Italy:** Announcement of budget austerity measures.
	Oct 16	**Denmark:** Comprehensive stabilization package: automatic wage indexation suspended; wage freeze until March 1983; tight fiscal policy; progressive dismantling of capital controls.
	Oct 21	**Ireland:** Proposal for elimination of budget deficits by 1986.
	Dec 30	**Belgium:** Selective price freeze extended until end of 1983.
1983		
	Mar 28	**France:** Austerity program aimed at reducing inflation via monetary restraint, restoring external balances via foreign exchange controls and reducing the public budget deficit by cutting expenditures and raising taxes.
	Apr 12	**Denmark:** Government announces further liberalization of capital movements to take place on May 1.
	Apr	**Denmark:** Government guidelines for an upper-limit of 2% for the annual wage increase in the new two-year wage agreement.
1985		
	Jan 1	**France:** Start of a two-year transition of monetary policy operating procedures from quantitative credit controls to a more market-based system of reserve requirements.
	Apr	**Denmark:** Government enforces a 2% legal upper limit for the annual wage increase in the new two-year wage agreement.
	Jul 22	**Italy:** Announcement of revenue measures to contain the increase in the budget deficit.
	Jul	**Italy:** Modification of wage indexation mechanism, *scala mobile*.
1986		
	Apr 7	**France:** Steps to slow nominal wage growth; plans to reduce government budget deficit; relaxation of exchange controls.
	Jun	**Denmark:** Wage indexation law (suspended in 1982) is abolished.

SOURCE: Weber (1991), 65–67.

TABLE 2.2. Annual growth in real compensation of government employees for the EMS's original participants (period averages)

	70–79 AVERAGE	80–89 AVERAGE	90–99 AVERAGE
Austria	5.03[1]	2.24	2.14
Belgium	7.44	0.03	2.86
Denmark	5.4[2]	1.85	2.03
France	NA	2.08	2.53
Germany	5.1	0.74	1.2
Ireland	NA	0.57[3]	6.02
Italy	NA	4.5[4]	0.97
Netherlands	5.53	−1.3	1.36

SOURCE: EU Commission AMECO Database (2014).
[1] Period average from 1977–1979; [2] Period average from 1972–1979;
[3] Period average from 1986–1989;
[4] Period average from 1981–1989.

was steered by right-of-center coalitions for three of the ERM's earlier converts (Belgium, Denmark, and the Netherlands), partisanship did not dictate adjustment in all EMS countries or the lack thereof in non-EMS countries. France's François Mitterrand[14] and Austria's Bruno Kreisky demonstrated that leftist governments could initiate the transition to a hard currency stance, while Margaret Thatcher battled British unions under an accommodating central bank. In countries where the conversion was initiated under right-of-center governments, non-accommodating central banks remained sticky once they left office; in Denmark, Poul Rasmussen's Social Democrats further institutionalized the Danish Central Bank's hard currency commitment with a formal separation of powers arrangement in 1993 (see chapter 4).

In monitoring inflation developments at the national level, non-accommodating central banks penalized employers in sectors that previously had greater leeway to pass rising labor costs on to prices. As central banks increased their commitments to anti-inflationary monetary policies, sheltered sector employers became more restricted in the wage settlements they could award. Terms within the sequential bargaining game outlined in figure 2.1, therefore, changed with a shift toward a non-accommodating monetary authority. With the rise of inflation-averse central banks, sheltered sector employers inherited a signaling device that conveyed their new commitment to wage moderation. Though the shift from a HIGH to LOW wage equilibrium in the sheltered sector was transitioned through the STRIKE LOW equilibrium, significant public sector industrial action failed to deter sheltered employers' low-inflation commitments in EMS's early converts.

Enhanced sheltered sector wage moderation led to significant reductions in national inflation rates, as inflation within (committed) EMS participants demonstrated remarkable convergence throughout the 1980s and 1990s.

While the ERM proved a convenient institution for sheltered sector employers to produce downward wage adjustments, this monetary arrangement was adopted heterogeneously across EMS participants, with some making difficult monetary transitions earlier, rather than later, in the regime. In 1992, the ERM crisis brought the future of the EMS and, monetary union itself, into question. After the Danes rejected the Maastricht Treaty in a national referendum, and the French barely accepting it in theirs, financial markets entertained doubts about the viability of the Treaty's grand design for monetary union. Severe currency speculation against weaker links ensued, prompting the exit of British pound, the Finnish markka, and the Italian lira from the ERM in 1992 (McNamara 2005, 146).[15] Following the crisis, the ERM's exchange rate bands were widened to $+/-15$ percent. This band widening suggested that national central banks may relax more serious commitments to low inflation in the enforcement of (German) monetary policy on their national wage-setters. However, the Maastricht inflation criteria replaced the now looser ERM constraint and introduced new rules, which continued to strengthen sheltered employers' capacity to withstand inflationary wage demands in collective bargaining.

EMU Conditionality and Maastricht: New Constraints on the Sheltered Sector

What Europe's common currency project lost, in terms of discipline, in the widening of ERM's fixed exchange bands, it immediately regained in the encompassing nature of the Maastricht criteria. The Maastricht criteria restored sheltered sector employers' bargaining strength via two channels. One, it imposed credible deficit limits onto candidate countries, which enabled public employers to proceed with public sector wage adjustment. Two, it further enhanced the inflation-averse stance of candidate countries' central banks. Contrary to the ERM, Maastricht outlined three nominal targets that candidates were obliged to fulfill; countries had to partake in the ERM for at least two years, they had to adopt an explicit inflation target (inflation could be no higher than 1.5 percent of the EMU's three lowest inflation performers), and they had to achieve nominal interest rate convergence. As a result of these nominal requirements, the Maastricht criteria prompted some countries to reform their banking laws and legally enhance central bank legal independence. Belgium, France, and Italy reformed their banking legislation, increasing the legal independence of their central banks near to that of the Bundesbank after 1992 (Polillo and Guillén 2005). Only in Finland did monetary non-accommodation continue to deteriorate after 1993, due to a severe recession, which initiated a 13 percent depreciation in the markka once it left the ERM in 1992. By the time the country rejoined the ERM in 1996, monetary conservatism had been restored.

Along with important banking system reforms, some EMU candidate countries that had not done so already, made significant advances in abandoning wage indexation during the 1990s or, in the case of Belgium, imposed *additional* (trade-related) ceilings on wage increases. Belgium introduced a law in 1996 establishing a pay-ceiling with its three largest trading partners—France, Germany, and the Netherlands—to limit pay rises in order to secure EMU entry, as well as safeguard its competitiveness after it had assumed the single currency (Pochet 2004). This institutional arrangement would prove advantageous to the country in maintaining wage competitiveness in the EMU period. In 1992, Italy abolished *scala mobile*, its automatic wage indexation system (Ebbinghaus and Hassel 2000). The mass abandonment of wage indexation in EMU candidate countries reduced the possibility of wage-price spirals. Because the penalty associated with failing to comply with Maastricht's inflation target, EMU exclusion, was important to policymakers, central banks were provided with new mandates to reduce inflation "for the sake of Europe," reinforcing sheltered employers' capacity to deliver wage moderation (Buti and Giudice 2002, 825).

For public employers, the Maastricht criteria provided an additional constraint on bargaining strategies with the public sector: a 3 percent deficit rule.[16] Fiscal rules can counter governments' temptation to yield to inflated wage proposals by increasing the costs associated with a high (public sector) wage equilibrium. Yet unlike central banks, which can be distinctly separated from the Treasury, fiscal rules as an institution suffer from credibility and agency capture problems, particularly if they are made, assessed, and enforced within the domestic political realm. Such problems can be addressed if penalties associated with reneging on fiscal targets are high and the targets are monitored by an external authority. For EMU candidate countries, the 3 percent Maastricht deficit criterion was unique in embodying both of these characteristics and did much to increase public employers' bargaining strength between 1992 and 1998. The penalty for reneging on the 3 percent deficit rule, EMU exclusion, was significant enough to compel governments to impose wage moderation on powerful public sector unions. Moreover, the Maastricht's penalties were transparent and its terms established a clear deadline for EMU entry (Buti and Giudice 2002). Countries seeking to join in the first wave, particularly those with histories of excessive deficits, were not in a position to negotiate more lenient terms. If consolidation was not achieved and public sector moderation was not imposed, the country in question would remain outside EMU.

A second advantage of the Maastricht criterion was the nature of its assessment. Rather than falling into the domestic realm, the European Commission was responsible for assessing whether countries had successfully fulfilled the 3 percent deficit rule. The simplicity and the (largely) unambiguous definition of the fiscal requirements allowed the Commission to effectively monitor candidate countries' fiscal positions and apply a homogenous interpretation of the rule. These two characteristics, in some sense, made Maastricht's deficit criterion a perfect fiscal rule. Jürgen Von Hagen, Andrew Hallett, and Rolf Strauch (2001) outline that much of the consolidation that occurred throughout EMU candidate countries during the 1992–1998 period could not be explained by a forecasting model of budgetary behavior, leading to evidence of a specific "Maastricht effect."

The adjustment to Maastricht's fiscal constraint proved difficult for even the core countries in the Deutsche mark bloc (Austria, Belgium, France, Germany, and the Netherlands), where difficult monetary adjustments and fiscal adjustments were undertaken simultaneously in the 1980s. Belgium introduced a finance bill in 1997 that not only cut welfare and increased taxes, but also placed ceilings on public sector pay rises.[17] In France, the Juppé Plan, aimed at meeting the EMU convergence criteria by limiting public sector pay, among other measures, drew considerable social unrest from unions, while in Germany, the introduction of austerity packages aimed at curbing public sector pay and public spending also evoked union opposition.[18] In Austria, public sector workers were forced to accept pay raises of 0.3 percent in 1996 (compared to 2.4 percent increases in the private sector and a 1.9 percent rise in inflation), due to austerity measures introduced in the 1996/97 budget aimed at complying with Maastricht.[19]

In economies where there was a lack of monetary and fiscal adjustment in the 1980s, cuts in public sector pay were more dramatic and fiscal adjustments in some cases involved a resurgence in national social pacts. In Italy, the Ciampi Protocol in 1993 reorganized the fragmented public sector pay system and implemented a series of caps on public sector pay (Ebbinghaus and Hassel 2000; Hancké and Rhodes 2005). In 1998, the Greek government passed a taxation bill that contained a controversial clause to curb collective-bargaining rights in loss-making public sector utilities, granting Parliament the ability to intervene and unilaterally legislate on restructuring in the event of a bargaining stalemate.[20] The Maastricht budgetary criterion in general, and German interests in particular, placed considerable pressure on Greece to comply with requirements for entry. After being refused outright from joining EMU's first wave, the

Greek government was forced to resort to more drastic public-savings measures to convince the European Commission that it was a capable second wave candidate.

During the 1990s, public sector unions were exposed to considerable wage austerity from governments intent on entering EMU's first wave. Conditions of the Maastricht budgetary criterion were absolute: failure to meet the 3 percent deficit limit would result in EMU exclusion, and governments could not secure exceptions. In retrospect, there may have been some instances of creative accounting, yet the negotiating strength of public employers in all candidate countries was clearly exhibited in the moderated wage settlements they imposed on the public sector workforce between 1992 and 1998. Both the Maastricht and EMS regimes were conducive to extending wage moderation onto sectors whose unions had little interest in exerting it by enhancing the credibility of sheltered employers' bargaining strength. The result was wage moderation, in both exposed and sheltered sectors within EMU candidate countries, and unprecedented inflation convergence among EMU's future member-states. The ERM, and Maastricht especially, standardized domestic inflation politics within Europe's corporatist and noncorporatist economies. Because domestic political elites in all EMU candidate countries had the desire to participate in deeper European economic integration, they were equally forced to comply with common macroeconomic rules in order to do so. While elites in what are now EMU's peripheral economies may have been more forgiving of inflation in the 1980s, EMU's entry requirements prompted them to mimic the anti-inflationary stances of their corporatist neighbors.

Monetary union, however, altered both institutions, and in doing so, removed commitment devices that prompted sheltered sector employers in (inflation prone) southern European economies to mimic their (wage moderation prone) northwest European counterparts. By rendering national central banks and the Maastricht criteria obsolete, sheltered employers entered a regime where their credibility toward upholding moderated wage settlements waned, reducing sheltered unions' perception in their employers' ability to challenge high wage proposals. However, sheltered employers in some countries, particularly those whose domestic politics were sympathetic to the economic dominance of their export sectors, were more fortunate than others; they were able to replace the ERM and Maastricht criteria with low-inflation, domestic collective-bargaining institutions that gave exposed sector wage-setters and governments the ability to set the natural wage bargaining agenda and veto sheltered sector wage negotiations. In other words, by 1999, Europe's diverse domestic institutional configurations and the politics that upheld them were allowed to organically diverge, creating a schism between EMU's corporatist and noncorporatist economies.

EMU's Macroeconomic Governance Vacuum: Sheltered Sector Employers on the Defensive

Conceptualizing the pre-EMU regime as an institutional arrangement that enhanced sheltered sector employers' bargaining power, particularly in the EMU South, helps explain the remarkable convergence in wage moderation and, in turn, national inflation between candidate countries in the 1980s and 1990s. As a result of inflation convergence, price competitiveness among EMU candidate countries became synchronized, explaining the lack of divergence in the EMU North and South's current account balances (see figure 1.1). Monetary union was not intended to alter Maastricht's or the ERM's non-accommodating design. The European Central Bank (ECB) was just as conservative, if not more so, with its strict 2 percent inflation mandate, as the central banks that shadowed the Bundesbank's anti-inflationary policy prior to 1999. For public employers, the Stability and Growth Pact (SGP), too, stipulated identical excessive deficit limits as the Maastricht budgetary criteria. Yet, while the content of EMU was similar to the EMS/Maastricht regime, the method by which it was enforced differed, producing important repercussions for sectoral wage governance within countries.

After 1999, wage-setters in tradable sectors continued to face competiveness constraints that limited unions' capacity to push for high wage settlements; some argued this competitive constraint was more magnified under a single currency where pricing between EMU countries was more transparent (Calmfors et al. 2001; Allington, Kattuman, and Waldman 2005). Sheltered sector unions, on the other hand, witnessed a decline in the monitoring power of institutions that enhanced employers' capabilities to enforce wage moderation. The major alteration in the non-accommodating monetary threat under EMU occurred in the influence of sheltered sector wage negotiations on the central bank's targeted inflation rate. Under the EMS and Maastricht regimes, sheltered sector wage settlements could influence national inflation and commitments to fixed exchange rates, as wage-setters within the sector constituted a significant proportion of the total labor force. Hence their influence on the central bank's target inflation rate was high. Under EMU, the weight of individual sheltered sector unions in the Eurozone aggregate inflation rate, which is the supranational European Central Bank's monetary policy target, was negligible,[21] and their wage settlements were unlikely to draw monetary reproach from the ECB. Because the ECB's mandate was to ensure price stability across the Euro-area as a whole, it had little incentive or ability to punish inflationary wage settlements in sheltered sectors of individual member-states. In transferring non-accommodating central banks from the national level (where they had the capacity to penalize sheltered employers for awarding high wage settlements) to the international level (where the ECB did not have this capacity), the EMU eliminated the monetary contraction threat against sheltered employers, who now had greater maneuvering room to pass rising labor costs onto prices. The subversion of this threat, which presented output repercussions for private service employers and political repercussions for the state, eliminated an important wage moderation commitment device for sheltered employers and would have important implications for sheltered employers' bargaining strength.

There were some attempts to incorporate further institutional constraints on the public sector in EMU's design. The SGP was created to enforce fiscal discipline in the Euro-area in order to safeguard the credibility of the single monetary authority (Buti, Franco, and Ongena 1998; Eichengreen and Wyplosz 1998). Unlike Maastricht, whose (limited) goal was to ensure budgetary retrenchment, the SGP was designed to foster sustainable fiscal policy within the medium and long run under EMU (Buti and Giudice 2002). While the pact itself was not specifically aimed at public sector trade unions, it was designed to continue to tie the hands of governments that may have otherwise been inclined to reengage in an expansionary fiscal policy. Like Maastricht, the SGP continued to be scrutinized by the European Commission, and hence its assessment remained outside the domestic realm. However, though the rules of the pact were the same, the costs of governments reneging on the fiscal rule were different from those of breaking the Maastricht deficit criterion. Before 1999, the threat of EMU exclusion and the rigid timeline for entry constituted a severe penalty for failing to address budgetary excess. Under the SGP, penalties associated with excessive deficits were reduced to fines and the time scale for compliance was lengthened: if member-states breached the 3 percent deficit limit under the SGP, they had two years to correct fiscal excesses before their mandatory deposits were transformed into financial penalties (Eichengreen and Wyplosz 1998). Hallerberg (2002) further outlines that the SGP was blunted by the fact that it could only be used *a posteriori* and could not coax states to take alternative fiscal action to avoid breaching the 3 percent limit *a priori*, like the Maastricht criteria could.

In comparing the ill-fated SGP to Maastricht, two components of the latter's success were lacking within the former. Both Maastricht's constraining calendar and the clear political incentive to join monetary union were absent (Buti and Giudice 2002; Johnston 2012). Once they gained membership, countries could not be excluded from EMU for excessive deficits or, more pertinent to Europe's sovereign debt crisis, for excessive national debts. In EMU's early years, scholars pointed to consolidation fatigue to explain why governments were unsuccessful in moderating fiscal expansions (Von Hagen 2003). Von Hagen (2002) outlined that fiscal expansion was especially prevalent in countries facing elections while Von Hagen and Wolff (2006) discovered that the SGP induced governments to employ "creative accounting" measures such as stock-flow adjustments to hide deficits, particularly during recessions. By 2003, the SGP had become widely violated, even by Germany, the country that was most insistent on its creation and enforcement (Hodson 2011, 58). In 2005, the Eurozone's largest members succeeded in eliminating the (corrective) financial penalty component behind the excessive deficit procedure (Alesina, Ardagna, and Galasso 2008; Hodson 2011, 58). The dubiousness of the SGP as a reputable fiscal rule, due not only to its lengthened implementation period but also its revised framework, did little to convince public sector unions that the state's collective-bargaining strength would remain unaltered under EMU. Path dependency also played an important role in reducing public employer strength. Maastricht's seven long years of fiscal consolidation could not be infinitely sustained, and its absolution, coupled with economic upswing in the late 1990s and early 2000s, reduced governments' incentives to carry on with austere bargaining strategies.

EMU's institutional regime made the deliverance of wage moderation more difficult for sheltered sector employers. In removing effective low-inflation commitment devices, EMU provided a less restrictive bargaining environment for sheltered sector employers, granting them greater leeway to absorb wage inflation into price increases. Relative bargaining power between sheltered sector employers and the unions they negotiated with increased in the unions' favor, as employers no longer faced the critical output and exclusionary penalties associated with price markups. Such capacity is revealed when looking at differences in annual wage growth between the manufacturing sector, on the one hand, and a composite of the health, education, and public administration sectors, on the other. Between 1979 and 1998, EMU10 candidate countries had an average wage growth gap of 0.56 percent a year in favor of the manufacturing sector, translating into a 5.6 percent wage gap between the two sectors over a ten-year period (EU KLEMS 2010). Between 1999 and 2007, however, this wage gap reversed itself, and annual wage growth in the health, education, and public administration sectors outpaced that in manufacturing every year during this period. Such developments did not arise in non-EMU countries where national-level, non-accommodating central banks remained intact. In Australia, Canada, Denmark, Japan, Sweden, the United Kingdom, and the United States, the gap between annual wage growth in manufacturing and in the health, education, and public administration composite improved, on average, from 0.26 percent a year in favor of the manufacturing sector between 1979 and 1998, to 0.34 percent in favor of the manufacturing sector between 1999 and 2007 (EU KLEMS 2010).

Growing bifurcation in sectoral wage settlements was largely confined to EMU countries, whose sheltered sector employers lost important institutions that increased their bargaining strength. However, the deterioration in sectoral wage relations exhibited large variations across EMU countries after 1999. In Ireland and Spain (whose EMU experiences with rising wage inflation are outlined more thoroughly in chapter 6), the deterioration was most pronounced; differences in annual wage growth between the education, health, and public administration composite and manufacturing grew by over 1.3 percent a year, translating into a 13 percent wage gap in favor of the sheltered sector over ten years (see figure 1.3, EU KLEMS 2010). In contrast, Austria and Germany witnessed higher levels of sheltered sector wage growth suppression under EMU, as manufacturing wage growth surpassed wage growth in education, health, and public administration by a greater extent after 1999 than under the EMS/Maastricht era. Connecting these developments to countries under heavy exposure to the current crisis, the rise in sheltered sector wage growth in EMU's peripheral economies (Ireland, Italy, Portugal, and Spain) between 1999 and 2007 was twice that of EMU's northern core (Austria, Belgium, Finland, France, Germany, and the Netherlands).

Though sheltered sector employers in EMU's core and periphery experienced EMU's governance vacuum, employers in the core appeared better equipped to manage it than their peripheral counterparts. National corporatist institutions gave wage-setters in the exposed sector and/or the state veto and agenda-setting powers in national wage bargaining and therefore acted as a crucial governance substitute for national central banks and EMU conditionality within EMU's northern economies, shielding them from the potential inflationary effects of sheltered sector wage growth after 1999. By facilitating the continuance of sheltered sector wage moderation under the single currency, these institutions helped EMU's core economies maintain price competitiveness and healthy current account surpluses before entering the crisis.

Promoting a Corporatist Comparative Advantage: EMU's Favoritism Toward Low-Inflation Labor Markets

EMU allowed differences in the domestic wage-setting politics governing inflation performance within corporatist and noncorporatist economies to unfold. EMU's predecessors harmonized inflation constraints across fragmented, non-corporatist and coordinated, corporatist labor market institutions. The removal of these constraints eliminated macroeconomic devices that delivered order to peripheral labor markets. Admittedly, wage inflation in EMU's southern economies did not return to their pre-Maastricht levels. Inflation rates within these economies were quite subdued compared to the 1980s. What destined the periphery toward persistent (price) competitive decline under EMU was not merely the removal of low-inflation-favoring domestic institutions, but more importantly, the establishment of a real exchange rate that penalized countries with *relatively* high inflation rates.

In an international system with multiple currencies, a country's real exchange rate (RER) is a function of a its nominal exchange rate, e, multiplied by the ratio of the domestic to foreign price level ($RER = e\frac{P_d}{P_f}$). Under a flexible exchange rate system, or permissive peg, a country's inflation rate does not directly impact the real exchange rate because the nominal exchange rate provides a buffer. National currencies that are prone to high inflation lose their relative value to currencies that are prone to low inflation, and these declining nominal exchange rates consequently blunt the impact of (high) domestic inflation on the real exchange rate. Under a hard peg, such as that provided by Maastricht or ERM's more restrictive +/−2.25 percent exchange rate band, countries lose their nominal exchange rate as an adjustment mechanism, but witness inflation convergence with their fixed exchange rate partners due to the common (low-inflation) monetary policies undertaken by national central banks. In removing both the nominal exchange rate and national central banks that promoted inflation convergence, monetary union transformed the real exchange rates of its member-states to a simple relative inflation ratio ($RER = \frac{P_d}{P_f}$). This ultimately meant that member-states that could persistently undercut their trading partners' inflation performance, *without* the assistance of national central banks, would realize persistent improvements in their real exchange rate. In other words, EMU was structured in such a way that countries that could not match or undercut their trading partners' inflation performances, even if their performance was an improvement from historical trends, would be destined for persistent competitive decline.

Sectoral wage politics help explain why some countries are better able to undercut their common currency trade-partners than others. Emphasized in the dual-sector framework, exposed sector employers (and unions) have clear incentives to exert wage moderation in order to enhance output and maintain employment. As a consequence of these common international trade competitiveness incentives, exposed sectors within countries sharing a common currency converge in their wage inflation behavior. Therefore, in light of *tradable goods* price convergence, what matters most for relative domestic inflation performance in a monetary union is the level of wage discipline in *nontradable* sectors. Real exchange rate developments are crucially linked inflationary pressures within the sheltered sector. This places wage-setters in the exposed sector in a precarious position vis-à-vis their sheltered sector counterparts: while the former have incentives to moderate wages in order to remain (price) competitive, the latter do not but are able to influence the employment status in the former if they set wages too high.

Under EMU, exposed sector wage-setters had to rely on national institutions to deliver wage discipline within their sheltered sectors. Because their wage coordination systems granted the exposed sector high political leverage in national wage bargaining, either directly or indirectly via the state, EMU's core economies were better equipped with disciplinary wage-bargaining institutions than peripheral ones. The core's wage-setting regimes that severely curtailed sheltered sector wage growth maintained the low-inflation rates that were needed to undercut its (noncorporatist) EMU trading partners. As a result of its persistently lower relative inflation rates, these countries had more competitive RERs and improving trade and current account surpluses under EMU. With their growing current account surpluses, the EMU core accumulated domestic savings, which made them external net creditors and therefore spared them from speculative crisis. EMU's peripheral economies, which did not have wage-setting institutions that could enforce persistent austere wage moderation within sheltered sectors, suffered opposing fates.

What political dynamics existed in the core's labor market institutions that allowed these countries to so severely moderate sheltered sector wage growth? Historically, and presently, the export sector carries significant leverage within the EMU core's domestic political realm because of its prowess in national economic success—this prowess is further enhanced internationally by product niches in high value-added goods (Hall and Soskice 2001). Export-favoring domestic politics align with wage coordination institutions that grant these actors (or the state acting in the exposed sector's interests) veto or agenda-setting powers in national bargaining. Recent scholarship in sectoral wage-setting politics (Brandl 2012; Johnston, Hancké, and Pant 2014) highlights that export-favoring coordination mechanisms come in three forms: "pattern bargaining" systems, where exposed sector firms act as trendsetters (Germany and Austria); state-imposed coordination regimes that grant the state unilateral power to deliver public sector pay outcomes in line with export-sector preferences (France and Belgium); and state-led wage pacts where social partners bargain in the state's *shadow of hierarchy* and the state has the unilateral *capacity* to establish productivity-based wage ceilings or, in times of crisis, wage freezes if social partners fail to negotiate wage restraint (Finland and the Netherlands in the early 2000s).

Under Germany and Austria's pattern bargaining system, the exposed sector (IG Metall in Germany and the Metalworking and Textiles Union, GMT, in Austria) establishes wage agreements first, which serve as upper limits for subsequent sectoral wage settlements (Traxler and Brandl 2010). Belgium, whose government had a history of repeated interventions in wage-setting in the early 1980s, formally institutionalized its state-imposed coordination system in its 1996 wage competitiveness law. While Belgian social partners are able to negotiate wages independent of the state, the 1996 law provides government with the legal capacity to impose ceilings on national wage settlements if they exceed the average established in Germany, France, and the Netherlands, Belgium's three largest trading partners (Pochet 2004). France's state-imposed coordination system is less formal than Belgium's and revolves more exclusively around public sector wage settlements than national wages. Similar to Germany and Austria's pattern bargaining system, the French government uses the collective agreements of large exporter firms, which act as non-negotiable benchmarks for the public sector (Hancké 2002).

Contrary to pattern bargaining and the state-imposed system, which grant exposed wage-setters or the state a more permanent monitoring role in wage-setting, state-led wage pacts lead to indirect, and often temporary, involvement by the state in wage-setting. In the Netherlands, whose coalition governments have historically endorsed and enforced low-inflation macroeconomic policies, these state-led pacts are the institutional means by which the state coerces social partners to deliver wage moderation when inflation spirals are imminent. Dutch state-led wage pacts have been used reactively by the state in response to sudden increases in inflation (as was the case with the 1982 Wassenaar Agreement and its early 2000s wage pacts, which are discussed more thoroughly in chapter 4). The terms of these state-led wage pacts involve either nominal wage ceilings or wage freezes, which are subject to legislative decrees if they are not met. State-led wage pacts are not usually permanent systems of coordination, as these pacts tend to be reactively used to respond to economic crisis. Nevertheless, when implemented, they can correct wage inflation across the entire economy, including sheltered sectors, even though such interventions may only provide temporary remedies.

Nonexport-favoring wage coordination systems either provide sheltered sector interests with greater political leverage or seriously undermine the exposed sector's capacity to exert its dominance/leadership in national bargaining due to fragmentation (Spain and Greece) or the lack of representation in peak-level institutions (multinational corporations in Ireland). These sheltered sector-favoring systems assume the following forms: peak bargaining coordination systems, where both exposed and sheltered sector unions are united under a confederal umbrella (Greece, Italy, Spain, and Portugal); uncoordinated regimes where sheltered sector wage-setters bargain independently with employers (the United States and United Kingdom); and nonstate-led wage pacts (or "state sponsored") coordination regimes, where the government helps to facilitate the conclusion of national wage pacts between union and employer peak-level confederations but lacks the power to directly intervene in wage-setting on the behalf of exposed sector preferences (Ireland). The predominance of the three types of coordination regimes in the EMU South are reflective of domestic politics that favor national economic champions that are more sheltered in nature (construction in Ireland and Spain; tourism in Greece, Portugal, and Spain; and the public sector in Greece, Italy, and Portugal). Ireland, whose economic model is centered around its export-oriented multinational corporations, is a deviation from this trend, although I highlight in chapter 6 how this "Celtic tiger" inherited a collective-bargaining system organized around the dominance of its public sector, due to its multinational firms' lack of representation in Ireland's peak union confederation.

Peak bargaining coordination systems led by highly politicized social partners are particularly problematic for (sheltered sector) wage inflation if peak-level union confederations are unable to unify sectoral conflicts within the labor movement. Peak bargaining is *shelter sector dominated* when sheltered/public sector unions hold greater membership than those in the export sector. Italy, Spain, Portugal, and Greece best conform to this system. As highlighted in greater detail in chapter 6, the cohesiveness of Spanish peak bargaining, and the ability of export sector interests to articulate their preferences within it, is further complicated by regional/provincial bargaining fragmentation. Though public and private sector unions in Portugal bargain under a united confederal umbrella, the General Confederation of Portuguese Workers (CGTP), Portugal's *public administration sector* has increasingly assumed the role of a trendsetter in peak bargaining since the 1990s.[22] Like Spain, the three different levels of bargaining (firm, sectoral, and peak-level) within Greece's confederal umbrellas have few systematic interlinks. Unlike Spain, however, Greek sectoral bargaining is highly fragmented along party-political lines and is further marred in the public sector by clientelistic relationships (Christopoulou and Monastiriotis 2014b). Despite these cases, peak-level bargaining can be conducive toward delivering sheltered sector wage restraint if the exposed sector's influence is upheld by its higher membership representation. *Export sector dominated* peak bargaining, for example, exists in Denmark, where the manufacturing sector's dominance within the Danish Confederation of Trade Unions (LO) has been maintained by the formation of the CO-Metal export cartel in 1992 (see chapter 4).

Wage inflation problems that stem from sheltered sector dominance in peak-level confederations are also present in nonstate-led wage pact systems

(Ireland). Unlike state-led pacts, where the state has an indirect role in monitoring inflationary wage settlements, nonstate-led pacts lack the presence of (threatened) government intervention in the event of high inflation or economic crisis. Nonstate-led wage pacts are delivered by peak-level confederations, but their conclusion and enforcement relies on the collective compliance of affiliates; the state has little capacity to ensure that concluded wage levels stay within or below agreed limits. Under EMU, Ireland's nonstate-led wage pacts were more aligned with the preferences of the public sector because the dynamic multinational sector is nonunionized and hence representatively absent in the Irish Congress of Trade Unions (Regan 2012).

Finally, uncoordinated bargaining regimes are more sheltered sector "neutral" than (shelter sector dominated) peak bargaining and nonstate-led wage pact regimes. If wage-setters in an uncoordinated regime individually agree on wage settlements that are equivalent to inflation (or average wage increases), differences in sectoral wage growth should be nil (Baumol and Bowen 1965). If, however, wages are set according to a neoclassical framework, where workers receive pay awards based on their productivity, these regimes may produce negative pay differentials between sheltered sectors and manufacturing, as the former tends to consist of service sectors where productivity growth is lower than in goods-based production sectors. Despite these two possible worlds, uncoordinated bargaining systems do not have the capacity to deliver the degree of national wage suppression that exist in the three export-favoring collective-bargaining regimes outlined previously, as fragmentation inhibits employers' capacity to coordinate and moderate wage growth in *all* sheltered sectors. The debilitation of export (and sheltered) sector union organizational capacity was the intended result of "union busting" initiatives undertaken by the neoliberal Regan and Thatcher governments in the 1980s. Moreover, these regimes have the capacity to be wage inflationary if *wage inequality* leads to disproportionate wage increases at the upper end of the income distribution. In the United States and the United Kingdom, these above-productivity wage increases are common in high-skill services such as finance and legal services. These six typologies of export and sheltered sector favoring coordination systems, and where they exist among developed economies under the pre-crisis EMU years, are detailed in table 2.3.

With the relinquishment of national inflation-averse central banks and the Maastricht criteria, countries with bargaining regimes conducive toward limiting sheltered sector wage growth (those in the left-hand column of table 2.3) witnessed the continuation of sheltered sector wage moderation under EMU. This resulted in low aggregate inflation and, thanks to EMU's exchange rate bias toward low inflation, a persistently competitive real exchange rate, current account surpluses, and ultimately increased net external lending. Countries that

TABLE 2.3. Wage moderation by bargaining regime and country (1999–2007)

EXPORT-SECTOR FAVORING COLLECTIVE-BARGAINING REGIMES	SHELTER-SECTOR FAVORING COLLECTIVE-BARGAINING REGIMES
Pattern bargaining: Austria, Germany, Japan, Sweden	*Peak-level bargaining*: – ED: Denmark (1999, 2001–2007), Finland (2001 & 2007), Netherlands (1999–2001, 2006–2007) – SD: Greece, Italy, Portugal, Spain
State-imposed wage laws/state coordination: Belgium, France	
State-led wage pacts: Denmark (2000), Finland (1999–2000, 2002–2006), the Netherlands (2002–2005)	*No coordination*: Australia, Canada, United Kingdom, United States
	Nonstate-led wage pacts: Ireland

SOURCE: Brandl 2012, Visser 2011, European Industrial Relations Observatory (various articles).
ED indicates export-sector dominated, SD indicates shelter-sector dominated.

possessed coordinated bargaining institutions that were not conducive to sheltered sector wage moderation (right-hand column of table 2.3) witnessed a deterioration in sheltered sector wage moderation under EMU's less-constraining institutional regime. The rise of sheltered sector wage inflation in these countries after 1999, though not excessive compare to pre-Maastricht levels, led to a rise in relative inflation (to the EMU North), an uncompetitive real exchange rate, and current account deficits that required net external borrowing to finance. In removing pivotal institutions that enabled sheltered sector employers to deliver wage moderation, leading to inflation convergence, and establishing a real exchange rate that was solely a function of relative inflation, EMU established a clear distinction between Europe's low-inflation corporatist "haves" and "have-nots." Countries with export-favoring institutions could continue with business as usual. More advantageous for them, competitiveness wise, they could also take advantage of sheltered sector-favoring corporatist institutions in the EMU South to enhance their external trade and lending positions in EMU's pre-crisis years.

Pairing the constraints in place under the EMS and Maastricht against the relative governance vacuum under EMU provides an institutional explanation for the persistent rise in current imbalances between the North and South under monetary union. Due to national commitments under the ERM and Maastricht, sheltered employers in both the EMU North and the EMU South possessed greater leverage in wage negotiations vis-à-vis unions, as the employment and EMU membership costs associated with wage inflation rose. The deliverance of sheltered sector wage moderation had important implications for inflation convergence and improved price competitiveness. Especially during the 1990s, when all EMU candidate countries made impressive inroads toward lowering inflation and public deficits, current account imbalances between the North and South were relatively contained. Sheltered sector employers in all countries were equipped with the same commitment devices, yielding unseen convergence in inflation rates across the North and South. The pre-EMU experience demonstrated that adoption of restrictive macroeconomic policies, via participation in international monetary and rules-based arrangements that enable sheltered employers to develop reputations for being "tough" wage negotiators, could suppress exposed/sheltered sector cleavages and harmonize the inflation performance of diverse wage-setting systems.

When the context such restrictive macroeconomic policies disappears—as it did under monetary union—potential for conflict reemerges. Since sheltered and public sector employers had greater leeway to pass rising labor costs onto prices, they became more inclined to concede to high wage demands made by the unions with which they negotiated. Yet such developments did not play out equally in all Eurozone economies. Economies with coordinated bargaining institutions that granted the exposed sector and/or the state an agenda-setting or veto role were able to use these institutions as a functional substitute for the orderly pre-EMU regime. Sheltered employers in EMU's peripheral economies, however, had neither the confined institutions of the EMS/Maastricht regimes nor the functional wage coordination institutions that could deliver a necessary check on sheltered sector wage growth. Sheltered sector wage moderation deteriorated relative to that in the EMU core. Relative inflation and current account imbalances emerged, threatening national economic stability.

The next chapter provides an empirical assessment of the two theoretical linkages explained here. First, the link between inflation-averse central banks at the national level and the Maastricht convergence criteria, on the one hand, and sectoral wage dynamics on the other, are tested using a panel analysis of seventeen OECD countries from 1980 to 2007. Using the same sample, the second part of the chapter analyzes the link between sheltered sector wage suppression and export success. I demonstrate that that export-favoring wage governance institutions helped maintain competitiveness for countries that possessed them, and that the effect of these institutions on export growth was particularly magnified under monetary union.

MONETARY REGIMES, WAGE BARGAINING, AND THE CURRENT ACCOUNT CRISIS IN THE EMU SOUTH

Empirical Evidence

Both institutional linkages outlined in chapter 2—that EMU led to a bifurcation in sectoral wage developments within its member states and that, despite this bifurcation, employers in northern EMU economies utilized corporatist bargaining arrangements to persistently undercut the trade performance of their southern EMU neighbors after 1999—are different in nature and require different empirical analyses to assess their validity. Given the complexity of the argument, I present these empirical analyses in two parts: first by examining the empirical association between EMU conditionality and *national* central banks' enforcement of low inflation, on the one hand, and sectoral wage dynamics on the other; second, by examining the empirical association between sheltered sector wage suppression and trade performance. I begin by presenting an empirical analysis of how EMU contributed to a prominent bifurcation in sheltered and exposed sector wages within its member states, setting the stage for inflation and real exchange rate divergence between the EMU North and South.

Falling into Line: The Dampening Effects of National Central Banks and Maastricht Conditionality on Wage Growth

Figures 1.2 and 1.3 provide a summary of sectoral wage dynamics for countries that participated in the EMS, Maastricht, and EMU regimes. Both the rise in sheltered sector wage inflation and wage growth, vis-à-vis the manufacturing sector, conspicuously emerges for the EMU10 near the introduction of the euro. However, both figures neglect the inclusion of other factors that could have contributed to the suppression of sheltered sector wage growth before 1999 in EMU economies, and exclude counterfactuals of sheltered sector wage dynamics in other economies that did not join monetary union in 1999. Here, I utilize a cross-sectional, time-series analysis of seventeen OECD countries[1] from 1979 to 2007 to test how EMU's altercation of economic penalties associated with sheltered sector wage inflation impacted sectoral wage differentials after 1998. For the sample end year, 2007 was selected because the onset of the debt crisis and the extraordinary pressure that markets and external creditors placed on peripheral sovereigns to cut wages mark the current crisis period as a sharp deviation from how employers would traditionally operate.

While both differences in sectoral wage inflation (inclusive of sectoral productivity) and differences in sectoral wage growth (exclusive of sectoral productivity) gauge wage suppression in the sheltered sector, wage growth differentials are selected as the primary dependent variable in the examination of the link between EMU regime change and sectoral wage bifurcation. This is done to focus on components of wage-setting that actors have formal control over. Employers and unions generally cannot bargain over the delivery of productivity increases, but they do bargain over the determination of wages. Furthermore, focusing only on wage growth differentials, rather than wage inflation differentials that include sectoral productivity differences, removes contamination problems of monetary union's influence on sectoral productivity dynamics in isolation of wages. EMU may alter sectoral productivity differences through trade integration's enhancement of exposed sector productivity—also known as the Balassa/Samuelson effect (Balassa 1964; Samuelson 1964). Including both wage growth and productivity growth in the conceptualization of sheltered sector wage suppression captures two wage inflation "effects," one operating through wage bargaining power and one through productivity. The use of productivity differentials as a control, rather than in the dependent variable itself, rectifies this problem.

One of the central assumptions of the theoretical framework established in chapter 2 is that exposed sector wage-setters have greater incentives to limit their wages relative to sheltered sectors. These incentives exist because, in the presence of greater competition and available substitutes of goods, price increases result in more substantial reductions in output and employment for the exposed sector. Due to these diverging incentives, wage developments in the exposed sector provide a helpful benchmark in assessing sheltered sector wage suppression. Wage developments in all sectors follow cyclical patterns according to growth and employment trends, and focusing on sheltered sector wage growth in isolation of wage developments in other sectors may not reflect wage militancy per se, but rather economic overheating or employment shortages. Selecting the manufacturing sector as a benchmark can help account for common developments in the *general* economy; wages in both the manufacturing and sheltered sectors are subject to common national economic shocks, and assessing sheltered sector wage growth relative to wage growth in the manufacturing sector partially accounts for these common cyclical trends. Yet merely anchoring sheltered sector wage growth to manufacturing does not overcome divergences in *sectoral* economic conditions, such as differences in sectoral labor demand and productivity growth. These factors, however, can be accounted for via the inclusion of relative sectoral controls (employment growth, productivity developments, etc.) in a formal regression model.

Figure 3.1 provides summary time-series data for differences in sheltered and exposed sector wage moderation for the EMU10—if differences are positive/negative, annual wage growth in the sheltered sector has surpassed/undercut that in the manufacturing sector. For EMU's peripheral economies, the EMS and Maastricht regimes were marked by considerable volatility in sheltered and manufacturing sector wage differentials. Ireland's success in reining in sheltered sector wage growth through the 1987 Programme for National Recovery agreement (see chapter 6) was visible in the marked decline in sheltered and manufacturing sector wage differentials in the late 1980s, while Italy's successes in reining in sheltered sector wage moderation through its abolition of *scala mobile*, introduction of public sector reforms, and the linking of wage increases to government macroeconomic targets (Levy 1999; Ebbinghaus and Hassel 2000; Baccaro 2003) was marked by a persistent lull in sheltered sector wage growth, relative to manufacturing wage growth, in the early and mid-1990s. In some EMU core economies, sheltered sector wage growth consistently remained below that of the manufacturing sector during the pre-Maastricht EMS period; sheltered sector wage suppression was particularly pronounced in Belgium and the Netherlands, where governments undertook measures in the early 1980s to severely curtail public sector wage growth. Under EMU, Ireland, Italy, Portugal, and Spain had, on average, positive wage growth differentials between the sheltered and manufacturing sector—indicating rising wage gaps in favor of the sheltered sector—while Austria, Belgium, Finland, Germany, and, to a lesser extent, France and the Netherlands had negative wage growth differentials between the sheltered and manufacturing sector on average—indicating rising wage gaps in favor of the manufacturing sector.

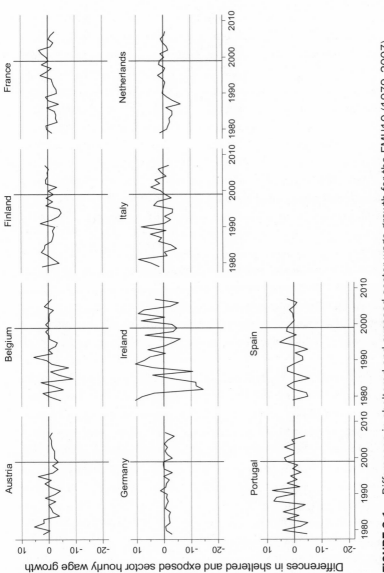

Differences in sheltered and exposed hourly wage growth

FIGURE 3.1. Differences in sheltered and exposed sector wage growth for the EMU10 (1979–2007)

Note: The solid vertical line delineates the start of European Monetary Union in 1999. The solid horizontal line delineates whether sheltered sector wage growth overshoots that in the manufacturing sector (in which case the value would be above the horizontal line) or whether sheltered sector wage growth undershot wage growth in the manufacturing sector (values below the horizontal line). Greece is omitted due to the lack of consistent data. Source: EU KLEMS Database (2010).

Conceptualizing Central Banks' Monetary Threats and Supranational Regime Change

Central bank inflation-aversion and the monetary threats they impose have been subject to a variety of conceptualizations and definitions in political economy. The most commonly used proxy is central bank independence (CBI). Central bank independence indices often are constructed to incorporate higher values to banks that are more inflation-averse than society/policymakers. Bade and Parkin's (1982) and Grilli, Masciandaro, and Tabellini's (1991) central bank independence indices assign higher values of independence to banks where the statutory requirement of the pursuit of monetary stability exists among its goals. Cukierman's (1992) legal central bank independence index, one of the most widely used in political economy literature, shares many similarities to the other two indices, yet presents two major advantages over them. First, its components are more detailed, including further information on the central bank's board and chairman's appointments and term, which better assess whether central bankers have the (independent) political capacity to conduct the bank's statutory monetary policy objectives. Second, Cukierman's index also includes a more detailed codification system of *instrumental* independence, including limitations on lending to the government, limitations of lending in terms of loan maturity, and limitations on the setting of interest rates on bonds.

Though the Cukierman central bank independence index is widely used as a proxy for monetary conservatism, it has two major disadvantages in the examination of the impact of central banks' inflation non-accommodation on sectoral wage dynamics. First, the index itself has limited variation over time. Across the seventeen countries used in the analysis here, central bank independence changes at most twice per country over the 1979–2007 period, while for several countries (Australia, Canada, Denmark, and the United States), legal central bank independence remains unaltered over the entire period. Second, the index is an input variable and may not successfully predict the *deliverance* of anti-inflation monetary policy over time. Torben Iversen explains that "central bank independence is neither a necessary, nor a sufficient, condition for commitment to a conservative monetary policy" (Iversen 1999a, 58). Central banks that adopt an anti-inflationary policy indirectly via membership in a fixed exchange rate system, where the anchor currency is anti-inflationary, or even directly via the use of an inflation target, rather than through the explicit statement of a price stability objective within a legal statute, are assigned lower central bank independence values than central banks where price stability is explicitly mentioned in its legal charter. This distinction in CBI coding values effectively penalizes central banks that strongly uphold commitments to price stability and low inflation yet do not have a price stability objective explicitly written into law. Likewise, the legal codification of price stability does not imply that central banks will deliver it. Countries with high levels of central bank independence can fall victim to high inflation if conservative monetary policies are defeated through expansionary fiscal policies, exhortation, and political threats (Iversen 1999a). Hence, what is required to truly gauge the degree of central bank non-accommodation toward inflation is not only an input variable, but also an output variable that measures markets' confidence in the fulfillment of a non-accommodating stance toward inflation.

In his measurement of monetary non-accommodation, Iversen (1999a) relies on movements in nominal effective exchange rates to gauge the degree of confidence in a conservative monetary policy. Dornbusch (1976) outlines that exchange rate movements serve as a suitable proxy for central bank commitment to low inflation. Under perfect capital mobility, monetary tightness, particularly in response to output decline, will raise confidence in a currency, leading to its gradual appreciation (explaining why core Deutsch mark countries in the 1980s had appreciating nominal exchange rates vis-à-vis their southern European trading partners, whose higher inflation rates eroded their currencies' value). If a central bank commits itself to an anti-inflationary policy stance, the success of such a commitment will be revealed over time in the form of a strong and (relatively) appreciating currency. Iversen (1999a) notes, however, two problems in using changes in the nominal effective exchange rate alone as a proxy for central bank non-accommodation toward inflation. First, exchange rates are sensitive to short-run speculative pressures, a problem that has serious implications for some sample countries during the 1992 Exchange Rate Mechanism (ERM) crisis. Second, they can "exaggerate" monetary policy changes because nominal exchange rates, especially outside of "hard-peg" fixed exchange rate systems, can be quite volatile. To address the first problem, Iversen utilizes (normalized) four-year period averages of changes in the nominal effective exchange rate. To address the second problem, he combines the effect of these four-year averages with the central bank independence index, which is more stable over time, by averaging the two (normalized) values. Iversen's final index, ranging from 0 to 1, provides a more effective proxy for monetary non-accommodation toward inflation than crude regime dummies, with higher values indicating greater inflation aversion of a central bank.

My measure for central banks' monetary threat toward inflation is constructed in an identical manner to Iversen's index, with three modifications. One, I use four-year *moving* averages rather than static averages, maintaining a larger sample size and a larger number of time units over the EMU period (if four-year static averages were used then EMU would be represented, at most, by two four-year periods). Two, the normalized nominal effective exchange rate is averaged with the Cukierman (1992) central bank independence index only,[2] as his is the most detailed and updated of the three that Iversen uses. Three, in order to capture EMU's altercation of the monetary threat on sheltered employers, the index is *weighted according to the sheltered sector employment share within an economy the central bank targets.* This is crucial to examining the impact of monetary union on wage developments, as EMU substantially decreased the weight of the sheltered sector in aggregate inflation developments. Countries with the European Central Bank (ECB) as their central bank after 1999 witnessed a lower *conditional* non-accommodation index, as sheltered sector wage-setters became too small to influence EMU aggregate inflation. Weighting Iversen's non-accommodation index in this manner produces a conditional monetary threat for sheltered sector employers; non-accommodating central banks matter to sheltered sector employers *only* if their size is significant enough to generate monetary response. If central banks, such as the ECB, are non-accommodating but the sheltered sector bears a minimal weight in their inflation reaction functions, sheltered sector employers come under less pressure from a monetary authority to reduce wage growth.

For countries under EMU, the ECB's non-accommodation index is weighted against national sheltered sector employment relative to total employment within the EMU economy (see figure 3.2, which presents the conditional central bank non-accommodation index for the seventeen OECD sample countries). Weighting the non-accommodation index captures the feasibility of a monetary threat against sheltered sector unions, because it accounts for their size in the relevant inflation aggregate. It also enables one to determine whether the EMU effect was heterogeneous according to country size. German unions, for example, may continue to observe wage moderation under EMU, given that they constitute a more notable (albeit much smaller compared to the EMS and Maastricht regimes) share of the (European) central bank's targeted labor force. A monetary threat should be less acute for sheltered sector employers in small states because these wage-setters carry minimal weight in the European Central Bank's reaction function.

Unlike central bank inflation aversion, Maastricht conditionality and monetary union regime change have received a more systematic conceptualization, generally via binary regime dummies (see Johnston 2012). This is largely due to candidate countries' homogenous urgency to fulfill Maastricht and the homogenous application of monetary union to candidate countries once they joined the euro. Here, Maastricht conditionality is defined via a simple dummy variable. EMU candidate countries (Austria, Belgium, Finland, France, Germany, Ireland, Italy, the Netherlands, Portugal, and Spain) received a coding of 1 for the

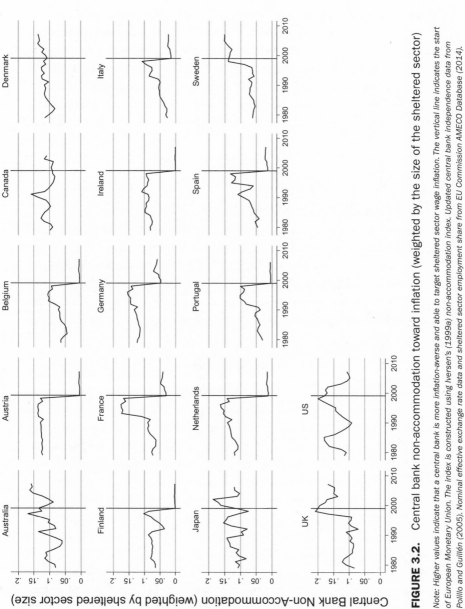

FIGURE 3.2. Central bank non-accommodation toward inflation (weighted by the size of the sheltered sector)

Note: Higher values indicate that a central bank is more inflation-averse and able to target sheltered sector wage inflation. The vertical line indicates the start of European Monetary Union. The index is constructed using Iversen's (1999a) non-accommodation index. Updated central bank independence data from Polillo and Guillén (2005). Nominal effective exchange rate data and sheltered sector employment share from EU Commission AMECO Database (2014).

years 1992–1998, and 0 if otherwise in order to delineate the presence of Maastricht conditionality. Non-EMU candidate countries (Australia, Canada, Denmark, Japan, Sweden, the United Kingdom, and the United States) receive a Maastricht regime coding of 0 for the entire 1979–2007 period. In addition to being incorporated into the central bank non-accommodation index, the "EMU effect" is also measured via a crude dummy variable (embodying the value of 1 for EMU countries between the years 1999–2007, and 0 if otherwise). However, given that this dummy variable and the monetary non-accommodation index assess the same monetary regime shift, these two variables do not simultaneously serve as explanatory variables of sheltered sector wage dynamics within a given regression model.

The Great Unraveling: Monetary Union's Perverse Effects on Sheltered Sector Wage Suppression

A standard neoclassical wage growth equilibrium model, where sectoral wage growth differentials are a function of sectoral productivity growth differentials between the sheltered and manufacturing sector, is used to analyze the relationship between EMU regime change and wage suppression in the sheltered sector. Appendix II provides full details on how all variables were measured and the sources from which data were taken. This baseline model can be summarized as follows:

$$w_{s,i,t} - w_{m,i,t} = \alpha_{i,t} + \beta_1 a_{s,i,t} - a_{m,i,t} + \beta_2 \text{Maastricht}_{i,t} + \beta_3 \text{EMU}_{i,t} + \beta_4 \text{MT}_{i,t} + \varepsilon_{i,t}$$

$w_{s,i,t} - w_{m,i,t}$ is the difference in annual sheltered sector and manufacturing hourly wages in country i in year t, as featured in figure 3.1; if this value is positive/negative, hourly sheltered sector wage growth overshoots/undershoots wage growth in the manufacturing sector. $a_{s,i,t} - a_{m,i,t}$ is the difference in annual changes in sheltered sector and manufacturing productivity, where sectoral gross value added per hour worked serves as a proxy for sectoral productivity. This variable should be positively associated with sectoral wage differentials, because if the sheltered sector realizes greater increases in productivity compared to the manufacturing sector, it should also realize greater increases in wages, as a neoclassical wage equilibrium model predicts. $\varepsilon_{i,t}$ is the error term.

Maastricht$_{i,t}$ and EMU$_{i,t}$ are institutional dummies indicating whether country is subject to the Maastricht criteria or to European Economic and Monetary Union, respectively, in year t. I begin first with a simple event analysis of the Maastricht and EMU regime dummies to assess whether there were significant differences in national sectoral wage dynamics under these different institutional arrangements (the baseline temporal category is the non-EMU/Maastricht period). These regime dummies are presented in model I of table 3.2. Monetary union should exhibit a positive relationship with sheltered and manufacturing sector wage growth differentials, indicating greater bifurcation between their wage developments, while the Maastricht dummy should either exhibit a negative association or a non-significant association with sectoral wage differentials, *relative to the non-EMU/Maastricht baseline period.*

$MT_{i,t}$ is the more detailed central bank non-accommodation index toward inflation for country i at time t, weighted by the size of a country's sheltered sector to the total economy over which a central bank presides. This conceptualization of EMU regime change, by its influence on the *monetary threat* posed by central banks, is presented in models II, III and IV of table 3.2. This monetary threat was enhanced for EMU candidate countries under the EMS and Maastricht periods and was weakened under EMU. For non-EMU countries, this threat would be enhanced if national central banks adopted a less accommodating stance toward inflation over time. The monetary threat should be significantly associated with lower or negative differentials between sheltered sector and manufacturing wage growth. This could be the result of one of two causes: 1) embodying dynamics of the EMS/Maastricht period, sheltered sector wage growth should undercut wage growth in manufacturing as central banks become more inflation-averse and/or 2) embodying dynamics of the EMU period, sheltered sector wage growth should surpass wage growth in the manufacturing sector as the ECB loses the capacity to monitor sectoral wage inflation in individual member-states.

Several economic and institutional controls were added to the baseline neoclassical wage growth equilibrium model. These include differences in sheltered sector and manufacturing sector employment growth and net public lending. A lag rather than the present value of differences in sectoral employment growth was included as a control in order to partially overcome endogeneity problems with the dependent variable—employment growth differentials also may be determined by wage growth differentials. Because much of the sheltered sector composite lies in the public sector, net government lending (as a percentage of GDP) was incorporated as a control within the regressions. A lag term of net public lending was used given endogeneity problems with the dependent variable—higher fiscal deficits may be caused by high wage growth within the (sheltered) public sector. Net public lending should be positively associated with sheltered and manufacturing sector wage differentials; past deficits (negative balances) should prompt (sheltered) public employers to limit present sheltered sector wage increases. GDP growth was specifically *excluded* given endogeneity problems with the dependent variable and multicollinearity problems with sectoral productivity differentials.

In addition to economic variables, several institutional controls were introduced that may affect bargaining power dynamics between the sheltered and manufacturing sector. These controls include wage-bargaining centralization, intersectoral wage coordination, partisanship, and relative sectoral union density. Given that centralization promotes wage compression between sectors (Kahn 1998; Wallerstein 1999), wage-bargaining centralization should have a positive association with sheltered and manufacturing sector wage growth differentials; sheltered sector unions should secure higher wage growth relative to manufacturing in more centralized regimes than decentralized regimes. Bargaining centralization, based on Iversen's (1999a) wage centralization index, ranges from 0 (no union centralization) to 1 (monopoly union centralization). Because bargaining centralization misses the important role of wage coordination between sectors as an institutional constraint on sheltered sector wage growth, an *export-favoring* wage coordination governance dummy, based on the six coordination regimes discussed in chapter 2, is also incorporated into the neoclassical wage growth model. Intersectoral wage coordination is crucial in explaining why the EMU core remained effective at limiting sheltered sector wage growth after 1999, as these countries possessed coordination mechanisms where either the export sector or the state could exert agenda-setting or veto powers over wage settlements in other sectors. Countries received a coding of 1 if they possessed one of the three export-favoring sectoral wage coordination institutions identified in chapter 2 (pattern bargaining, state-imposed coordination, or state-led wage pacts) during a given year, and 0 if national wage coordination was uncoordinated, conducted exclusively by peak-bargaining confederations, or facilitated by nonstate-led wage pacts.

Descriptive statistics, presented in table 3.1, indicate that on average, export-favoring sectoral coordination regimes were more effective at limiting sheltered sector wages relative to those in the manufacturing sector across the seventeen OECD country panel. Pattern bargaining systems, state-imposed wage coordination, and state-led wage pacts, on average, kept wage growth in the sheltered sector below that of the manufacturing by 0.66 percent, 1.14 percent, and 0.41 percent, respectively, every year, translating into 6.6 percent, 11.4 percent, and 4.1 percent wage gaps, respectively, in favor of the manufacturing sector over the span of a decade. Peak bargaining systems, whether (representatively) dominated by export sector unions or sheltered sector unions, uncoordinated wage-bargaining regimes, and nonstate-led wage pacts, were less effective at limiting sheltered sector wage growth compared to their export-favoring coordination counterparts, as indicated by their narrower and, in the case of sheltered-sector dominated peak bargaining and nonstate-led wage pacts, positive wage growth gaps between the sheltered and manufacturing sector.

TABLE 3.1. Differences in sheltered sector and manufacturing sector annual wage growth by bargaining regime (1979–2007 average)

EXPORT-SECTOR FAVORING COLLECTIVE-BARGAINING REGIMES	SHELTER-SECTOR FAVORING COLLECTIVE-BARGAINING REGIMES
Pattern bargaining: −0.66% annual difference	*Peak-level bargaining*: – ED: −0.40 annual difference – SD: 0.32% annual difference
State-imposed wage laws/state coordination: −1.14% annual difference	*No coordination*: −0.29% annual difference
State-led wage pacts: −0.41% annual difference	*Nonstate-led wage pacts*: 0.24% annual difference

ED indicates export-sector dominated, SD indicates shelter-sector dominated. Data from EU KLEMS Database (2010).

Partisanship, measured as the proportion of legislative seats occupied by right-wing parties, was also incorporated as an explanatory variable given the predominance of the sheltered sector composite in the public sector. Rightist legislatures should be negatively correlated with sheltered (public) sector wage growth, and hence differences in public sector and manufacturing wage growth, as right parties are less inclined to raise the public sector wage bill compared to left parties. Finally, the ratio of membership of the three largest public sector affiliates to the three largest exposed-sector affiliates in a country's largest union confederation serves as a rough proxy for the ratio of sheltered sector to exposed sector union density.[3] This indicator should be positively correlated with sheltered and manufacturing wage growth differences—greater representation of public sector affiliates in a country's largest union confederation should provide sheltered sector unions with greater political leverage to push for higher wage increases for their members. Data on the ratio of public to exposed sector membership in a country's largest union confederation, which originates from Traxler and Brandl (2010), is only available over three-year average periods from 1985 to 2002. Therefore, the empirical model that includes this control (model IV, table 3.2) is conducted using three-year static averages for sixteen OECD countries (data for Ireland is unavailable) rather than for yearly data.

An ordinary least squares (OLS) regression model with panel corrected standard errors (PCSE) and a panel-specific Prais-Winsten first-order autoregressive transformation was utilized due to the presence of panel heteroskedasticity and first-order autocorrelation (Beck and Katz 1995).[4] Country dummies were included to control for country-specific omitted variables that are relatively invariant over time,[5] although a random effects estimator was used when the export-favoring wage coordination dummy was included as a control (model III, table 3.2). This was done because five countries (Canada, Ireland, Spain, the United Kingdom, and the United States) witnessed no change in the possession of an export-favoring wage coordination regime; consequently, their sectoral wage coordination regime dummies would exhibit perfect collinearity with their country dummies, causing the variable to lose explanatory power in the presence of high collinearity. Though (country) fixed effects have been criticized for their absorption of level effects in dependent variables (see Kittel and Winner 2005 for an excellent critique), differences in sectoral wage growth follow heavily stochastic processes in the majority of panels, as can be seen in figure 3.1.

Beginning with model I, table 3.2, the empirical result for the EMU dummy suggests that wage growth in EMU's sheltered sectors, relative to wage growth in manufacturing, was on average *0.7 percent higher per year* in countries that participated in monetary union, relative to non-EMU and pre-Maastricht EMS participants. Over a ten-year period in EMU, this would equate to a sectoral wage gap of 7 percent in favor of the sheltered sector, relative to the era of national central banks outside of Maastricht. The Maastricht dummy was not significantly associated with increasing or decreasing sectoral wage growth differentials, indicating that wage growth gaps between the sheltered and manufacturing sector were not significantly different between the Maastricht and non-EMU period, although Wald tests of Maastricht and EMU dummy equivalence indicated that the EMU coefficient was also significantly higher than that for the Maastricht dummy. Maastricht's lack of significance, at least relative to the pre-Maastricht EMS years, is not entirely unanticipated, as most of the EMS's original participants, including Ireland in 1986, made difficult downward adjustments in sheltered sector wages before 1992 (Kelly 2003).

The shelter sector weighted central bank (inflation) non-accommodation index was also significantly associated with reduced wage growth differentials between the sheltered and manufacturing sector, regardless of whether fixed or random effects were used. Providing a frame of reference to examine the magnitude of the monetary threat effect, the average weighted central bank non-accommodation index was 0.083 in the pre-Maastricht EMS period for current EMU member states, growing to 0.113 in the Maastricht years. Given the range of coefficients on the weighted central bank non-accommodation index in table 3.2 (3.7 to 6.9 for the entire seventeen OECD country sample), this would imply that current EMU member-states witnessed a reduction in sheltered and manufacturing wage growth differentials of 0.3 percent to 0.6 percent per year during the pre-Maastricht EMS period (equating to a 3 percent to 6 percent wage gap in favor of manufacturing over a decade) and of 0.4 percent to 0.8 percent per year during the Maastricht years (equating to a 4 percent to 8 percent wage gap in favor of the manufacturing sector over a decade). The transition to EMU was more extreme. The average decrease in the weighted monetary threat in the transition to EMU, due solely to the reduced weight of national sheltered sector wage-setters in the ECB's reaction function, was 0.106 in absolute terms, with large states witnessing smaller absolute reductions and small states witnessing larger reductions. Using the range of beta coefficients on the monetary threat in table 3.2, this implies that under the EMU period, annual sheltered sector growth increased by a magnitude of 0.4 percent to 0.7 percent per year vis-à-vis manufacturing wage growth (producing a 4 percent to 7 percent wage gap in favor of the sheltered sector over the course of a decade), due to the reduced weight of sheltered sector bargaining actors in the ECB's reaction function. These increases would have been subtler for larger countries (i.e., Germany), although the predicted relative increase—0.36 percent to 0.65 percent per annum—is still notable.

In regards to the other economic and institutional variables, only differentials in sectoral productivity growth and the export-favoring coordination regime dummy consistently retained their significance and exhibited the expected relationship with relative sheltered sector wage growth suppression. Rising productivity differentials in favor of the sheltered sector were positively associated with rising differentials in sheltered and manufacturing sector wage growth. The export-favoring wage coordination regime dummy was significantly associated with reduced sheltered sector and manufacturing wage growth differentials. Results from model III, table 3.2, suggest that countries with export-favoring wage coordination regimes yielded roughly 0.4 percent lower annual wage growth differentials (a 4 percent wage gap in favor of the manufacturing sector over a ten-year period) than countries with coordination regimes favoring the sheltered sector. While partisanship, net government lending, and bargaining centralization held the expected associations with sheltered sector and manufacturing wage growth differentials, these variables failed to exhibit significance and, in the case of net government lending, only held significance in one of the three models in which it was included.

The results indicate that EMU, whether embodied as a crude regime dummy or as a detailed measure of its monetary threat, was associated with widening wage growth gaps in favor of the sheltered sector. While wage growth under Maastricht was not significantly different compared to non-EMU participants and the pre-Maastricht EMS years, this dummy exhibited a significantly lower magnitude relative to the EMU dummy. Such results supplement the theoretical predictions of EMU's influence on sectoral wage relations provided in chapter 2. With the removal of Maastricht's conditionality and, more crucially, the significant reduction of sheltered sector wage-setters' weight in the central bank's inflation reaction function, EMU removed pivotal constraints that sheltered employers used

TABLE 3.2.   The influence of EMU and central banks' monetary threat on sectoral wage differences

INDEPENDENT VARIABLES	I	II	III	IV
Maastricht Dummy (1 if present)	0.327 (0.420)			0.251 (0.560)
EMU Dummy (1 if present)	0.700** (0.310)			
Monetary Threat (Weighted)		−4.494** (1.901)	−6.637*** (2.176)	−3.774** (1.849)
Difference in Sectoral Productivity Growth	0.408*** (0.051)	0.407*** (0.051)	0.372*** (0.040)	0.178** (0.079)
Difference in Sectoral Employment Growth (lag)	0.027 (0.054)	0.029 (0.055)	0.051 (0.047)	−0.065 (0.046)
Net Government Lending (lag)	0.041 (0.043)	0.056 (0.049)	0.063** (0.031)	
Partisanship	−0.008 (0.007)	−0.006 (0.005)		
Wage Centralization	4.554 (3.052)	4.526 (3.011)		
Export-Favoring Wage Coordination Dummy (1 if present)			−0.393* (0.233)	
Public/Exposed Union Density				0.352 (0.260)
Constant	0.993 (0.987)	1.61 (1.015)	1.638*** (0.256)	0.705 (0.753)
Estimator Used	FE	FE	RE	FE
Time Effects	None	None	None	None
Number of Countries	17	17	17	16
Observations	409	409	445	87
Unit of Analysis	Year-on-Year Changes	Year-on-Year Changes	Year-on-Year Changes	3-Year Static Averages
R Squared	0.288	0.291	0.235	0.389

Dependent variable is the difference in sheltered and manufacturing sector real hourly wage growth. Model used was an ordinary least squares (OLS) estimator, including a panel-specific Prais-Winsten AR1 term, for 17 OECD economies from 1979 to 2007 (model IV is limited to 16 OECD economies from 1985 to 2002—Irish data is missing). FE denotes fixed effects and RE denotes random effects. For fixed effects models, N-1 country dummies were included but not shown. Panel corrected standard errors are in parenthesis. *, **, and *** indicate significance on a 90%, 95%, and 99% confidence level.

to deliver wage suppression. Employers' negotiating strength, and the wage growth outcomes they delivered vis-à-vis the manufacturing sector, improved under the EMS and, particularly in peripheral Europe, under the Maastricht years, because sheltered sector wage excess carried monetary and membership penalties. Once EMU entry was obtained, sheltered sector adjustment was turned on its head. With the monetarist threat removed from the national level and no further possibility for membership exclusion, sheltered employers entered EMU on the defensive.

Sheltered sector employers in EMU's core countries, however, were able to use their export-favoring, coordinated wage-setting institutions, which had been embedded in their labor markets long before the arrival of the Maastricht criteria, to maintain (severe) sheltered sector wage moderation under monetary union. Sheltered employers in EMU's northern countries could substitute these coordination institutions for the EMS monetary threat and Maastricht conditionality, once they were removed after 1999. Export-favoring sectoral wage coordination regimes were not homogenously distributed across EMU member-states. Given their political (and institutional) legacies in building and promoting export-based growth models, EMU's core economies possessed a low-inflation, institutional comparative advantage in their wage-setting institutions, which EMU implicitly favored with its *exclusively inflation focused* real exchange rate.

The EMU periphery, with its legacy of conflictual and sheltered sector-favoring bargaining institutions, witnessed a more abrupt change in labor market politics under EMU. Though sheltered sector wage inflation did not return with a vengeance, except in Ireland (see chapter 6), sheltered sector employers in the EMU South were unable to produce the comprehensive level of wage moderation that they had under Maastricht or that their northern counterparts continued to produce under EMU. The result was a bifurcation in sectoral wage growth developments between the EMU North and South. Using their export-favoring sectoral wage coordination institutions, EMU's core economies kept inflation low and their real exchange rates competitive, while the loss of sheltered sector wage moderation in EMU's peripheral economies led to higher relative inflation, worsening their real exchange rates and external balances. Exacerbated by its new and strictly inflation-based real exchange rate calculus, EMU fueled the competitive divergence that led to its current crisis.

National Corporatist Institutions and Wage Suppression under EMU

Results in table 3.2, model III, suggest that countries with sectoral wage coordination regimes that allow wage-setters from the exposed sector to exert influence in national wage-setting also witness lower differentials between sheltered and manufacturing sector wage growth. Though all EMU countries witnessed a reduction in inflation-averse central banks' monitoring power and should have been subject to increases in relative sheltered wage growth, these increases were mitigated in countries where sheltered employers operated under export-favoring wage governance institutions. Such institutions, and the domestic politics that underpinned them, would have important implications for trade flows and external borrowing under monetary union. If Eurozone countries were successful in curtailing sheltered sector wage growth, producing low inflation, they would realize a persistently more competitive real exchange rate vis-à-vis countries sharing the same currency. Consequently, they would also witness larger expansions in their export shares and current accounts, and by the balance of payments identity, reductions in the capital account (reduced external borrowing), which would shield them from speculative pressure that followed the 2008 global financial crisis.

Operationalizing Export Competitiveness

Export-favoring, wage-bargaining institutions were a pivotal stopgap for the potential rise in sheltered sector wage inflation under monetary union. Because these institutions promoted low inflation through sheltered sector wage suppression, they also helped to magnify competitive real exchange rates under a common currency. Here, I exhibit the influence of these wage-coordination institutions, and the sheltered sector wage suppression they produced, on export performance. I select two measures of sheltered sector wage suppression: the annual difference in sheltered sector and manufacturing hourly wage growth, which served as the dependent variable in the empirical analysis described previously, and the export-favoring coordination regime dummy that was used as an institutional control. Both variables provide different means of assessing the presence of sheltered sector wage moderation; the difference in sheltered and manufacturing wage growth is an output variable that measures whether countries were successful in producing wage moderation in the sheltered sector, whereas the export-favoring coordination regime dummy provides a (theoretical) institutional context under which sheltered sector interests should be less able to exert their (inflationary) wage-setting preferences at the national level.

Growth in a country's export share serves as the dependent variable, which operationalizes national "competitiveness." The export share, rather than the current account, was selected to operationalize competitiveness because it is the main channel in the current account through which corporatist institutions promote the "trade success" of core EMU economies (hence, their typology as export-led growth regimes). Previous accounts of the trade success of (small) corporatist countries highlight the predominance of the export sector in national GDP (Katzenstein 1984, 1985; Rodrik 1998). Countries with low inflation, and hence a more competitive real exchange rate under EMU, should witness greater export expansion than those with an uncompetitive real exchange rate. *Growth* in the export share was selected as the primary dependent variable rather than the *level* of exports to GDP for two reasons: first, time stationarity, a central assumption for time series within panels, is violated for export share levels, which are consistently increasing for all countries for the time period under examination; second, the use of (country) fixed effects in models where the dependent variable is expressed in levels is more problematic as country dummies may largely crowd out level effects. Unsurprisingly, Germany witnessed the highest export share growth under the pre-crisis EMU period; Germany's export share grew, on average, by 6.2 percent each year, while in Austria, Belgium, Finland, France, and the Netherlands, export shares grew by 4.6 percent, 1.5 percent, 3.9 percent, 1.7 percent, and 3.5 percent a year, respectively. Ireland was the best export performer of the EMU periphery, but failed to achieve export growth performance on par with the core's best performers. Irish export shares grew by 1.6 percent each year, on average, under the pre-crisis EMU period, whereas export share growth in Italy and Portugal was, on average, 1.4 percent a year. Spain was the only country to witness export growth decline under the pre-crisis EMU period; export shares declined by 0.4 percent yearly, on average (EU Commission AMECO Database 2014).

Differentiating EMU's "Haves" from its "Have-Nots": The Influence of Sectoral Bargaining Politics on Export Success

Similar to the analysis of EMU regime change's influence on sectoral wage differentials, a pooled OLS cross-sectional, time-series regression is used to gauge the relationship between sheltered sector wage suppression and export performance.[6] The baseline model for the examination of sheltered sector wage suppression on export success can be summarized as follows:

$$\Delta(X/GDP_{i,t}) = \alpha_{i,t} + \beta_1(SheltWageSup_{i,t-1}) + \varepsilon_{i,t}$$

$\Delta(X/GDP_{i,t})$ is the year-on-year change in country i's export share at time t and $SheltWageSup_{i,t-1}$ is the degree of sheltered wage suppression in country i at time $t-1$. Two separate analyses are conducted: one where differences in sheltered and manufacturing sector wage growth serve as a proxy of employer success in limiting sheltered sector wage settlements (results presented in table 3.3), and one where the export-favoring coordination regime dummy measures the institutional conditions that grant export wage-setters and the state veto powers in sheltered sector wage formation (results presented in table 3.4). For the sectoral wage differential independent variable, the lagged difference is used to avoid endogeneity problems with the dependent variable, as well as multicol-linearity problems with terms of trade shocks and changes in the real exchange rate that are incorporated as economic controls.

The same seventeen OECD country panel, from 1979 to 2007, is used to test the relationship between these two proxies and export growth. Non-EMU countries are included to analyze possible interaction effects between sheltered sector wage suppression and EMU (model IV, table 3.4). If the interaction be-tween the EMU dummy and corporatist institutions were considered for EMU member-states alone, it may be possible that the outcomes are driven by common post-1999 time shocks unrelated to monetary union. The inclusion of non-EMU countries provides a counterfactual to developments happening in EMU countries after 1999. For the analysis where the difference in sheltered and manufacturing wage growth serves as the primary independent variable of interest (table 3.3), country dummies are used to account for omitted time invariant country-specific effects.[7] For empirical models where the export-favoring wage coordination re-gime dummy is used as the primary independent variable of interest, country dummies are purposefully excluded due to the relatively static nature of this in-stitutional dummy.

A number of economic controls were included, given their predicted effects on export performance. These variables include terms of trade shocks, total factor productivity growth, and real exchange rate shocks. Though the influence of sec-toral wage dynamics on export performance operates primarily via the real ex-change rate, real exchange rate shocks are included as a separate control to account for real exchange rate movements that may be influenced by developments other than wages (such as the prices of nonlabor factor inputs like oil or other natural resources). Real exchange rate shocks should be correlated with export decline; as increases in nonlabor factor prices place upward pressure on domestic inflation, export performance should worsen. Like real exchange rate shocks, terms of trade shocks, which are the change in the ratio of export prices to import prices, should be negatively associated with export growth; as export prices increase relative to im-port prices, exports should decrease. Given terms of trade's strong association with the real exchange rate, both were separated as controls in different models to avoid multicollinearity. Terms of trade shocks were also excluded from the export-favoring wage-governance dummy regressions, given their slight, but significant, correlation with the dummy variable across all panels. Real interest rate shocks were purposefully excluded from the analysis given their relationship by identity with real exchange rate shocks, via the interest rate parity condition.[8]

Several institutional controls that may influence export performance were also included in the empirical analysis. These institutional variables include: the level (not change) of social benefits as a percentage of GDP to account for

Rodrik's (1998) hypothesis that highly open countries have large welfare states as an insurance mechanism against (export) market risk; the proportion of legislative seats held by right parties to account for the fact that these parties may be more likely to pursue pro-trade policies that favor export growth; wage-bargaining centralization; and the employment share of the sheltered sector to account for Garrett and Way's (1999) hypothesis that larger sheltered (public) sectors may produce greater wage inflation and hence hamper macroeconomic outcomes, including export growth.

Results in table 3.3 demonstrate the robustness of the influence of relative sheltered sector wage growth on export performance. Differences in sheltered and manufacturing sector wage growth are consistently and significantly associated with export decline. Taking the average marginal effect from table 3.3 (-0.17), a 1 percent increase in the spread of sheltered and manufacturing sector wages is associated with a 0.17 percent a year decline in export share growth. By linking results from table 3.2 to table 3.3, it becomes possible to understand why EMU's northern economies inherited such an *institutionally* competitive position after 1999 relative to their southern neighbors. Though both groups of countries were subject to the EMU shock that weakened sheltered employers' bargaining strength, the EMU North continued to (severely) suppress wage growth differentials between its sheltered and exposed sectors through its export-favoring, wage-setting institutions. This sheltered sector wage and, in turn, inflation suppression enabled these countries to benefit from EMU's low-inflation bias, boosting their export performance relative to those in EMU's southern rim.

Similar results for the influence of sheltered sector wage suppression emerge when using the export-favoring wage governance dummy as an institutional proxy for its deliverance. Countries with export-favoring wage governance institutions witness, on average, 1 percent to 1.15 percent higher growth in their export shares every year than countries without these institutions, implying a 10 percent to 11 percent relative expansion in their export shares over the course of a decade. In addition to the direct effect, the export-favoring wage governance dummy also exhibits an interactive effect with monetary union (model IV, table 3.4), implying that monetary union *magnified* the influence of these wage governance institutions on export growth.[9] While the hierarchical export-favoring governance dummy term just lacks significance (p-value=0.109), its interaction with the EMU dummy is significantly associated with export share growth. This suggests that the influence of export-favoring wage governance on export performance may be conditional on the monetary regime. According to model IV (table 3.4), countries with export-favoring wage coordination institutions witness a 1.7 percent annual boost in export share growth, or a 17 percent relative boost over the course of a decade, *but only if they are in monetary union.* In

TABLE 3.3. The influence of sheltered sector wage suppression on export growth

INDEPENDENT VARIABLES	I	II	III	IV	V	VI
Difference in Sheltered and Manufacturing Wage Growth (lag)	-0.129** (0.057)	-0.19*** (0.057)	-0.176*** (0.067)	-0.124** (0.055)	-0.224*** (0.057)	-0.20*** (0.067)
Total Factor Productivity Growth	-0.168 (0.146)	-0.328** (0.160)	-0.163 (0.194)	-0.262* (0.141)	-0.172 (0.163)	-0.211 (0.186)
Terms of Trade Shocks	-0.354*** (0.066)	-0.51*** (0.077)	-0.469*** (0.076)			
Real Exchange Rate Shocks				-0.27*** (0.034)	-0.23*** (0.033)	-0.26*** (0.038)
Social Benefits (% of GDP)	0.617*** (0.127)			0.645*** (0.119)		
Partisanship		-0.042** (0.016)			-0.024 (0.016)	
Wage Centralization		-3.596 (5.181)			0.967 (4.737)	
Sheltered Sector Employment Share			0.046 (0.044)			0.008 (0.046)
Constant	-3.999** (1.593)	2.308 (1.792)	-1.107 (1.969)	-5.71*** (1.571)	0.873 (1.668)	-0.262 (1.810)
Number of Countries	17	17	17	17	17	17
Observations	412	435	470	412	436	471
R Squared	0.381	0.406	0.365	0.433	0.383	0.381

Dependent variable is the year-on-year change in the export share (X/GDP). Model used was an OLS estimator, including a panel-specific Prais-Winsten AR1 term, from 1979 to 2007. N-1 country dummies and time dummies included but not shown. Panel corrected standard errors are in parenthesis. *, **, and *** indicate significance on a 90%, 95%, and 99% confidence level.

TABLE 3.4. The influence of export-favoring wage governance institutions on export growth

INDEPENDENT VARIABLES	I	II	III	IV
Export-Favoring Wage Coordination Regime Dummy (1 if present)	1.150** (0.456)	1.071** (0.503)	1.306** (0.531)	0.789 (0.492)
Total Factor Productivity Growth	−0.12 (0.140)	−0.033 (0.160)	−0.109 (0.187)	−0.175 (0.136)
Real Exchange Rate Shocks	−0.210*** (0.033)	−0.197*** (0.034)	−0.214*** (0.040)	−0.209*** (0.031)
Social Benefits (% of GDP)	0.199*** (0.073)			0.193*** (0.074)
Partisanship		0.013 (0.008)		
Wage Centralization		1.668 (1.067)		
Sheltered Sector Employment Share			0.024 (0.032)	
EMU Dummy (1 if present)				−1.881* (1.045)
EMU Dummy* Export-Favoring Wage Coordination Regime Dummy				1.711** (0.856)
Constant	−3.263*** (1.205)	−1.966*** (0.739)	−1.367 (0.928)	−2.976** (1.210)
Number of Countries	17	17	17	17
Observations	414	437	471	414
R Squared	0.362	0.337	0.332	v

Dependent variable is the year-on-year change in the export share (X/GDP). Model used was an OLS estimator, including a panel-specific Prais-Winsten AR1 term, from 1979 to 2007. N-1 time dummies included but not shown. Panel corrected standard errors are in parenthesis. *, **, and *** indicate significance on a 90%, 95%, and 99% confidence level.

other words, countries that possessed institutions that suppressed sheltered sector wage growth witnessed an exclusive corporatist comparative advantage under their pre-crisis EMU tenure.

Other control variables either perform as expected (terms of trade shocks and real exchange rate shocks are associated with export share contraction while social benefits as a percentage of GDP are associated with export share expansion, per Rodrik's hypothesis) or fail to hold significance (bargaining centralization). Total factor productivity growth possessed an unexpected negative beta coefficient, although it lacked significance. Partisanship also behaved unexpectedly in model II, table 3.3, with more legislative seats held by right parties indicative of export decline, although it failed to retain its significance when real exchange rate shocks were controlled for. Contrary to the results of Garrett and

Way (1999), sheltered sector employment share exhibits an insignificant relationship with export share growth, indicating that it is not the size of the public
sector that matters per se, but whether its wage demands can be controlled by the
exposed sector or the state.

Results provided in this chapter lend empirical support to the institutional linkages outlined in chapter 2. Monetary union, both when represented as a crude
dummy and a continuous indicator that assesses the relaxation of central banks'
monetary power after 1999, is significantly associated with rising wage growth
differentials between the sheltered and manufacturing sector. Echoing Von
Hagen, Hallett, and Strauch (2001), who recorded a distinct "Maastricht effect" in
fiscal consolidation throughout the 1990s, sheltered sector wage suppression within
monetary union's member-states exhibited a distinct "EMU effect" throughout the
2000s. Despite this EMU effect, however, sheltered sector employers in countries
with coordination regimes that favored the export sector continued to produce
wage moderation once EMU came into play. Domestic politics in the EMU
North prioritized low inflation, and this priority had been long embedded in its
labor market institutions, which curtailed the power of their sheltered (public)
sector unions. Hence, while sectoral wage bifurcation emerged across the majority of the EMU10 after 1999, it emerged quite heterogeneously across member-
states, becoming more prominent in the EMU South and less so in the North.

This bifurcation in sectoral wage-setting after 1999, and its dominance in the
EMU periphery relative to the EMU core, has important implications for the divergence in national current accounts under the pre-crisis EMU era. Countries
in which wage developments in sheltered sectors were heavily suppressed relative
to those in the exposed sector reported more pronounced export share gains.
As highlighted in model IV, table 3.4, the export-enhancing effect of intersectoral coordination institutions that limit the power of sheltered sector interests in
national wage bargaining was further magnified under monetary union, where a
real exchange rate expressed solely as a function of relative inflation makes it
impossible for countries to hide wage inflation, however small it is, in nominal
exchange rate devaluations/depreciations. The consequences of extreme sheltered wage suppression in the EMU North, and the South's incapacity to mimic
these developments, are the combination of current account surpluses and capital account deficits for creditor nations and current account deficits and external
borrowing in debtor nations. The crisis of EMU may therefore primarily be a
result of not only the removal of institutions that enabled sheltered sector employers to deliver wage moderation, but also the differences in wage-setting systems between countries in northwestern Europe and southern Europe, in which

the former have been able to deliver significant wage moderation through their export-favoring wage coordination institutions while the latter, which lack export-favoring coordination mechanisms, are unable to do so.

In the next three chapters, these two institutional linkages are further scrutinized via structured case study comparisons. Emphasizing employer and union dynamics within the public sector, I draw on the experience of six countries during the ERM, Maastricht, and EMU periods: Denmark, Germany, Ireland, Italy, the Netherlands, and Spain. In chapter 4, the link between monetary union regime change and sectoral wage bifurcation is explored by comparing the pre- and post-EMU experiences of Denmark and the Netherlands. Despite the fact that both countries were subject to similar economic and institutional conditions within the public sector (decentralization and labor shortages) that should have produced wage inflation, inflationary public sector wage settlements arose only in the Netherlands after EMU entry was secured. Successive Danish governments, both on the left and right of the political spectrum, utilized a hard currency policy constraint in public sector wage negotiations in order to withstand inflationary wage demands from health and education sector unions during the 2000s. Dutch negotiators, on the other hand, were not so fortunate. While they could continually refer to the urgency of Maastricht to stifle public sector wages in the 1990s, the removal of Maastricht's exclusionary penalties and De Nederlandsche Bank's monetary threat impaired the state's ability to moderate public sector settlements, as the Netherlands' major public sector union, Abva-Kabo, aggressively and successfully pursued its political objective to narrow the public/private wage gap during the early 2000s. The Balkenende coalition eventually reined in public sector wage developments via promoting (state-led) wage pacts that delivered *national* wage ceilings and freezes in 2003, 2004, and 2005. This temporal reversion back to these familiar wage pacts halted the Netherlands' deteriorating inflation and real exchange rate performance, and declining current account surpluses.

4

NATIONAL CENTRAL BANKS AND INFLATION CONVERGENCE

Danish and Dutch Corporatism Inside
and Outside of Monetary Union

Denmark and the Netherlands provide a convenient microcosm to examine the relationship between national level, inflation-averse central banks and EMU regime change, on the one hand, and sheltered sector wage suppression, on the other. Motivated in part by the benefits of a stable exchange rate for their export-growth models, both countries transitioned to an inflation-averse monetary regime early under the European Monetary System and their governments initiated difficult wage adjustments in the public sector to facilitate this transition. Likewise, these two countries share similar features of trade unionism and collective-bargaining organization, making them very comparable. Both countries are small, have high trade shares, and share traditions of corporatism that influence pay and working conditions for the majority of the labor force. Trade union density is higher in Denmark, where union density averaged 70 percent of the labor force between 2000 and 2010, compared to 20 percent in the Netherlands; however, bargaining coverage for both countries is over 80 percent (Visser 2011). Sector-wide bargaining predominates in both countries, with company bargaining also enforcing guidelines established at the sectoral level.[1] Furthermore, as accentuated in table 2.3, Dutch and Danish intersectoral coordination was, and still is, conducted via export-dominated peak-association bargaining during much of the late 1990s and early 2000s (although the Netherlands switched, periodically, to state-led wage pacts in the early 1990s and the early 2000s). More specific to sheltered (public) sector industrial relations, the Netherlands and Denmark were subject to trends of decentralization and labor shortages within their sheltered (public) sectors throughout the late 1990s and early 2000s.

During the early 1990s, both the Dutch and Danish governments delivered moderated public sector wage settlements. Yet despite both countries macroeconomic and corporatist similarities, Abva-Kabo, the Netherlands' largest public sector union, and other public sector union affiliates in the Dutch Trade Union Confederations were successful in securing generous wage settlements from the Kok and Balkenende coalition governments during the late 1990s and early 2000s. By contrast in Denmark, the Social Democratic and Danish Liberals coalitions enforced strict wage moderation on the public sector, as public employers used a variety of bargaining tactics to quell dissent among nurses, teachers, and municipal employees who repeatedly demanded double-digit pay increases during various bargaining rounds in the late 1990s and 2000s. In both Denmark and the Netherlands, employers and governments endorsed the primacy of wage moderation in upholding their export growth models. Despite these similar low-inflation preferences, however, only Denmark witnessed the persistence of (public sector) wage moderation in the late 1990s and 2000s. In this chapter, I highlight that the presence of a non-accommodating central bank and credible fiscal rules promoted "adaptive" governance in Denmark, granting public employers greater steering capacity over bargaining through target-based macroeconomic objectives.

Through its monetary union opt-out, the Danish state retained a national-level, non-accommodating monetary threat that granted public employers an effective wage moderation commitment device. Danish governments were vocal in using this macroeconomic constraint during public sector pay bargaining, explaining to unions and the public at large the importance of maintaining low and stable inflation. (Low) inflation-minded Dutch governments, however, could not rely on this policy constraint after their entry into EMU was guaranteed in 1998. Led by Abva-Kabo, Dutch public sector unions effectively secured generous wage settlements for their members, placing upward pressures on national wage growth and inflation. In 2001, near the peak of the Dutch inflation/wage bubble, Dutch Finance Minister Gerrit Zalm publicly lamented that he had few macroeconomic instruments to halt rising prices and wages in the country—under EMU, monetary contraction was simply out of his control.[2]

Resorting back to their tradition of (export-favoring) state-led wage pacts, the Dutch were eventually able to deliver public sector wage moderation through social partners' consent to a 2.5 percent *national* wage ceiling in 2003 and *national* wage freezes for 2004 and 2005. A comparison of the Dutch and Danish experience in the 2000s demonstrates how national-level, inflation-monitoring central banks can assist employers/governments in delivering sheltered sector wage moderation within a bargaining regime where conflicting sectoral interests amalgamate under a peak-bargaining umbrella. In Denmark, public employers used Danmarks Nationalbank's aversion to low inflation as a hand-tying device in wage-setting. In the Netherlands, where this constraint was lacking, the Dutch state was forced to make various concessions on its social policy reform agenda to motivate Dutch social partners to adopt restrictive wage pacts in order to stop the country's wage/price spiral.

Comparing Denmark and the Netherlands: Hotbeds for Sheltered Wage Inflation

Both Denmark and the Netherlands experienced institutional and economic developments in the 1990s and 2000s that were conducive toward sheltered sector wage inflation. Institutionally, both countries witnessed steady decentralization trends in collective bargaining, although several scholars identify these decentralization trends as "organized" (Traxler 1995a; Visser 1998a; Rhodes 2001; Regini 2000). In the Netherlands, the 1982 state-led wage pact, the Wassenaar Agreement, initiated the process, with consent from both unions and employers, while public sector decentralization was initiated in the late 1980s (Visser 1998a). Wage-setting was first devolved to sectors and then firms. Since Wassenaar, controlled decentralization has continued via time irregular social pacts. These (state-led) pacts substituted informal consensual norms, moral suasion, and interagency trust-building for formal centralization (Visser 2002). As a consequence of decentralization, Dutch companies have successfully incorporated flexible pay elements into contracts, reducing the influence of collective agreements. By 1999, flexible pay elements were included in 15 percent to 30 percent of remuneration packages in the private sector, contributing to a widening private/public sector pay gap.[3]

Decentralization in Denmark proved inevitable after social partners failed to conclude national collective agreements in the late 1970s (Lind 2000; Iversen 1996). Centralized pay-setting made way for sectoral bargaining in Denmark, as it had in the Netherlands. In the 1990s, company-level bargaining became increasingly predominant. Negotiations within the private sector involved the establishment of minimum, rather than actual, pay growth levels, assigning a key bargaining role to local negotiators. In 2004, 62 percent of private-sector employees under the Danish Confederations of Trade Unions' (LO) and the Confederation of Danish Employers' (DA) bargaining umbrella were covered by sectoral minimum wage settlements, whereas only 16 percent were covered by traditional pay determination (Stokke 2008, 8–9). Decentralization in public sector bargaining intensified in 1997, when a new framework was introduced allowing for local negotiation over pay package elements based on qualifications and job performance.[4]

Economically, both countries were primed for wage inflation due to substantial declines in unemployment during the 1990s (in Denmark, unemployment fell from 9.6 percent in 1993 to 4.3 percent in 2000, whereas in the Netherlands it fell from 7.1 percent in 1995 to 3.1 percent in 2000) and the emergence of labor market bottlenecks (EU Commission AMECO Database 2014). An estimated 997,000 private sector and 2,000 public sector jobs were created in the Netherlands between 1980 and 1996, a 19 percent increase; most were part-time positions in the service sector (Auer 2000, 15).[5] Amid slowing economic growth in 1999, the Dutch labor market continued to witness high vacancy rates, particularly in the education and health sectors (Borghans and Kriechel 2007). Danish employment creation was equally impressive; unemployment dropped from 127,000 to 69,000 between 1994 and 1998 alone (Van Oorschot and Abrahamson 2003, 298). Nine percent and 10 percent of private sector companies and public institutions, respectively, had difficulty recruiting staff in 2000; for public sector institutions, this percentage increased to 13 percent in 2001, with shortages also concentrating in the health and education sectors.[6]

Despite their similar developments in decentralization, unemployment, and labor shortages, Denmark and the Netherlands experienced different trends in wage inflation after 1999. Examining three-year moving averages of Blanchard's wages in efficiency units (WEUs, figure 4.1), the Netherlands produced impressive degrees of wage moderation during the 1980s in its adjustment to a low-inflation regime and consistently outperformed Denmark in aggregate wage moderation. By the late 1990s, however, Dutch national wage inflation rose steadily and, for the first time since the early 1980s, significantly overshot Danish wage developments (see figure 4.1). In 2001 and 2002, Dutch *nominal* hourly wage growth exceeded productivity growth by nearly 5 percent (EU KLEMS 2010; EU Commission AMECO Database 2014). Such numbers may appear trivial compared to the 1980s and early 1990s, yet they produced an acute sense of crisis in a country that prided itself on its low-inflation performance. By May 2001, Dutch inflation had reached 5.4 percent, the highest in the Eurozone for that month.[7] The Dutch government eventually resorted to social consultation and offered substantial welfare concessions to unions to produce a two-year wage freeze. Finance Minister Gerrit Zalm admitted that such concessions would inhibit the government from adhering to the 3 percent limit of the Stability and Growth Pact (SGP), but that such measures were necessary for the stabilization of inflation.[8]

A sectoral analysis of wage developments is helpful to understand where this national wage inflation divergence originated from. Figure 4.2 provides three-year moving averages of Blanchard's wages in efficiency units for the manufacturing and sheltered services composite between 1980 and 2007: values

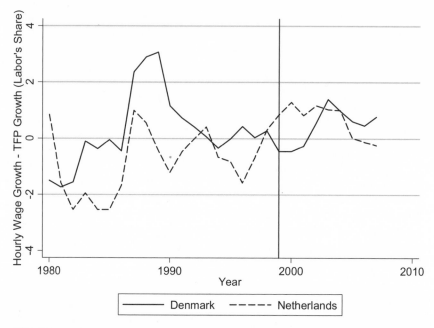

FIGURE 4.1. National wages in efficiency units (real hourly wage growth minus labor productivity growth), three-year moving averages (1979–2007)

Source: Nominal compensation per hour worked (for all industries) taken from EU KLEMS (2010). Data on labor's contribution to total factor productivity and inflation taken from EU Commission AMECO Database (2014).

below zero indicate that sectoral labor productivity exceeds sectoral real hourly wage growth, a deflationary effect, while values greater than zero indicate that sectoral real wage growth exceeds sectoral labor productivity growth, an inflationary effect. Between 1980 and 2007, the Dutch manufacturing sector consistently outperformed Danish manufacturing in the production of wage moderation. The Dutch sheltered sector, on the other hand, exhibited similar wage inflation trends, relative to Denmark, as those at the national level near the introduction of the euro. Dutch sheltered sector wage moderation (far) exceeded that in Denmark during the 1980s and much of the 1990s. By 1999, however, Dutch sheltered sector wage inflation outstripped that in Denmark, peaking in 2001. The mimicking of aggregate Dutch wages (in efficiency units) in the late 1990s and early 2000s to wage developments in the sheltered sector is not coincidental; the sheltered (public) sector composite holds roughly 30 percent of total employees in both countries.

Pay-related industrial conflicts arose in the health and municipal sectors in both Denmark and the Netherlands in the late 1990s, yet the outcomes from these conflicts were in contrast. After EMU entry was guaranteed in 1998, inflationary

FIGURE 4.2.   Sectoral wages in efficiency units (real hourly wage growth minus labor productivity growth), three-year moving averages (1980–2007)

Source: EU KLEMS Database (2010); inflation data from EU Commission AMECO Database (2014).

wage settlements emerged in the Dutch health, social care, and education sectors, where workers received pay settlements double those reached in the private sector. Such pay increases are expected amid staff shortages and decentralization and on their own are not especially puzzling. What is puzzling is that such developments did not arise in Denmark, which also witnessed staffing shortages in its health and education sectors in the late 1990s. Unlike their Dutch counterparts, the nursing union Dansk Sygeplejeråd (DSR), teachers' union Danmarks Lærerforening (DLF), and the healthcare bargaining cartel were unable to secure pay settlements above the private sector from center-right *and* center-left Danish coalition governments throughout the late 1990s and 2000s.

How can one make sense of the divergent trends in public sector wage-setting in Denmark and the Netherlands in the early 2000s? Relying on the institutional framework established in chapter 2, I argue that this divergence resulted from different exposure to EMU entry. Non-accommodating monetary authorities and fiscal rules enabled public employers to credibly "signal" their commitment to fiscal conservatism to public sector unions. However, signaling a non-accommodating reputation is only effective if the conditions that make it credible are present over an infinite horizon. If these conditions are limited to a finite timescale, the "receiving" player is rational to change behavior once the conditions disappear (Osborne and Rubinstein 1994, 239–243). EMU's removal of national level non-accommodating central banks and the Maastricht deficit criterion, two institutions that enhanced the Dutch government's traditionally fiscally conservative and inflation-moderating reputation, enabled public sector unions' to manipulate fiscal consolidation fatigue and the public/private sector wage-divide to push for higher wages.

In remaining outside EMU, the Danish government left its disciplinary commitments and policy instruments intact. Denmark was not legally bound to the Maastricht criteria because of its opt-out; hence the necessity to adhere to Maastricht did not equally apply. However, Poul Rasmussen's Social Democratic coalition formally institutionalized the commitment toward budgetary stability in 1993, in a separation-of-powers agreement with the Danish Central Bank.[9] In the agreement, the government consented to deliver sustainable fiscal practice (in domestic and foreign borrowing), which had informally been in operation since the early 1980s, so as not to impede on the central bank's objectives (Danmarks Nationalbank 2003, sections 1.5.2 and 4.4.2). The institutionalization of this rule provided a legal basis behind the Danish government's fiscally austere reputation, and the voluntary abstention from EMU allotted the reputation-enhancing policy an infinite time horizon. In the face of aggressive wage demands, the Danish state remained committed to fiscal prudence in the name of low inflation, isolating these unions from other negotiations in order to limit their bargaining influence.

The Dutch and Danish government utilized a hard currency peg to the Deutsch mark as a signaling mechanism for their shift to a conservative fiscal policy. While this shift may have reflected already-predetermined government preferences for low inflation, commitments to narrow exchange rate bands within the Exchange Rate Mechanism (ERM) forced public sector wage-setters to alter their wage demands in response to the government's transition to a non-accommodating regime. Unions' (reluctant) acceptance of this transition resulted in a significant wage-setting shift during the 1980s in both countries, which is outlined in greater detail in the next section. In the Netherlands, this wage shift, in both the private and public sector, was facilitated by the Wassenaar Agreement in 1982. Wassenaar introduced a prolonged era of voluntary wage moderation in Dutch collective bargaining, although in the public sector, government was more coercive in its imposition of deflationary wage settlements. In Denmark, the transition was state-imposed. After a decisive policy reversal in 1982 by Poul Schülter's Liberal-Conservative coalition, wage moderation was delivered through government intervention in collective bargaining. With government abandoning its commitment to full employment, trade unions were forced to adapt.

Social Partners Adjusting to Monetarism in the 1980s

Dutch Wage Setting under a Hard Currency Commitment

Weber (1991, 68) and McNamara (1998, 141) identify the Netherlands as the only country, other than Germany, that entered the ERM with a credible hard currency policy in place.[10] Under the currency snake, social partners and government realized the incompatibility of high wage increases and deficit monetization with a non-accommodating monetary policy. As labor costs rose faster than those in Germany, the central bank increased interest rates to maintain its monetary commitment. Though a successful inflation record was achieved, it was done at the expense of employment and sustainable public borrowing, given the higher interest rates on government bonds.

Christian Democrat (CDA) Dries van Agt's center-right coalition implemented numerous legislative measures to limit wage increases during the late 1970s and early 1980s. In July 1979, it abolished wage indexation on earnings, introduced cuts of 0.2 percent to 0.7 percent in social security benefits, and reduced the minimum-wage calculation index by 3 percent.[11] In late 1980, government passed another law to decrease pay indexation from 2.7 percent to 0.7 percent and reduce holiday bonus pay by 1 percent.[12] Despite these efforts, or perhaps because of them, by 1982 the Netherlands was confronted with chronic economic conditions and depressed domestic demand. Between 1979 and 1982, Dutch unemployment increased from 6 percent to 10.3 percent, the budget deficit doubled, and GDP slightly contracted (EU Commission AMECO Database 2014). Such developments produced an acute perception of crisis, and it was widely felt that government must act decisively (Hemerijck and Vail 2006; Visser 1998b). In June 1982, Van Agt's coalition collapsed, and the CDA and the Liberals (the People's Party for Freedom and Democracy—VVD) diverged from their former socialist partners to campaign for civil servants pay and social security benefits freezes.[13] CDA's electoral success in 1982 under an expenditure-reduction platform indicated the severity of the situation.

Upon entering office, Ruud Lubbers's CDA/VVD coalition suspended cost-of-living indexation for wage agreements and social benefits and froze the minimum wage and public sector wages (Hemerijck and Vail 2006). Such severe forms of intervention moved unions and employers closer to together, producing the historic Wassenaar Agreement in December 1982. Government's threats of intervention were crucial in convincing employers, who had little enthusiasm for a central agreement, to consent to it. High unemployment improved employers' bargaining position over unions, whose organizational power became fragmented due to rivaling sectoral factions. Employers had little incentive to reduce working time, a central union demand. Lubbers's threat of imposing a reduction in working hours in return for wage moderation, however, altered employers' noncooperative stance (Visser 1998a). Dutch employers resolutely opposed the government dictating terms, and in consenting to tripartism that produced the Wassenaar Agreement, employers avoided persistent government intervention in bargaining, which was becoming commonplace within Belgium and France. The accord lacked a concrete figure for wage restraint; rather, wage growth was to be kept below productivity and unions were to resist price-compensation. In return, employers agreed to working-time reductions (Hemerijck 2003).

Government unilateralism was not the only political pressure behind Wassenaar's creation; export sector factions within peak-level union confederations also vocalized support for the deal. After suffering severe job losses in the 1970s, the Dutch Trade Union Federation's (FNV's) largest union affiliate, the manufacturing Industries' Union (IB) reversed its stance on income redistribution and adopted a policy of wage moderation in 1979 (Visser 1998a, 279). The union placed increasing pressure on FNV to draft a central agreement whose primary terms included wage moderation; however, it was unable to force FNV's hand due to opposition from public sector affiliates. With further increases in unemployment between 1979 and 1982, however, IB's position gained support. IB's U-turn was critical in convincing FNV leadership to support a central accord with employers, and Wassenaar's terms echoed its newly adopted policy stance.

Though IB had convinced FNV to sign the agreement, Wassenaar, technically, applied to collective bargaining in the private sector only. Government's imposition of Wassenaar's terms onto the public sector took more time than the private sector's adaptation and was largely driven by government unilateralism. In 1983, the Dutch government introduced a three-month public sector pay freeze and cut teachers gross earnings by 1.65 percent.[14] By the end of the year, government announced a 3.5 percent nominal pay reduction for 700,000 public employees in 1984.[15] Such proposals sparked outrage among public sector unions, who organized their largest postwar strike. They possessed few allies, however, and faced powerful veto players in the union movement—namely, from the exposed-sector manufacturing Industries' Union. Government refused to deviate from its proposed cuts and, in December 1984, public services unions conceded to a 3 percent nominal pay reduction after six weeks of industrial action (Visser 1998a, 280). After 1984, adjustment to a non-accommodating macroeconomic regime was complete, resulting in a prolonged period of wage moderation in the private and public sector.

Many Dutch industrial relations scholars (Hemerijck 2003; Enderlein 2006; Hemerijck, Van der Meer, and Visser 2000) describe the chain of events between the Netherlands' central bank's enforcement of a hard currency policy and the conclusion of the Wassenaar Agreement in 1982 as causal rather than coincidental. The hard currency regime brought the end to inflationary wage settlements, as private sector unions realized the increased unemployment costs of wage militancy and public sector employers realized the increased fiscal costs of public sector wage excess once the possibility of monetizing the deficit was removed. The accord produced several political victories. Its creation marked the triumph of government over unyielding employers, as well as exposed-sector unions against those in the public sector. Its implementation marked the triumph of public employers over public sector unions. Finally, Wassenaar's economic outputs were unprecedented. Real unit labor costs fell by 6.9 percent between 1982 and 1990 (EU Commission AMECO Database 2014). Such results were spurred by restraint produced in the public sector, where real wages fell in absolute and relative terms. The real public sector wage bill declined, on average, by 1.3 percent *per annum* for *each year during the 1980s*, while public sector wages fell behind those in the private sector by 10 percent between 1982 and 1990 (Visser 1998a, 281).

Danish Wage Setting Responds to State-Imposed Austerity

Like the Netherlands, Danish sheltered (public) sector adjustment to a low-inflation monetary regime was driven largely by state unilateralism, yet this transition occurred slightly later than in the Netherlands due to the Social Democrats' reluctance to abandon Keynesian macroeconomic demand management. Frequent re/devaluation in ERM's early years was reflective of Anker Jørgensen's Social Democratic government's hesitation in committing to a conservative macroeconomic policy. To their credit, the Social Democrats undertook several measures in the late 1970s to ease the economic crisis. They introduced numerous incomes policies to reduce Denmark's high inflation, which in 1979 was double that of the Netherlands. Given their pro-labor stance, however, the Social Democrats often sought consent from unions for their imposition; because of the unions' veto power, the effectiveness of these proposals was limited (Damgaard 1989).

Jørgensen also reduced price-indexation on wage increases, but fell short of removing it completely (Lind 2000, 137). Such measures should have limited wage increases. In practice, however, new bonus-pay systems, introduced first in the engineering sector, made reductions in indexation obsolete in addressing inflation. Bonus-pay in the private sector created frictions in Denmark's central-ized bargaining regime, as government employees demanded similar compensa-tion mechanisms to maintain their purchasing power. In the 1970s, the Social Democrats paid for inflationary settlements with tax increases and modest cuts in public expenditures, while simultaneously limiting the inflationary impact of private sector wage settlements through currency devaluations (Damgaard 1989). By 1980, however, the political scope for further tax increases was exhausted, and the Social Democrats turned to deficit spending (Iversen 1996, 417). The financ-ing shift was apparent in budgetary figures; between 1979 and 1982, Denmark's budget deficit increased from 0.7 percent to over 8 percent of GDP (EU Commis-sion AMECO Database 2014).

It soon became evident that Keynesian management and the commitment to full employment were unviable under a fixed exchange rate regime with limited capital controls. By 1982, unemployment was 11 percent (OECD Annual Labor Force Statistics 2010). Unlike the Netherlands, however, Denmark also entered the ERM with a high inflation rate. High relative inflation meant that the krone could only hold its value against the mark if a significant interest rate premium kept capital within the country. In 1979, nominal interest on long-term govern-ment securities was 16.7 percent in Denmark, compared to 7.6 percent in Ger-many and 9.2 percent in the Netherlands (EU Commission AMECO Database 2014). The stifling effect that high interest rates had on investment made em-ployers keen advocates of a transition to an anti-inflationary policy.

In October 1982, Poul Schlüter's Conservative Party responded to the crisis and formed a coalition government between elections with the Liberals, Center Democrats, and the Christian People's Party. Schlüter's government was unwilling to compromise with unions and transition to monetarism marked the introduc-tion of government unilateralism. Once in office, Schlüter's business-friendly coalition wasted no time in introducing reforms. It unilaterally introduced a comprehensive stabilization package affecting monetary, fiscal, and incomes poli-cies. Pay indexation was suspended outright without consultation from unions; government suspended indexation again in May 1984 and removed it completely in 1985.[16] Government also temporarily repealed public sector pay indexation to private sector wages, later reducing it from 100 percent to 80 percent.[17] It rejected devaluations as an instrument of monetary policy and dismantled all remaining capital controls (Damgaard 1989; Weber 1991). Social welfare bene-fits were cut, a waiting day for the collection of sickness benefits was introduced, and employer and employee contributions to unemployment insurance were increased (Scheuer 1998, 162).

Denmark's primary employers' confederation (DA) welcomed the new ini-tiatives from the conservative regime. The unions, which not only felt attacked by the policies but also by being excluded from the consultation process in creating them, were bitterly opposed. They responded to the stabilization package with increased wage militancy; in 1983, nominal earnings in Denmark grew by 9.3 percent, the highest under the ERM period (EU Commission AMECO Database 2014). Government responded via legislative intervention. Schlüter introduced legislation imposing below-inflation pay increases for both private and public sector workers in 1985 and 1986; private/public sector workers received a maximum pay increase of 2 percent/1.75 percent in 1985, and 1.5 percent/ 1.25 percent in 1986. Strikes and lockouts ensued, involving some 300,000 private sector workers, the majority of which were affiliated to the low-skilled (sheltered) services union (SiD).[18] While the Danish Confederation of Trade Unions (LO) lodged numerous complaints with the International Labour Organization over Schülter's transgressions, it did little to halt the coalition's monetarist drive.[19]

Denmark's shift toward a non-accommodating regime was also indirectly responsible for initiating decentralization in bargaining. Contrary to the Netherlands, where union confederation leadership consented to decentralization, Danish trade union leadership opposed employers' calls for decentralized bargaining in the early 1980s. Some have attributed this opposition to SiD's political leverage within the federation.[20] Government's union-unfriendly policies, however, offered employers significant leverage on the issue. After government's intervention in 1985, the DA rejected centralized bargaining and undertook steps, similar to employers in Sweden, to pursue separate negotiations with the high-skilled Metal Union. Manufacturing employers and CO-Metal persevered over SiD's opposition, forming a separate bargaining cartel within the LO/DA framework in 1987. Scheuer notes that the formation of this bargaining cartel was made easier due to SiD's belligerent reaction toward government in the 1985 bargaining crisis (Scheuer 1998,162). In light of SiD's confrontational position, other LO affiliates became more sympathetic toward the Metal Union's wishes. The decentralized 1987 CO-Metal settlement was copied in other bargaining units, although government continued to impose lower wage increases on the public sector (Scheuer 1998, 163).

After 1987, public and private sector unions had fully adapted to the non-accommodating regime. Transition involved little compromise, given Schlüter's business, rather than labor, sympathies. When labor was uncooperative in the early and mid-1980s, Schlüter responded with fiscal contraction in order to mitigate inflationary pressures. As unemployment rose drastically in the second half of the decade, Danish unions changed gears, focusing on price stability rather than increasing purchasing power. By 1990, budget surpluses returned, inflation reached 2.5 percent, and public sector pay was moderated (EU Commission AMECO Database 2014). During the 1980s, the real public sector pay bill grew, on average, by 1.85 percent a year, compared to 5.4 percent annually for the 1970s (EU Commission AMECO Database 2014). However, these improvements in pay-bill moderation in the public sector came at the expense of unemployment, which by 1990 was above 8 percent and rising. It was not until 1994, when unemployment began to fall and growth improved, that LO *continually* consented to wage moderation (Lind 2000, 138).

Fiscal Constraints Preserving Wage Moderation in the 1990s

The early 1990s marked continued wage moderation in Denmark. High unemployment and low inflation provided Danish public employers leverage over unions regarding the continued exertion of pay restraint. In the Netherlands, trade unions held greater political leverage with the return of buoyant economic growth. The period marked the return of political confrontation between unions, employers, and government as public sector unions' tolerance to wage moderation waned. Abva-Kabo, representing almost 30 percent of FNV's 1.2 million membership in 1995, voiced its discontent with the public/private sector pay gap that had emerged throughout the 1980s and made the bridging of this gap its main bargaining priority (Visser 1998a, 281). Yet Dutch public employers continued to thwart the ambitious wage demands of the public sector unions, citing the fiscal borrowing requirements imposed by the Maastricht deficit criterion. Maastricht did not pose a similar threat to Danish public sector unions, whose government received an opt-out from its terms after the failed 1992 referendum. Instead, the Danish state created its own legal mandate through a separation-of-powers agreement with the central bank. Both countries relied on different legal mandates in the 1990s, yet they produced similar outcomes; wage moderation continued in the private and public sector throughout the decade.

A Temporary Lid for a Boiling Pot: The Convenience of Maastricht

In the early 1990s, Dutch unions, employers, and government were divided on the necessity for continued wage moderation. Between 1988 and 1990, robust growth was restored—real GDP growth averaged 4 percent per annum over the three years—as were healthy business profits (EU Commission AMECO Database 2014). Unions raised their aspirations and demanded further reductions in working time. FNV's public sector affiliates, Abva-Kabo in particular, made the recovery of wage decline a top priority. Employers refused to budge on working hours, and consequently, labor pushed for generous wage settlements.

Though private employers witnessed substantial profit growth in the late 1980s and early 1990s, government had reason to request further restraint. In 1990, the deficit remained over 5 percent of GDP, due in part to the strain social security placed on public finances. The Christian Democrats expected leeway from the unions. Yet reforms to the ballooning social security deficit put them at odds. In April 1992, government abolished benefit indexing to private sector pay, which unions resisted strongly.[21] Employers too were opposed to government's handling of the social security crisis, claiming that it had done little to halt the rise in spending, which placed upward pressures on employers' contributions. The deadlock reached the breaking point in 1991, when employers announced, for the first time in postwar history, that they would abstain from the traditional bipartite meeting in the Foundation of Labor as well as the tripartite spring meeting in the Social Economic Council (SER) (Hemerijck, Van der Meer, and Visser 2000, 264). The employers' walkout marked the beginning of crisis in Dutch concertation, which, given the looming economic lull in Europe, could not have come at a worse time. By 1991, domestic growth slowed, taxes and wage inflation were on the rise, and, due in part to the Bundesbank's war with the German Finance Ministry over financing of reunification, interest rates were increasing.

Renewed attempts at consultation were pursued simultaneously with intervention threats by government. Attempts at concertation revolved around the SER's revival in 1992, which itself revolved around the need to fulfill the Maastricht criteria (Hemerijck, Van der Meer, and Visser 2000, 265). In the late 1980s, the tripartite body was marginalized, given the shift to bipartism via decentralization, and its organizational role was reduced to delivering opinions on policy (Rhodes 2001). Hence, when the Minister of Social Affairs proposed that government, unions, and employers reach a "joint orientation" on two policy realms in the summer of 1992, SER members quickly rose to the occasion, producing the two frameworks in six months.[22] Government requested the board's opinion on the division of labor between the government and social partners in achieving policy objectives and on the sustainability of the Dutch model under EMU (Hemerijck, Van der Meer, and Visser 2000, 266). The move was welcomed by social partners who, by 1992, viewed the conclusion of another Wassenaar-like accord as inevitable. Alexander Rinnooy Kan, president of the Dutch employers' association VNO, described a central agreement that would address the rising spiral of taxes, prices, and pay as "urgently needed" and relented that both unions and the cabinet must be involved.[23] Government, too, exhibited its shadow of hierarchy to force a central agreement; in autumn of 1992, the Dutch

Social Affair Minister sent an economy-wide wage freeze bill to Parliament, forcing negotiators' to produce a deal. By September, FNV adopted an "employment before pay" policy, against its public sector affiliates' wishes, and government made it clear that any central agreement's terms must fulfill the Maastricht criteria.[24]

SER's unanimous decision on EMU was a crucial signal toward the deliverance of a central agreement. In its November 1992 report "Convergence and the Consultation Economy," the tripartite body claimed that not only was entry into EMU paramount to the Netherlands' economic future, but also that the Dutch system of consultative corporatism would become an important asset once EMU removed other macroeconomic adjustment policies (Visser 1998b, 301). The SER concluded that Maastricht's fulfillment required the delivery of wage moderation by social partners and reduced social security spending from government.[25] The decision, coupled with the looming threat of a government-imposed wage freeze, mobilized social partners. In November 1992, trade union confederations and employers' organization representatives agreed on the exchange of wage moderation for working-time reductions and outlined steps to further decentralize Dutch bargaining. With two-thirds of Dutch collective agreements expiring in March 1993, a two-month pay pause was agreed, and the National Confederation of Christian Trade Unions's (CNV's) moderate pay policy of maintaining purchasing power, no more and no less, was adopted by FNV.[26]

Public sector unions contested the fulfillment of wage moderation. Government announced in its June 1993 budget plans to introduce 8 billion guilders worth of savings (roughly £2.84 billion) in order to bring the Dutch deficit in line Maastricht's 3 percent deficit rule.[27] Due to the urgency to comply with Maastricht, Prime Minister Lubbers claimed that pay increases for civil servants would be severely limited. Unlike their private (and exposed sector) counterparts, public sector unions were in opposition, maintaining the move would deliver a pay-cut. Public sector unions had good reason to protest the pay freeze: in the private sector, average pay increases of 2.8 percent were concluded, and though meager, were on par with inflation.[28] Government refused to budge from 1 percent. With projections of 720,000 additional unemployment benefit claimants in 1994, Lubbers was desperate to avoid any worsening of public finances and encouraged his Social Affairs Minister to send a second wage-freeze bill to Parliament.[29] With threats of further intervention, civil servant and municipal employees unions agreed to no consolidated pay increases for 1994. In December 1993, a formal central accord was signed between all major union federations and employer organizations. Later known as the "New Course" accord, the agreement maintained that the scope for pay increases in most sectors was limited. FNV abandoned its 2.5 percent wage target to renegotiate old agreements.[30] In return, employers would provide funds for vocational training and employment creation and government withdrew its legislated wage freeze.

Maastricht played a critical role in restoring wage moderation to the Netherlands in the early 1990s. Government had few economic indicators with which to cry "crisis." In comparative perspective, the only indicator that bore resemblance to its early 1980s counterpart was public borrowing. In this respect, Maastricht could not have come at a better time. Its urgency, coupled with the SER's unanimous approval that EMU entry was paramount, mobilized government in addressing the deficit. Government continually referred to the criteria when limiting public sector wage growth throughout the 1990s. Aside from the nominal pay freeze introduced in 1994, government secured a two-year wage freeze from the healthcare sector in the same year, covering some 280,000 workers.[31] In 1995, it limited civil servants pay growth to 1.25 percent over two years in return for a two-hour reduction in the working week and holiday concessions.[32] In December 1995, the Minister of Education negotiated a (retrospective) year agreement that offered a 1.75 percent pay increase; the deal was short-term, delaying potentially costly negotiations on early retirement and social security benefits within the education sector.[33] Between 1982 and 1990, the Lubbers coalitions reduced the deficit from 6.2 percent to 5.3 percent of GDP (EU Commission AMECO Database 2014). By 1998, however, public sector pay restraint coupled with high economic growth paid off and the deficit, 0.9 percent of GDP, was nearly eliminated (EU Commission AMECO Database 2014).

Maastricht was a convenient solution to the corporatist crisis in the early 1990s and mitigated the effects of labor market overheating and decentralization on wage inflation. Yet Maastricht, while a convenient solution, was also a temporary one. Once EMU entry was guaranteed, government could no longer refer to its terms to impose wage moderation on social partners. Consequently, 1999 provided a perfect storm for the reemergence of wage inflation. Unemployment was at a record low, growth was high, EMU entry was secured, decentralization reduced the influence of union confederations on local bargaining, and most important, after fifteen years of consistent wage moderation, public sector unions convinced confederation leadership to abandon pay moderation. With few cards left to play, the Dutch government entered EMU on the defensive.

A Long-Term Plan: Denmark's Permanent Institutionalization of Fiscal Constraints

While the first Danish "no" to Maastricht unleashed uncertainty about monetary union's future within financial markets, it had little impact on Danish industrial relations. The true political test of government's continued willingness to impose restraint on the public sector emerged in January 1993 with the formation of a between-elections center-left coalition, led by Poul Rasmussen's Social Democrats. The new government had political and ideological ties to trade unions, suggesting that a sympathetic policy line toward organized labor would follow.[34] Yet Rasmussen's center-left coalition, surprisingly, continued its predecessor's commitment to sustainable fiscal policy. Once in power, his government formally institutionalized sustainable borrowing practice in an agreement with the Danish Central Bank. The borrowing norms were informal practice under Schlüter; Rasmussen merely wrote them into law.

The 1993 agreement outlined that "monetary policy is aimed at keeping the krone stable vis-à-vis the European Currency Unit [ECU], where any specific Danish requirement to stabilize the cyclical development *is to be accommodated via fiscal policy*" (author's emphasis, Danmarks Nationalbank 2003, section 4.4.2). The accord provided continuity in the Danish Central Bank's hard currency stance and the Finance Ministry's respect of this monetarist stance via sustainable borrowing practices. Still, its creation was important for two reasons. One, it formally recognized that (high) public borrowing impeded on the Central Bank's objectives, and legally stressed the need for fiscal policy to accommodate low inflation rather than unemployment. Two, it was created by a *center-left* coalition, signifying that a non-accommodating fiscal stance was accepted among the traditional political allies of the unions.

Rasmussen's symbolic agreement was a legal guarantee that fiscal authorities would accommodate the Central Bank's objectives. Like all policies of commitment, however, Rasmussen needed to signal credibility. Institutionalizing his predecessor's policies was insufficient; Rasmussen also had to mimic them to convince a skeptical public (and trade unions) of his anti-inflationary stance. The 1993 bargaining round provided his coalition government with a reputational opportunity. In March, the Finance Minister signed a "modest and responsible" two-year agreement for 210,000 state employees, providing direct, nominal pay increases of 1.5 percent (0.75 percent per annum) for the duration of the agreement, with an additional 1 percent for training and annual leave.[35] The total agreement was less costly than that concluded under the Conservatives in 1991, although lower inflation also merited a lower nominal wage increase.[36]

For the 1995 bargaining round, public employers were in a less advantageous position. Unemployment was falling, GDP growth was increasing, and bottlenecks and staff shortages arrived in the public sector. Government, in a minority coalition after the November 1994 election, announced a nominal pay target of 2 percent.[37] In autumn 1994, most LO-affiliates accepted the need for moderation in 1995. There were two notable exceptions to this view, however. SiD, representing low-skilled services workers, and DSR, the nurses' union, remained unconvinced about restrained pay growth, since their rank-and-file had accepted pay rises below the national average in 1993.[38] The latter proved particularly difficult to negotiate with, demanding a 10 percent to 15 percent pay increase.[39] Fearing the influence of such demands on other public employees, the Danish government isolated negotiations with hospitals from public sector negotiations. With little compromise between DSR and hospital employers, the (State) Official Concilia-tor postponed industrial action until late April, limiting DSR's influence over public sector pay negotiations.[40] Once industrial action was permitted, DSR was the only union without an agreement. The nurses pursued strike action in early May, yet given their isolation, government was able to intervene and impose on them the 3.5 percent pay-increase (over two years) public sector settlement.[41]

DSR challenged government again in 1997, this time with other public sector unions that also sought pay increases on par with the private sector.[42] As in 1995, the nurses' demands for high pay increases threatened to paralyze bargaining. Public employers relied on peer pressure from other public sector unions to secure a moderate deal. Government's refusal to settle separate agreements with nurses made other public sector affiliates unsympathetic toward DSR's lack of wage solidarity. Under pressure from the municipal employees union (the Asso-ciation of Local Government Employees, KTO), which was one of the two public sector bargaining cartels (the other being the Association of Danish State Em-ployees, StK), DSR relented and accepted the general agreement in late January.[43] The 1997 agreement was another major success for Rasmussen. The two-year agreement provided a 2.9 percent nominal pay increase over the lifetime of the contract. Terms were also outlined to reduce seniority bonuses and measures were introduced to decentralize public sector pay bargaining via a "Ny Løn" ("New Wage") system, a major concession for government.[44] Effective from January 1, 1998, public employers could experiment with new decentralized, negotiated allowances based on job functions, qualifications, and results.[45]

Rasmussen's sustainable fiscal policy commitment was not without contro-versy. In 1997, Hans Jensen, the president of LO, expressed concerns that the Social Democrats were sidelining unions from the policy-concertation process. Government, he argued, had become more unilateral on policies; in cases where Rasmussen believed that LO or DA was stalling the political process, he often acted without regard to social partners.[46] This not only applied to public sector pay and government's labor market policies, but also, in 1998, to private sector pay. The bargaining round, which involved the renewal of several major agree-ments only within the private sector, reached a stalemate between manufacturing unions and employers when, due to insufficient annual leave and pay conditions, trade union members rejected the drafted settlement between Dansk Industri (DI) and CO-Industri union negotiators. A general strike involving 500,000 workers erupted in April, the largest incident witnessed for thirteen years.[47] Government quickly intervened, passing legislation two weeks later that imposed a settlement resembling that reached by negotiators.

Rasmussen's intervention was a radical departure from the traditional Social Democratic line on voluntary bargaining. The legislation itself required a break in his minority coalition government; with left-wing parties of his coalition refusing to condone intervention, he sought, and received, support from right-wing parties.[48] After tensions had calmed, Rasmussen indicated that intervention would not be a habitual process as long as social partners acted "responsibly." However, the episode demonstrated that even private sector trade unions were not exempt from government's macroeconomic objectives. Under an accommodating macroeconomic policy, unions could secure rents from robust growth and business profits. Once a non-accommodating government places formal limits on inflation, like Rasmussen's government had done in 1993, "trade unions are not allowed to claim their part of the economic surplus" (Lind 2000, 155).

Through its public sector interventions in 1995 and 1997 and private sector intervention in 1998, Rasmussen's coalitions demonstrated their commitment to institutionalized borrowing norms. Under Rasmussen's tenure, public sector bargaining outcomes remained nearer to government's pre-bargaining recommendations rather than those proposed by trade unions. With one exception, annual wage increases in the public sector were consistently below those in the private sector between 1992 and 1998 (Lind 2000, 142). Maastricht imposed little constraint on the Rasmussen government. However, with the establishment of a legal borrowing mandate, Rasmussen pursued similar public sector wage policies as his Dutch counterpart.

Though Maastricht was more pressing for Dutch public employers, it held a major caveat: after 1998, its penalties were significantly reduced. Denmark's EMU opt-out, on the other hand, possessed continuity. The 1993 borrowing norm contained no deadline, ensuring continued commitment to fiscal discipline. Private and public sector bargaining in Denmark continued as it had during the 1990s, reflecting the preservation of the status quo. In the Netherlands, EMU entry marked a shift from adaptive to reflexive governance; government shifted from influencing bargaining with concrete targets (i.e., exchange rate bands and the Maastricht criteria) toward assuming a backseat approach, providing social partners with the freedom to establish their own policy objectives. The Dutch state was unable to stave off inflationary wage demands from public sector unions, as there was no economic crisis or political mandate that required continued restraint. Rather, government could only mobilize itself after these wage settlements led to high inflation and the deterioration of Dutch price competitiveness.

Continuity and Change: The Sustainable Danish vs. the Finite Dutch Monetary Constraint

Economic and collective-bargaining conditions suggested that the emergence of wage inflation in Denmark and the Netherlands was inevitable in the late 1990s. Yet only the latter witnessed sheltered (public) sector wage inflation. By opting out of EMU, Denmark preserved national policy instruments (the commitment to a hard currency policy enforced at the national level) which enabled government to pursue wage moderation. For the Netherlands, entry into monetary union removed this commitment and reduced the penalties of breaching a 3 percent deficit limit. The removal of these constraints, coupled with favorable economic conditions and decentralized bargaining, created an environment conducive to the emergence of public sector wage inflation. In the Dutch government's shift from adaptive, rules-based governance in the collective-bargaining sphere toward reflexive governance under EMU, public sector unions were able to manipulate wage coordination against public employers; unions in public subsectors with stable labor supplies mimicked wage developments in the health and social care sectors where labor shortages were acute. In Denmark, government's continued use of removed unilateralism in bargaining enabled public employers to manipulate wage coordination against unions; state, municipal, and health employer negotiators were forced to employ innovative tactics to isolate nursing and teachers unions, imposing moderate settlements on them so as to prevent the spread of inflationary wage settlements throughout the public sector.

Government on the Defensive: Monetary Union and Reactive Governance

In the Netherlands, Abva-Kabo initiated its campaign to increase public sector pay before Dutch entry into monetary union. In late 1997, its leadership proclaimed that the union's bargaining priority was to increase members' purchasing power over the medium-term. This claim was not one to be taken lightly. By 1998, Abva-Kabo contained 30 percent of FNV's membership and was the second largest trade union in the Netherlands (Visser 2000, 365). Abva-Kabo also had public sector allies. The Dutch Public and Health Sector Workers' Union (CFO), the public sector affiliate of CNV, expressed a similar desire to reduce the disparity between public and private sector pay during the 1998 bargaining round. CFO entered the bargaining round with a 4 percent wage demand while Abva-Kabo, the larger of the two public sector unions, established a 5 percent target; the days of zero to 2 percent annual pay increases, their leadership claimed, were over.[49]

On May 3, 1998, the Netherlands was selected as one of EMU's eleven original entrants. The announcement provided Abva-Kabo and its allies with the political leverage to pursue their pay agenda. The public sector, particularly the healthcare and welfare services sectors, witnessed generous settlements in 1998. Despite FNV's calls for a maximum 3.5 percent increase, healthcare unions reached a one-year settlement, providing a 4.35 percent pay increase, a 10 percent increase in salary for student-nurses, and the establishment of a £12 million fund to improve childcare facilities.[50] The settlement for 380,000 workers was closer to unions' original demands for 4.5 percent increase in pay than it was to employers, who demanded 0.5 percent and required arbitration by Prime Minister Wim Kok after threatened strike action.[51] To ease tensions, Kok conceded an additional 500 million guilders to the health budget to pay for the increased wage bill. Hospital, welfare sector, and care workers continued their calls for generous wage increases in 1999 and 2001. In 1999, a twenty-three-month agreement for 175,000 workers was concluded, providing for a consolidated increase of 5 percent, plus two 1 percent nonconsolidated bonuses at the end of 1999 and 2000. Like in 1998, the agreement was closer to unions' original demands (3 percent to 4 percent per annum) than what employers wanted (0.5 percent).[52]

By 2001, a report was published by the Labor Inspectorate outlining that, between January 1 and May 10, 2001, public sector settlements contained greater wage increases than private sector settlements. Workers in the care sector received, on average, 7.5 percent annual pay rises while those in the welfare sector received 5.25 percent.[53] By the end of 2001, after failed arbitration attempts by the Health Minister, a collective agreement was concluded for the healthcare sector providing for a 7.4 percent pay rise over sixteen months (roughly 5.55 percent per annum). Abva-Kabo's success was attributed to the political pressure that several "relay strikes," resulting in the canceling of hundreds of surgical operations, placed on government.[54] Teachers, too, received a generous settlement in 2001. Though the agreement provided for a basic pay increase of roughly 3 percent over eighteen months, they received two (considerable) increases in their thirteenth-month bonuses, worth 1.5 percent of pay in 2001 and 3.75 percent of pay in 2002. Similar thirteenth-month bonuses were introduced in law enforcement and the healthcare sector in 2001; in both sectors, government consented that individuals working longer than thirty-six hours a week would be awarded a 12 percent wage increase.[55]

Abva-Kabo's bargaining strategy not only involved ambitious demands over its bargaining domain but also increased pressure on FNV to modify its moderate national wage targets. Such influence meant that the union's demands impacted not only public sector negotiations, but also private sector ones. In January 1998, FNV established a 3.5 percent maximum pay limit for sectoral negotiations; by

October, Abva-Kabo convinced FNV leadership to revise this limit to 4.5 percent for 1999, despite warnings from FNV's own economists that 3.25 percent was more reasonable.[56] This upward-adjustment strategy was also deployed for the 2000 bargaining round. By September 1999, FNV proposed a 3 percent wage increase for the following year. Yet Abva-Kabo, again, successfully pressured the confederation to revise its target to 4 percent, nearer to Abva-Kabo's 4.5 percent target.[57] By late 2000, average collectively agreed pay rose by 3.7 percent, higher than FNV's initial 3 percent pay target. In 2001, the confederation's leadership remained committed to a 4 percent pay target, despite overheating warnings from the Dutch Central Bank, employers, Kok's government, and the OECD.[58] In the face of pressure from its largest union affiliates, FNV negotiators demanded wage settlements in excess of their traditional wage formula, which was based on inflation and productivity developments, such that "during the economic boom, [FNV was] no longer so concerned about getting the facts straight" (Van der Meer, Visser, and Wilthagen 2005, 357).

By mid-2001, it became apparent to government and employers that wage excess was causing problems. In May and June, the president of the Dutch Central Bank, the Minster of Social Affairs, and the Finance Minister all made public appeals for wage restraint while the country's metalworking employers' organization called for a pay freeze (Becker 2005, 1090).[59] Government and employers had good reason to fear unions' pay offensives. In May 2001, the Netherlands had the highest inflation rate (5.4 percent) of all eleven Eurozone member-states and the country's competitive position vis-à-vis its European trading partners, measured by real exchange rate developments, had fallen by 7 percent between 1998 and 2001 alone.[60] Pay agreements that concluded in 2001 provided for an average pay increase of 4.5 percent, higher than FNV's 4 percent target (in services the average pay increase was 5.3 percent), suggesting that public sector unions had little intention of reducing their pay demands.[61]

Despite the growing threat of a wage-price spiral, government, for the first time since Wassenaar, was powerless. In 1980, government relied on the economic crisis to convince unions of adopting wage moderation. In 1992, it referenced Maastricht to guarantee further restraint. Yet in the early 2000s, neither condition was present; growth was slowing, but unemployment was low, and Maastricht was obsolete. Finance Minister Gerrit Zalm publicly lamented that he had few instruments to halt rising prices: international contributors, such as energy prices and the depreciating dollar, were beyond his control, and given EMU, the Netherlands no longer possessed an independent monetary policy with which to negotiate wage moderation.[62] Government presented an official memorandum to Parliament in 2001, where the cabinet admitted it possessed no criteria for methods of intervention (Van der Meer, Visser, and Wilthagen 2005, 349).

Because the 1987 Wage Formation Act prohibited government intervention in bargaining, except under extreme circumstances, ministers could only publicly criticize Dutch unions and wait for crisis. Notwithstanding a threatened global economic slowdown after September 11 and stagnating domestic GDP growth, FNV continued to press for 4 percent wage increases in 2002. CNV pursued a more moderate approach for 2002, proposing a pay bandwidth of 2.25 percent to 4 percent, yet its chair Doekle Terpstra claimed that 4 percent would be more appropriate for the public sector.[63]

To the relief of employers, general election results in May 2002 brought the return of a business-friendly center-right coalition, led by Jan-Peter Balkenende's Christian Democrats.[64] It was Balkenende's reformist agenda, not his aggressive stance toward unions, that became a crucial negotiating tool. FNV and CNV agreed to consider a wage ceiling once government clarified its plans for reform. Balkenende's coalition made last-minute concessions, agreeing to limit the cutback in social protection, social insurance, and curtailment of early-retirement policies if unions reduced their wage demands (Van der Meer, Visser, and Wilthagen 2005, 357). In November 2002, a centrally agreed wage ceiling of 2.5 percent was agreed on by both FNV and CNV. Government, in turn, set aside €1 billion for 2003 to ease social security contributions for employers and employees.[65] As a result of the ceiling, pay growth dropped to 2.8 percent in 2003. Some areas in the public sector continued to secure significant wage increases; employees in the disabled care sector, for example, achieved a 6.3 percent settlement, despite the suggested 2.5 percent cap.[66] However, pay increases throughout the public sector as a whole were decreasing; by late 2003, average public sector pay increases were 3.1 percent, down from 4 percent in 2002.[67]

In 2003, government again convinced the unions to produce a second social agreement in return for several concessions on its reform proposals. In October 2003, Dutch social partners agreed to a two-year wage freeze in 2004 and 2005. In return for their efforts, unions secured several concessions from government: a one-year postponement of its plan to stop tax advantages for early retirement and pre-pension arrangements; the withdrawal of a plan to deduct redundancy payments from unemployment benefits; the abandonment of the disability insurance "partner test," in which government planned to retract disability benefits to people whose partners were earning; and an increase in government spending of €200 million to reduce the cost of sickness insurance premiums in 2004.[68] Finance Minister Zalm claimed that, though the initial costs meant the Treasury could not adhere to its own budget rules in the short-term (in 2003, Dutch public borrowing breached 3 percent), such imbalances would be offset by the wage freeze over the medium-term.[69]

Several Dutch industrial relations scholars claim the 2002 and 2003 pacts were reminiscent of their predecessors; Dutch response to crisis had not diverged from its old ways (Becker 2005; Van der Meer, Visser, and Wilthagen 2005). However, two characteristics set the two 2000s pacts apart from those reached in the 1980s and 1990s. First, the 2002 and 2003 agreements involved little concessions from employers; rather, exchanges involved primarily unions and government. Perhaps it is appropriate that the state bore the burden of deal-making. Public sector unions initiated the wage-price spiral, both through their own settlements and through the pressures they placed on FNV and CNV. Hence, restraint in the public sector required concessions from the state, not private employers. Concessions made by government, however, were not sustained indefinitely. Disability insurance continued to plague public finances, and for several concessions in the 2003 agreement, Balkenende was only able to postpone, rather than withdraw, his reforms. Such caveats help explain the second characteristic that distinguishes the 2003 agreement from its predecessors: its short-termism. By late 2006, FNV, CNV, and the Federation of Managerial and Professional Staff Unions (MHP) yet again abandoned wage moderation. The country's economic recovery made it difficult for union leadership to request further restraint from its rank-and-file.[70] Abva-Kabo, too, resorted back to its wage catch-up policy. In November 2006, it demanded a 5 percent annual wage increase for 120,000 government officials, while the Minister of Internal Affairs, Johan Remkes, offered no more than 2 percent. After a series of relay-strikes, a three-year agreement was signed, providing for a 10.5 percent pay increase (3.5 percent per annum), plus a 5.4 percent increase in the thirteenth-month bonus for 2009.[71]

The fate of wage moderation after 2005 should not be surprising, given the institutional premise of monetary union. Unlike Wassenaar or "New Course," public employers could not utilize an external hand-tying device such as a hard currency policy that targets national wage developments or the Maastricht criteria. Government and employers conveniently relied on the latter, in a period where low unemployment and decentralized bargaining should have produced wage inflation. Securing long-term wage restraint from unions, in the absence of these institutions, evaded Dutch employers until the 2008 financial crisis, when government was able to capitalize on these events and gain the upper hand in imposing public sector wage moderation. The successes of the social pacts at delivering wage moderation proved more temporary than those struck under the auspices of a hard currency policy or the Maastricht criteria, and capacities at delivering wage moderation, especially in the public sector, proved cyclical, given the reactive nature of pay-setting to economic crises.

Consequences of Opting-out: Controlling Public Sector Pay outside EMU

Danish public employers' governance style during the 1990s cannot be considered purely "adaptive." The derogation from Maastricht meant that Danish authorities were not subject to Maastricht's specific targets; rather, its hard currency policy subjected Denmark to broader policy goals such as maintaining "low" inflation and "sustainable" borrowing levels. However, the EMU-period also cannot be classified as one of "reflexive" governance for Denmark, where public employers encouraged bargaining parties to establish their own objectives. In the 1999, 2002, 2005, and 2008 public sector bargaining rounds, Danish authorities undertook preemptive action against ambitious wage demands from teachers and nurses (in 1999 and 2002), the healthcare sector (2005 and 2008), and municipal employees (2008), successfully mitigating wage settlements. Hence, "adaptive" and "reflexive" forms of governance are insufficient in describing Danish public sector bargaining during the 2000s. Rather, the governance style can be better explained by "removed unilateralism." Government allowed unions and public employers to negotiate independently. Yet, if moderate wage settlements were not concluded, it unilaterally imposed more moderate terms on militant unions, preventing possible mimicking effects in other sectors.

For the first time in a decade, 1999 witnessed the return of budgetary surplus to Danish public accounts. Public employers were intent on maintaining this record and effectively negotiated moderate pay increases in 1999, securing further pay decentralization in exchange for additional paid holidays. Two general, three-year agreements were reached for 200,000 state employees and 640,000 municipal employees after one month of negotiations.[72] They provided a 6 percent general wage increase (2 percent per annum), one extra holiday per year, and in line with the 1997 agreement, further bargaining provisions for the "Ny Løn" decentralized pay system.[73]

Though agreements were quickly concluded for the state and municipal sectors, members from the nurses' and teachers' unions, DSR and DLF, rejected the general municipal (KTO) package, the former on grounds of pay and the latter on working time. With strike action scheduled for May, Poul Rasmussen publicly announced that if the Official Conciliator failed to build bridges, he would enter a "trail of strength" with union leadership and unilaterally impose the KTO package on them via government-sponsored legislation. On May 21, 1999, the Danish Parliament passed legislation to impose the public sector pay deal on nurses, ending the nine-day industrial action. DLF reentered negotiations with government in May, reaching an agreement on June 3. The settlement provided for a slight reduction in the previous increase in teaching hours, although DLF was forced to concede a pay-cut, neutralizing the agreement.[74]

The 1999 public bargaining round was Rasmussen's minority coalition's last. November 2001 brought an election victory for Anders Fogh Rasmussen's Liberal Party, who entered a center-right coalition with the Conservatives, Danish People's Party, and the Christian People's Party. The incoming center-right government did not deviate from its predecessor's macroeconomic policy goals, although Rasmussen's coalition voiced its intent, in summer 2002, to introduce structural reform in the public sector. In light of the orientation of economic policy toward low inflation and sustainable government borrowing in the 1980s and 1990s, the new government had little intention of weakening the Danish bargaining model, in fear of inflationary consequences that such a move could unleash.[75]

Unions in the central government bargaining cartel (the State Public Servants' Trade Union, CO II, and the Association of Danish State Employees, StK) and the KTO municipal bargaining cartel made above-inflation wage increases a bargaining priority for 2002, as well as the continuation of the 80 percent public sector pay indexation to pay developments in the private sector. DSR went further, seeking a general wage increase that provided for 100 percent private-sector pay indexing, as well as the elimination of the pay gap between the private and public sector. Rising labor shortages enhanced KTO's and DSR's bargaining position. In late 2001, 13 percent of public sector institutions, compared to 6 percent of private companies, expressed difficulty in recruiting staff, with the healthcare and education sectors possessing the majority of vacancies.[76] KTO's and DSR's demands did not bode well for the new government's budgetary ambitions, which campaigned on a platform of reducing taxes and expenditures. Rather than resorting to legislation, however, Government's ability at producing wage moderation in 2002 was dependent on negotiation tactics and timing.

Negotiations in the state sector began in early January 2002. Finance Minister Thor Pedersen was keen to settle before January 29, the start-date for municipal negotiations, so he could limit their influence on the state sector. To speed negotiations, Pedersen assured StK and CO II that government's planned public expenditure cuts would not result in redundancies. Along with government's retreat from further development of the "Ny Løn" system, StK and CO II consented to a moderate, three-year pay settlement on January 27. The agreement provided a 6 percent wage increase (2 percent per annum), plus two extra holidays (in line with what had been agreed in the 2000 private sector settlements), and a continuation of the 80 percent private sector indexation mechanism. The agreement, in total, cost government 7.55 percent, identical to the 1999 agreement under the Social Democrats' minority government.[77]

The state sector settlement provided a convenient ceiling for municipal employers—namely, Kommunernes Landsforening (KL) and Amtrådsforeningen (ARF). Fearing the influence of the Danish nurses' union (DSR) on the wider municipal sector, both KL and ARF adopted a "centralize and conquer" approach for municipal negotiations. Traditionally in municipal sector bargaining, the Association of Local Government Employees (KTO) held individual union ballots for a unifying agreement, rather than a single cartel-wide ballot, which enhanced the veto power of DSR and DLF. However, in January 2002, KL and ARF declared that they would not accept an agreement unless KTO provided a single cartel-wide ballot. The declaration was one that KTO could not easily refuse; if the unions proved uncooperative, the Official Conciliator would intervene and impose the state sector agreement on local authorities.[78] KTO consented to the single ballot initiative, yet municipal talks collapsed in February because of opposition from DSR and DLF. Negotiations were transferred to the Official Conciliator, which drafted an agreement similar to the state sector. Overall, the three-year agreement provided for a 7.55 percent increase for employers, setting aside 5.5 percent for a general wage increase, 1.87 percent for local bargaining, and the remainder for two extra holidays.[79]

The agreement, put to ballot in April, was overwhelming rejected by nurses (74 percent rejection rate), secondary school teachers (75 percent rejection rate), and primary school teachers (95 percent rejection rate). However, because the municipal agreement was put to a centralized ballot, such notable rejections were overshadowed by the majority, who approved the settlement by a narrow 51.9 percent.[80] Employers achieved a major victory over a potentially destabilizing public sector bargaining round. With unemployment below 5 percent, Rasmussen's center-right coalition presided over highly coordinated negotiations, producing a moderate agreement in line with government's budgetary plans. Recentralization in the municipal sector proved highly unpopular among DSR and DLF members, who again were forced to accept a generalized agreement.

Employers achieved another victory in 2002, yet it came at a price: a rift emerged within the KTO cartel, where major health unions, led by DSR, broke away in November 2003, forming their own separate healthcare cartel.[81] The healthcare unions' mutiny cost KTO 100,000 of its 640,000 members.[82] However, the new cartel failed to dictate terms to public employers in 2005, due in part to employers' use of similar coordination and timing tactics between state and municipal negotiations. Government employed a "divide and conquer" approach in 2005, conducting the timing of negotiations in a similar fashion as in

2002 (concluding the less confrontational state and municipal negotiations first and the more difficult healthcare negotiations afterward), and then dictating the terms of municipal and state agreements to the healthcare cartel. In February 2005, moderate three-year agreements were again produced in the municipal and state sector, with little confrontation involved in bargaining. In the municipal sector, the KTO's demand for a 5.6 percent direct pay increase over three years was met, as were employers' demands that the "Ny Løn" decentralized pay system be maintained. The total three-year agreement, factoring in wage costs and funds secured to improve working conditions, cost employers 9.3 percent, which though higher than the 2002 settlement, did not exceed wage growth in the private sector. In the state sector, a general wage increase of 5.76 percent over three years was agreed on, with 1.2 percent of the wage bill being earmarked for Ny Løn.[83]

Demands for the healthcare cartel in 2005 were more ambitious. Led by DSR, the cartel sought pay rises above those reached by municipal negotiations and the abolition of the Ny Løn system. Given the speedy conclusion of the municipal agreement, ARF and KL positioned KTO and the healthcare cartel against each other. KTO's president, Dennis Kristensen, proclaimed that in the event of a higher wage settlement in healthcare, he would renegotiate KTO's settlement. Kristensen's sentiments sparked indignation among the healthcare negotiators, who understood that employers would rely on the Official Conciliator to extend coverage of the municipal settlement rather than risk reopening negotiations with KTO. In the end, the healthcare cartel secured a 9.3 percent package, identical in value, pay, and working-time terms to KTO's agreement.[84] The only concession granted was the elimination of the Ny Løn system in exchange for the establishment of a wage scale with eight pay grades.[85] The cartel's separatist strategy to achieve higher wage increases failed, leading to bitterness among its member unions.[86]

Public employers in Denmark limited wage excess in the healthcare and education sectors with greater success than their Dutch counterparts. The Ministry of Finance witnessed its largest surpluses in over thirty years in 2005 (5.21 percent of GDP), 2006 (5.16 percent), and 2007 (4.78 percent). Wage growth in the private sector was also moderate, despite low unemployment; the average annual increase in wages was 2.9 percent and 3.2 percent, in 2005 and 2006, respectively.[87] Interest rates, too, were at record lows, and tax relief on mortgage lending led to a real estate and consumption boom (Becker 2005, 1090). Adding greater stimulus to the economy, Rasmussen's center-right coalition introduced a tax freeze for 2006 and 2007. The economic and political climate suggested that significant wage increases loomed on the horizon. In 2006, many unions under LO's umbrella, particularly public sector unions, hinted that subsequent bargaining rounds would bring considerable wage increases.[88]

Rasmussen's government was in a difficult bargaining position leading into the 2008 bargaining round. For the first time in his tenure, all major public sector union cartels threatened strike action if their wage demands were ignored. Given their inflation commitments to the Danish Central Bank and its tax-freeze, Rasmussen was confined in public expenditure options, placing greater pressure on public employers to negotiate moderate settlements. Moreover, private employers warned government that high wage increases in the public sector would lead to a wage spiral in the private sector, further threatening inflation objectives.[89] The employers' organization, the DA, secured moderate settlements in manufacturing and industry in 2007 and did not want "inappropriate" public sector agreements to generate conflicts in subsequent private-sector bargaining rounds.[90] Rasmussen responded decisively, earmarking €800 million in the 2007 federal budget to improve education and training opportunities for public employees. With union pressure still high, he called an early election for November 13, 2007, so as to avoid any political fallout from the possible imposition of an unpopular public sector settlement.[91] His political gamble was rewarded with a victory for his party and coalition partners, and his new Finance Minister, Lars Løkke Rasmussen, entered the bargaining round with the last-resort option of a unilaterally imposed settlement.

Løkke Rasmussen's bargaining position was also enhanced by a 2007 structural reform within the public sector. The legislation was not intended to influence government's position against public sector unions, but rather to promote organizational efficiencies so that municipalities could realize operational economies of scale (Andersen 2008). The legislation reduced the number of municipalities; replaced thirteen counties with five regions that had oversight over healthcare, public transport, and environmental planning; and transferred full responsibility for collection of taxes and debt collection to the central government (Bundgaard and Vrangbæk 2007, 495–496). The latter was pivotal in negotiations with the healthcare cartel in 2008, as the recentralization of revenue collection enabled the Finance Minister to dictate levels of municipal and healthcare expenditure.

The state sector settlement was the first reached in 2008. The total value of the three-year deal, 12.8 percent as agreed by Løkke Rasmussen in the 2008 budget proposal, provided for a 9.67 percent pay increase, with the remaining funds being used for local negotiations on pensions, extra-care days, and other benefits. Municipal negotiations involved greater conflict. KTO initially demanded a minimum 13.1 percent three-year deal. Fearing the effect of the minor increase on healthcare negotiations, Løkke Rasmussen maintained that a 12.8 percent wage increase could not be exceeded under any circumstances, leaving KL and ARF with little choice but to reject KTO's demands. By the third negotiation round and Løkke Rasmussen's refusal to earmark any additional funds to the municipalities, KTO relented to a 12.8 percent settlement in early March. The three-year settlement was equal in value to that achieved in the state sector, with greater concentration on pay: a 7.53 percent general wage increase was agreed, 4.5 percent was allocated to local negotiations, and the (small) remainder covered fringe benefits and increases in holiday allowances.[92]

The resolution of the healthcare settlement, whose negotiations proved most difficult, was concluded in June after two months of industrial action. Nurses demanded a minimum 15 percent, three-year settlement, which was promptly turned down by employers. As in municipal negotiations, Løkke Rasmussen used his enhanced budgetary veto powers to establish a 12.8 percent ceiling for the healthcare sector, bringing regional budgets in line with those for the municipalities and the central government. The eventual agreement provided a 13.3 percent, three-year settlement, although not all occupational groups received this figure. Nurses and home-care workers received the full 13.3 percent settlement, while most other groups received slightly less than 12.8 percent, negating the scope of the 0.5 percent increase. DSR was satisfied with the agreement, although leadership criticized Løkke Rasmussen for restricting the negotiating space: "[The agreement was] the best possible result taking into account that negotiations were controlled by the Minister of Finance," DSR President Connie Kruckow said.[93] Løkke Rasmussen's hard-line in what was expected to be an explosive bargaining round enabled Denmark to adhere to its budgetary objectives in the face of a tax-freeze. In 2008, the country's fiscal surplus was 3.4 percent of GDP, marking the tenth year since Denmark last experienced a deficit, placing it in a healthy fiscal condition entering the European sovereign debt crisis.

The institutionalized commitment to a hard currency policy committed Danish authorities to fiscal austerity amid labor market shortages. Using efficient employer coordination practices to the detriment of public sector unions, via different negotiation strategies of isolation ("divide and conquer"), recentralization ("combine and conquer"), and hold-out ("trial of strength"), both the Social Democrats and the center-right Liberal coalition were proactive against public sector unions' pay demands. Though it remained questionable whether public employers would continue their success in sidelining DSR, DLF, and the healthcare cartel after 2005, the 2007 public sector reform enhanced the Finance Minister's power over municipal and regional budgets. With budgetary powers recentralized, Løkke Rasmussen dictated municipal and regional bargaining outcomes in accordance with government's borrowing obligations through top-down employer coordination. Through the reform, government secured greater leverage over state *and* municipal bargaining.

Though both the Netherlands and Denmark possessed intersectoral wage coordination regimes identified as less conducive to controlling sheltered sector inflation, sheltered (public) employers in Denmark were able to utilize macroeconomic constraints—a non-accommodating inflation-averse central bank that could monitor national inflation developments—to deliver sheltered sector wage moderation. Dutch public employers lacked these institutional constraints, and after the rise of public sector wage inflation in the early 2000s, reverted to wage-moderation-inducing, state-led wage pacts in late 2002 in order to deliver national wage ceilings and pay freezes. This temporary rise in Dutch public sector wage inflation hinged on the transition to monetary union. A hard currency policy, and later Maastricht, offered the Dutch government external rules to impose wage restraint on the public sector. EMU was the end-game to such rules. Maastricht's finite time-horizon meant that adaptive, rules-based governance also would be temporary. The removal of a non-accommodating monetary policy and entry targets ushered in a period of reactive governance, where unions yielded greater control over bargaining outcomes. Familiar fixes to wage inflation—wage pacts—were eventually employed, but their success at producing moderation was temporary.

Danish public employers, on the other hand, remained resilient against public sector unions, despite their peak-bargaining coordination regime. With borrowing rules institutionalized in 1993, the Danish government was required to adhere to the Danish Central Bank's currency policy via a neutral fiscal stance. The 1993 agreement lacked specific targets, yet its time-horizon was infinite. The Danish government treaded more carefully in public sector negotiations after 1998, isolating militant unions that risked the initiation of a wage-price spiral. The retention of a hard currency policy, and the fiscal discipline required to sustain it, has served Denmark well, particularly leading into the current European debt-crisis. The IMF credits the country's currency peg with producing a "remarkable" fiscal policy performance over the past two decades while the European Commission highlighted that Denmark's comfortable fiscal position entering the financial crisis provided it maneuvering room to implement a discretionary fiscal expansion in 2009 (IMF 2008b; EU Commission 2009).

The Dutch case suggests that little bodes well for candidate countries that seek to moderate public sector wages in the absence of a national monetary policy and fiscal targets. Yet while differences between public sector and manufacturing wage growth have grown in most EMU member-states since 1999, some countries, notably those in the north of Europe, continued to limited public sector wage growth. How have these countries continued to produce extreme sheltered sector wage moderation with the removal of inflation-averse central banks and Maastricht's nominal and fiscal rules? This question is the subject of chapter 5. Using a contextualized case comparison of Germany, Italy, and the Netherlands, I highlight the influence of intersectoral wage coordination institutions on sheltered sector wage moderation and inflation performance under monetary union. While Italy entered the 2008 financial crisis with a current account deficit, both Germany and the Netherlands entered the crisis with significant current account surpluses. Yet the latter two countries took very different paths to arrive at this outcome. Chapter 5 argues that the current account balances of Germany, Italy, and the Netherlands are partially influenced by public employers' capacity to uphold intersectoral coordination institutions with the exposed sector.

STRENGTH IN RIGIDITY

Public Sector Employment Reform
and Wage Suppression in Germany,
the Netherlands, and Italy

One of the central themes of this book is that EMU's northern economies possessed export-favoring corporatist institutions that severely moderated sheltered sector wages under EMU. These institutions enabled the North to continually (and arguably unfairly) undercut their southern neighbors in inflation performance, which upheld their competitive real exchange rates after 1999. Yet thus far, these wage setting institutions have merely been described and not thoroughly unpacked. This chapter provides a more detailed oversight of how, in some countries, public sector employers and the state undertook actions that upheld export-favoring national collective bargaining models, delivering sheltered sector wage moderation under a common currency. Here, the focus is on what types of power dynamics, bargaining structures, and legal pretexts *public* sector employers used to counter wage inflation pressures from public sector unions.

Debate on bargaining structure and the types of bargaining institutions that deliver wage moderation is extensive. The general consensus is that highly centralized and highly coordinated wage systems produce greater wage restraint than moderately centralized and lowly coordinated ones (regarding centralization, see Bruno and Sachs 1985; Marks 1986; Bean, Layard, and Nickell 1986; Calmfors and Driffill 1988; Wallerstein 1990; regarding coordination, see Soskice 1990). Yet much of this literature treats centralization and coordination as a given, ignoring the role of employers in upholding or eroding these systems. The Swedish, British, and Danish experiences during the 1980s demonstrate that employers can instigate institutional change by dismantling centralization (Brown and Walsh 1991; Iversen 1996; Swenson and Pontusson 1996; Thornqvist 1999). For employers in high-skill, export-driven industries, decentralization offers the flexibility to attract skilled workers with higher wages to positions whose required skill-sets are expensive but necessary to acquire.

Sheltered sector employers' preferences for decentralization, notably those in the public sector, have received less attention. Since the late 1980s, bargaining decentralization in the public sector has occurred in many countries, including the Netherlands and Italy, via the introduction of flexible pay systems and greater autonomy for lower-level collective bargaining. These trends, reinforced by a New Public Management (NPM) dogma, were motivated by governments' desire to introduce incentive structures to monopolistic public providers, harmonizing employment and pay conditions in the public sector with those in the private sector. Historically, public sector employees have enjoyed a privileged employment status regarding pensions and protection against dismissal. In many countries, however, these privileges came at the expense of bargaining rights: civil servants and contract public employees possessed no formal right to collectively bargain, granting the state unilateral authority to establish pay conditions and considerable capacity to limit public sector wage growth. Extending the debate about employers' dissolution of centralization to the public sector and using an analysis of Germany, Italy, and the Netherlands, I argue in this chapter that "liberalization/decentralization"[1] efforts undertaken by public employers created perverse effects on public sector wage-setting after EMU removed the monetary threat and conditionality constraints that public employers used to deliver wage moderation prior to 1999.

Germany and Italy shared several economic and sectoral characteristics that should have enhanced public sector employers' capacity to deliver wage moderation in the years succeeding EMU entry. Yet only German state negotiators imposed severe wage restraint on public sector employees, keeping the German public sector strictly aligned to Germany's manufacturing-centric pattern bargaining system. Italian and, for a brief period of time, Dutch public employers catered to unions' bargaining demands upon EMU entry. The extreme suppression of wage growth in Germany's sheltered sector was a key driver of the country's depressed inflation rate, which provided Germany with the most competitive (beggar thy neighbor) real exchange rate within the Eurozone after 1999 (between 1999 and 2008, Germany's real exchange rate declined by 15.2 percent while Italy's increased by 12.2 percent; EU Commission AMECO Database 2014). Extreme wage suppression in Germany cannot solely be attributed to its inflation-phobic domestic politics. Highlighted in chapter 4 and in the sections to follow, the Dutch government, which was just as low-inflation minded as Germany's, was not as able to act on its inflation preferences in the early 2000s because it lacked Germany's rigid sheltered sector wage-setting structures.

In this chapter, I argue that divergence in public sector pay and employment reform may account for the heterogeneity in public sector wage growth between these three countries. In Germany, the state resisted the liberalization of pay and employment conditions in the public sector. This institutional rigidity allowed public employers to retain important veto powers in wage determination for civil servants, enabling them to limit public sector wage increases under EMU. In keeping public bargaining institutions rigid, like their Danish counterparts did in their 2007 structural public sector reform (see chapter 4), German federal, regional, and municipal employers thwarted wage-push strategies by opportunistic public sector unions, upholding Germany's export-centric pattern bargaining system.

Governments in Italy and the Netherlands, in contrast, embraced the introduction of incentive payments and flexible wage bargaining to the public sector. Yet these "private sector like" bargaining frameworks granted civil servants legal bargaining status enjoyed by employees in the private sector, and removed veto powers from state negotiators. Consequently, such reforms curtailed employers' capacity to (unilaterally) control public sector wage growth. In the absence of a rigid public sector bargaining structure, unions were able to initiate a *sheltered sector-favoring* pattern bargaining system, where wages negotiated in public subsectors with generous incentive payments or labor shortages were used as targets for those without. The urgency to comply with Maastricht quelled public sector wage inflation, a by-product of such flexible systems, in Italy and the Netherlands during the 1990s. However, after 1999, Italian and Dutch public employers were simply unable to deliver the extreme level of sheltered sector wage suppression that their counterparts in Germany did. Italian public employers were completely unable to govern public sector wage developments like their German counterparts prior to the 2008 Brunetta reforms, which granted the state greater steering capacity in wage determination during the global financial crisis. The Dutch government, on the other hand, tackled wage-price spirals in the public sector earlier using state-led *national* wage pacts. Public sector employment reform, though intended to facilitate cost-savings within *nonwage components* of public employment (notably pensions), placed upward pressures on public sector wages by enhancing public sector unions' bargaining status, which had important implications for national inflation and relative price competitiveness under EMU.

Reversal of Fortunes: German, Italian, and Dutch Wage Performance under EMU

Germany, Italy, and the Netherlands entered EMU under very different competitive positions than they did when entering the debt crisis. Between 1992 and

1998, Italy and the Netherlands produced consistent current account surpluses (figure 5.1) while Germany produced persistent current account deficits. Under EMU, however, the German and Italian positions dramatically reversed, with Germany producing sizable current account surpluses and Italy producing consistent current account deficits (although not to the extent of those produced in Spain and Ireland, which will be discussed in chapter 6). In the Netherlands, after a notable decline in the current account balance in the late 1990s/early 2000s, current account surpluses surged in 2003—conspicuously the same year when the first negotiated national wage pact came into effect.

The argument presented in chapter 2 provides an explanation as to why Italy, identified by many as possessing weak or nonfunctional corporatist institutions (Bruno and Sachs 1985; Calmfors and Driffill 1988), managed to turn its economic misfortunes around in the 1990s and produce economic outputs (wage moderation) typically associated with corporatist wage bargaining structures. Italian public employers used the Maastricht inflationary and budgetary criteria, as well as a more serious monetary threat from the Bank of Italy, which was granted greater independence and an inflation mandate during the 1990s, to restrain wage growth. As a result of these constraints, Italy witnessed recoordination/recentralization in collective bargaining via a resurgence of national social pacts that helped reduce inflation and the fiscal deficit (Hancké and Rhodes 2005; Hassel 2003). Between 1992 and 1998, real wages in the sheltered sector declined *every year* in Italy (on average by 0.6 percent a year) while Germany and the Netherlands witnessed persistent sheltered sector wage growth (on average by 1.4 percent and 1.25 percent a year, respectively). However, like trends in the current accounts, this position reversed itself in the pre-crisis EMU years. From 1999 to 2007, Italian sheltered sector real wage growth averaged 1.7 percent a year. While not excessive, these wage developments exceeded the 0.7 percent yearly average real wage increase in Italy's manufacturing sector. In Germany, on the other hand, hourly real wages in the sheltered sector declined by 0.3 percent a year. In the Netherlands, after the inflationary run in the sheltered sector in the early 2000s, sheltered sector wage growth slowed in the mid- to late-2000s, producing an average sheltered sector real wage increase of 1.25 percent yearly for the 1999–2007 period.

What can account for this relative competitiveness reversal between Italy and Germany? General economic conditions do not explain why their current account behavior would diverge so significantly in the pre-crisis EMU years. Both were low growth economies, with similar deficit spending and Stability and Growth Pact (SGP) violation records between 1999 and 2007. General unemployment rates in both countries were relatively high and above the EU15 average—Germany had an average unemployment rate of 9.3 percent between

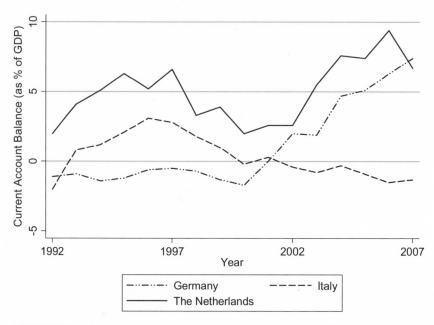

FIGURE 5.1. Current account balances, as a percentage of GDP, for Germany, Italy, and the Netherlands (1992–2007)

1999 and 2007, while Italy's averaged 8.4 percent (EU Commission AMECO Database 2014). Employment growth in the sheltered sector composite was paltry for both countries, increasing by roughly 4 percent between the euro's introduction and 2007, well below the average 12 percent sheltered sector employment growth rate for the EU15 (EU KLEMS 2010). Moreover, public sector union strength cannot account for the divergence witnessed after 1999, because it was higher in Germany than it was in Italy. In the late 2000s, roughly 40 percent of the Italian public sector belonged to a trade union (Fulton 2013a) whereas 60 percent of employees in the German public sector were unionized, largely through the civil services union confederation, Deutscher Beamtenbund (DBB), which is independent of Deutscher Gewerkschaftsbund (DGB), Germany's main union confederation (Fulton 2013b).

One notable difference between the two countries was the structure of bargaining institutions that facilitated (or failed to facilitate) the coordination of wage moderation along sectoral lines. Germany possesses a rigid pattern bargaining coordination system, which has been identified by several scholars as heavily conducive toward the production of not only aggregate wage restraint (Traxler and Kittel 2000) but specifically sheltered sector wage restraint (Traxler and Brandl 2010; Johnston, Hancké, and Pant 2014). In Germany's pattern bargaining system, IG Metall, the (exposed sector) Metalworkers Union that assumed its leadership role in German collective bargaining in 1956 (Manow 2000), negotiates wage settlements with employers first, and other sectors then mimic its wage settlements. Yet unlike other classic models of centralized bargaining, German industrial relations do not uphold wage compression. Cross-class alliances between manufacturing unions and the German Employers Association (BDA) and the Confederation of German Industries (BDI) have blocked solidaristic wage growth in sheltered sectors and, during the 2000s, the development of a statutory minimum wage for low wage sectors (Palier and Thelen 2010, 125). Consequently, though manufacturing settlements are used as a wage benchmark, nonmanufacturing German employers generally impose lower wage settlements onto services sectors employees in accordance with their lower productivity increases. In the public sector, the strict employment relations that govern the German civil service, the *Beamte*, have been crucially important in assisting public employers to deliver the high degree of wage suppression that reinforces the low-inflation competitiveness of the German pattern bargaining system.

Italian employers, in contrast, negotiate with unions under a (highly fragmented) peak-level association bargaining framework. Prior to the July 1993 agreement, union confederal leaders possessed no formal power in controlling the decisions made by leaders of (public sector) affiliate unions (Baccaro 2002). Sectoral relations within Italian union confederations have been described as politically divided, exchanges between unions and employers are more confrontational, and with the notable exception of the Maastricht period, employers and governments lacked the ability to contain wages due to the absence of framework bargaining (Pérez 2000; Baccaro 2002). Italy made impressive strides in limiting aggregate and sheltered sector wage growth between 1992 and 1998, and even (unsuccessfully) during the 1980s. In 1983, a tripartite agreement imposed several wage ceilings on sectoral collective bargaining. In 1984, government attempted to produce a similar agreement with the intention of limiting inflation, yet the Italian General Confederation of Labour (CGIL), Italy's largest union confederation, refused to sign the agreement (Baccaro 2002).

During the 1990s, Italy witnessed a more prominent shift in controlling wage growth via the unilateral imposition of a non-accommodating monetary policy in a fragmented bargaining environment. The abolition of *scala mobile*, the wage indexation system, in 1992 and the institutionalization of national incomes policies and national-level bargaining in the July 1993 agreement did much to improve Italy's inflation performance and price-competitive position during the 1990s (Regini 1997; Rhodes 1998; Ebbinghaus and Hassel 2000). Pérez (2000) outlines that one crucial instigator of this shift toward centralized wage

control was export sector employers: in a fragmented and moderately decentralized bargaining environment in the 1980s, exposed sector employers realized
that they were unable to produce their desired levels of wage restraint because
sheltered sector wage settlements set the pace of inflation. In 1993, Confindustria,
Italy's largest employer federation, helped to institutionalize a centralized locus of
collective bargaining at the national level, a proposal that was initially opposed by
unions that wanted some degree of power retained for lower bargaining units
(Pérez 2000, 451). Consenting to the need to qualify for EMU, however, Italian
unions signed onto the deal and, in 1994 and 1997, significantly curtailed their
wage demands, asking for wage increases that were minimally above inflation
(Pérez 2000).

Despite these impressive strides in Italian collective bargaining, several
scholars attributed Maastricht's pressures in spurring such events as an aberration rather than a permanent institutional shift (Hancké and Rhodes 2005; Hassel 2003). Once Maastricht's constraining terms of conditionality were lost with
EMU entry, the belle époque of Italian labor relations quickly waned. Sectoral
union labor relations once again soured, especially between the export and public
sector, as unions organizing local government and healthcare employees were
able to escape the 1998–2001 national agreements and pursue higher wage settlements that facilitated local level wage drift (Bordogna 2002; Dell'Aringa, Lucifora, and Origo 2005). Problems of the reemergence of fragmented bargaining
under EMU were further exacerbated by privatization efforts in public utilities
in the late 1990s.[2]

In regards to civil servants, wage push problems began to resurface for employees of Italian ministries for the 1998–2001 bargaining agreement: ministe-
rial workers received an (above inflation) pay settlement of 4.7 percent over a
two-year period, prompting Confindustria to express serious concerns over
how these settlements would affect wage demands within private sector negotiations.[3] Such wage developments, though not on par with those in the 1980s,
are notable when comparing differences in sheltered and manufacturing sector
real wage growth between 1992 and 2007. Prior to the euro's introduction, wage
growth in Italy's sheltered sector was consistently below that in the manufacturing sector (except in 1996 and 1997), and the degree of sheltered sector wage suppression relative to the manufacturing sector was far more magnified in Italy
than in Germany and the Netherlands (figure 5.2). However, under the pre-crisis
EMU years, Italian sheltered sector wage growth immediately surpassed that in
manufacturing—in 2001 by as much as 4 percent a year—while sheltered sector
wage growth in the Netherlands (after 2001) and Germany was surpassed by that
in the manufacturing sector.

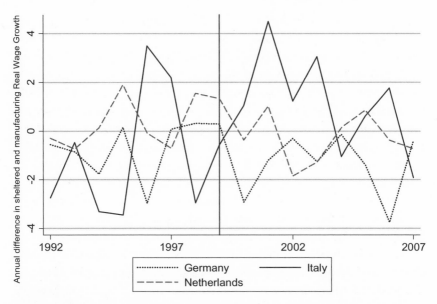

FIGURE 5.2. Annual differences in sheltered sector and manufacturing real wage growth (1992–2007)

Note: Positive differences indicate wage growth in the sheltered sector has overshot wage growth in the manufacturing sector, while negative values indicate the opposite. Vertical line delineates the introduction of monetary union in 1999.
Source: EU KLEMS (2010).

Maastricht's aberration was not limited to southern Europe. Monetary union's introduction spurred far higher public sector wage inflation in Ireland (see chapter 6) and brief public sector wage inflation in the Netherlands, a country that was unique in fulfilling the institutional stabilization prerequisites required for monetary union (Enderlein 2006). This early 2000s blip in public sector wage inflation was a strong deviation from previous Dutch macroeconomic policy, which has been geared to ensuring that exports of goods and services systematically exceeded imports (E. Jones 2003a, 210). Only in two countries (Austria and Germany, both possessing export-centric pattern bargaining coordination regimes and rigid bargaining statues in the public sector) did employers manage to *consistently* suppress wage growth in the public and services sectors relative to that in manufacturing under the new supranational monetary regime.

Why were German public employers able to deliver consistent public sector wage suppression after 1999 while this capacity was limited in Italy and for some of the 2000s in the Netherlands? Exposed sector industrial relations alone cannot explain Germany's success—Germany's largest public sector union, DBB, exists outside of the DGB umbrella and pursues parallel "discussions"[4] with public employers. Rather, to understand how public employers are able to reinforce sectoral coordination institutions that favor the export sector, is it important to examine bargaining mechanisms that grant them veto or agenda-setting powers in public sector wage negotiations. In Germany, these veto powers and rigid bargaining structures remained largely unaltered during the 1980s, 1990s, and 2000s. When employment and public sector pay reforms were introduced in the Civil Service Law Reform of 1997 and the 2005 TVöD general framework, they were highly restrictive and closely monitored by the state. Governments in Italy and the Netherlands, on the other hand, largely surrendered these veto powers in wide-sweeping public sector liberalization employment and pay reforms in the 1980s and 1990s. Consequently, both governments were unable to contain public sector wage inflation in the manner that their German counterparts were able to once EMU entry was guaranteed. While Italian public employers and the state more broadly possessed little coordination capacity to unify fragmented bargaining in the public sector, the Dutch government was able to fall back on reactive national wage pacts in the early 2000s that imposed wage ceilings and restored nationwide wage moderation.

Before discussing the specific nature of these diverse public sector bargaining institutions and how they conform (or do not conform) to an export-led system of collective bargaining, I first dissect the general nature of bargaining incentives and employment structures within the public sector. Unlike employees in sectors exposed to competition, public sector workers possess a more guarded employment status, which makes their employment less susceptible to inflationary wage increases. However, not all public sector unions bargain with weak employers. Some countries possess more rigid public sector bargaining institutions that grant the state greater capacity to impose low wages, to the advantage of the export sector. Others severely lack this capacity. Ironically, countries that fall into the latter camp are also those that *generally* have attempted to harmonize collective bargaining and pay conditions in the public sector with those in the private sector.

The Precarious Case of the Public Employee: Collective Bargaining in the Public Sector

Historically, public sector employees have enjoyed a privileged employment status regarding pensions and protection against dismissal, although in recent years the generosity of these employment conditions has been reduced across the OECD. Several scholars have observed that such privileged working conditions incentivize public sector employees to "shirk at work," and that incentive structures are necessary to enhance efficiency and promote organizational best practice (Hood 1995; Dunleavy et al. 2005). Others have attributed public sector unions' wage incentives to solidaristic factors (Pontusson, Rueda, and Way 2002). Despite possible altruistic objectives of promoting wage compression, public sector unions employ wage strategies that are more commonly associated with "selfish" motivations behind rent-seeking, which are exacerbated by the public sector's sheltered status (Iversen 1996; Garrett and Way 1999; Franzese 2001). Public sector unions are relatively sheltered from competitive pressures for two reasons. First, in most developed countries, public services are overwhelmingly provided by the state. Though some private substitutes may exist, with varying degrees of exposure depending on the country and service in question, the state retains a near monopoly on the provision of these services, particularly for social groups that do not have the economic means to resort to (private sector) alternatives. Second, public services are generally necessities (i.e., health and social care services, education, refuse collection, policing) rather than services whose consumption can be delayed for a protracted period of time. Consequently, demand for these goods tends to be fixed or in some cases (i.e., education) acyclical, granting public sector wage-setters further pricing power in wage negotiations.

Combining the lack of market constraints with the public sector's higher mobilization capacity, some scholars conclude that this sector remains one of the last strongholds where Olsonian collective action problems in modern wage-setting persist. Garrett and Way (1999) introduce a unique interaction to the Calmfors-Driffill (1988) hypothesis, which identifies a hump-shaped relationship between union centralization and unemployment/inflation along such Olsonian lines. In the absence of strong public sector unions, the relationship between centralization and unemployment/inflation conforms to the Calmfors-Driffill model, where only unions in intermediately centralized regimes, who are strong enough to extract high wage increases yet small enough not to bear the full cost of inflation, engage in wage push.[5] If strong public sector unions exist, however, greater centralization deteriorates economic performance, as these unions exacerbate wage militancy within union confederations and fail to internalize their wage externalities. Exposed sector unionism, in other words, is a necessary condition for the internalization of externalities within the labor movement.

Such arguments about public sector wage-setters suggest that European governments attempting to rectify or avoid public deficits may be in a perilous bargaining position, making it difficult for them to impose pay restraint. This is especially problematic under the context of monetary union, where governments of member-states also lack the constraining monetary and conditionality institutions that effectively tied their hands in the EMS and Maastricht regimes. While these theories provide a useful construct for understanding collective action problems in public sector wage bargaining, they fail to account for the heterogeneity in public sector wage growth that one can observe between Germany, Italy, and the Netherlands in the EMU era. Since entering the EMU in 1999 and replacing the fiscal yoke of Maastricht with the weaker Stability and Growth Pact, Italy has conformed well to the above arguments on public sector trade unionism. Annual public sector wage growth exceeded total national productivity growth by 1 percent per annum, on average, in Italy between 1999 and 2007, leading to a public sector wage and national labor productivity differential of 9 percent within the nine-year period (EU KLEMS 2010). Italy also had the third highest *relative* public sector annual wage growth (measured as the difference between public sector and manufacturing wage growth) among the EMU12, behind Ireland and Portugal, over the same period, indicating that public sector unions secured more generous settlements than their manufacturing counterparts. Wage differentials between the Italian public and the manufacturing sector widened by 8.6 percent in the nine years following EMU entry and preceding the global financial crisis (EU KLEMS 2010). Public sector wage-setters in Germany, on the other hand, do not conform well to the conventional wisdom about public sector bargaining. Annual public sector real wage growth lagged well behind national labor productivity growth; between 1999 and 2007, Germany was the only EMU country to see average *negative* public sector real wage growth *in the absence of productivity developments* (EU KLEMS 2010). Public sector wage growth also lagged substantially behind that of manufacturing, leading to an 11 percent widening of the wage gap between the sectors in nine years, the second largest sectoral wage gap between the manufacturing and sheltered sector among the EU15, behind Austria.

Much of industrial relations literature attributes Germany's impressive record of wage moderation within its sheltered sectors to its stable (and exposed sector led) pattern bargaining system of wage coordination and domestic politics that favor low inflation. German employers have been identified as crucial actors in the maintenance of this system, given their complacency in the economic outputs (specifically, coordinated wage moderation) associated with a collective pattern bargaining structure. Crouch (1999) attributes complacency to the excessive costs of changing the system. Though German employers would have more freedom to innovate under an Anglo-American model if they could deviate from constraints posed by trade unions and their own employers' associations, they prefer "sulking" under the current system because it would require too much conflict to abolish these institutions (Crouch 1999, 42). Others claim that Germany's largest and most prominent firms tolerate greater inflexibility because the German industrial relations system continues to generate production benefits; namely, a pool of skilled labor with specific skill-sets that are otherwise costly to acquire (Hall and Soskice 2001). Thelen (1993) and Thelen and Kume (2006) argue that while employers in the United States and United Kingdom may prefer labor market deregulation, employers in Germany and Japan cling to traditional industrial relations arrangements because their specialized production strategies rely on labor coordination, worker investment in skill acquisition, and peaceful working relations at the company level. As employers in other centralized bargaining systems (notably those in Sweden and Denmark) become active instruments of institutional change, German employers have grown accustomed to their rigid institutions, due to the costs associated with reforming them.

These arguments provide a rich account of employers' preferences for decentralization and institutional preservation, yet it is biased toward the perspective of manufacturing employers. Neglect of employers' preferences for decentralization in the *private services* sector is understandable, given the lack of union and employer organization within this sector across most OECD countries. However, neglect of public employers' decentralization preferences remains puzzling, especially in light of the fact that this sector is one of the last strongholds of union organization within most advanced democracies. Wage bargaining in the public sector should be more centralized relative to that in the private sector, given that unions interact with a more homogenized group of employers (central and regional levels of government), although in some public sector services that have quasi-public status, employers may also be affiliated with private employers' associations. The state's relative monopoly on public services, however, does not imply that the sector is immune from bargaining fragmentation. Covered extensively in the New Public Management literature (see Dunleavy 1985; Dunsire and Hood 1989; Hood 1991), many governments introduced flexible pay systems during the 1980s, 1990s, and 2000s that allowed greater individualized pay bargaining in order to establish incentive structures for civil servants.

Under what conditions are public sector unions successful in extracting wage gains from governments within a monetary environment where sheltered employers lack external constraints to impose moderation? Surprisingly, little attention has been given to the organizational role of employers within the public sector; rather, public sector union power is the most emphasized characteristic of wage militancy. Yet public sector union organization is neither a sufficient nor a necessary condition for understanding the heterogeneity in public sector rent capture. As the example of Germany shows, public sector unions can be highly organized (60 percent of the German public sector belongs to a union), but can still be forced to accept moderated wage settlements if public employers are cohesive and can rely on legal statues to credibly threaten unilateral intervention in pay-setting. Not all EMU member-states possess these unilateral bargaining structures that grant an overwhelming advantage to employers. Of the three countries analyzed here, those that introduced employment and pay reforms to align public sector employment conditions with those in the private sector exhibit the loosest configuration of pay-setting powers for public employers. Governments' decisions to flexibilize pay-setting within the public sector may have produced perverse feedback effects in public sector wage moderation, by granting well-organized public sector unions greater capacity to secure more generous wage settlements within a more fragmented bargaining environment. As selective governments attempted to modernize public sector pay-setting, they implicitly removed their veto power in wage negotiations with unions. Turning New Public Management theory on its head, I argue the strategies of employers in introducing public employment restructuring, particularly related to incentive/efficiency pay and bargaining rights, can better explain why some of EMU's northern economies were able to deliver such high degrees of public sector wage moderation under monetary union, while the economies of southern Europe could not.

Blunting Government's Sword of Damocles: Public Sector Employment Reform and Wage Inflation

The attraction of New Public Management theory to bureaucrats and policy-makers lay in the motivation to enhance efficiency and competition within all facets of the public sector. Before the 1980s, public sector employment relations in many EU countries were highly centralized, revolving around one major bargaining unit. *Sovereign employer models*, which applied largely to career civil servants, were prevalent in several European countries, including Germany, Austria, the Netherlands (prior to 1989), Italy (prior to 1993), and to a lesser degree France, Belgium, Denmark, and Spain—although, as outlined in chapter 6, Spain too abandoned its sovereign employer model in the 1990s (Bordogna 2008, 384). Under this employment model, public employees lack formal bargaining

STRENGTH IN RIGIDITY   123

rights and the state is permitted to unilaterally impose its preferred pay settle-ment via legislation at any time.

Within the sovereign employer model, the state's capacity to determine pay conditions lies within unilateral privilege. This privilege enables public employers to dictate wage growth in the public sector via two power levers: one is *the shadow of hierarchy*, where governments can threaten public sector unions with with-drawing from negotiations (a "sword of Damocles" bargaining tactic); the other power lever is *direct action*, where governments follow through on withdrawal and unilaterally impose their preferred pay settlement (a tool frequently used by the Dutch state in the late 1970s and early 1980s). Such privilege is based on the unilateral regulation of employment relationships in the public sector by law or decree. This powerful veto grants the state a unique capacity to centralize public sector wage relations with a fragmented bargaining context; there are no formal pay negotiations and if nonbinding consultations take place where public em-ployees request generous wage settlements, the state has the authority to impose its preferred wage decision on all public employees.

Unilateral privilege, while granting governments considerable veto power over public sector wage negotiations, has often been supplemented with generous nonwage benefits to public employees and civil servants, namely generous pen-sions and strict job dismissal regulations. Indeed, many European governments, when introducing public sector pay reforms in the 1980s and 1990s, willingly shed unilateral privilege in exchange for reducing the generosity of public sec-tor pensions and dismissal provisions. Such political "horse-trading" had impor-tant implications for the public sector wage bill, especially under the EMU, when the strong conditionality of the Maastricht deficit criteria was replaced with the more weakly enforced deficit rules of the Stability and Growth Pact (see Johnston 2012).

Public sector pay and employment reforms gained prominence as the shift to neoliberal policies highlighted the importance of government deficits, the effi-ciency of public services, and the size of the state. Public employment was a natural target, given the public sector wage bill's significant share in state expen-diture and public sector employees' generous employment terms. Three integrat-ing themes of public sector reforms were introduced in several OECD countries during the 1980s and 1990s with a view to enhance the efficiency of public services: 1) *disaggregation*, which divided large public sector hierarchies into a multiform structure, which is similar to decentralization within private sector bargaining; 2) *competition*, which involved a shrinking of administration and a diversification of suppliers; and 3) *incentivization*, which rewarded employees for achieving performance targets (Dunleavy et al. 2005). The harmonization of public employment conditions with those in the private sector, however, led to a trade-off between bargaining representation and employment conditions. Harmonization of employment *conditions*—pensions, dismissal rules, criteria for promotion—were perceived as a cost improvement, as these terms are more generous in the public sector than in the private sector. However, the generosity of these terms yielded advantages for governments, given their *coupling* with unilateral privilege, which severely restricted public employees *wage* negotiation strategies.

Public sector reforms were assumed to produce cost-savings by reducing the generosity of public sector employment conditions. Yet given that these conditions were inherently linked with unilateral privilege, public sector modernization also invoked the forfeiture of this right of government, by linking bargaining conditions with those in the private sector. Consequently, in countries where these employment and pay reforms took place, public sector unions were able to gain an advantageous legal footing in wage negotiations, enhancing possible wage push strategies. Cost-savings resulting from nonwage reforms could now be offset within the wage-setting realm of public sector employment relations, as reformist governments were presented with a new negotiating environment where highly organized public sector employees possessed greater statutory wage-bargaining leverage.

Extensive reforms were made in a number, though not all, of EU countries throughout the 1990s and 2000s in order to harmonize public sector employment conditions with those in the private sector. Despite these efforts, disparities in public and private employment conditions persist across the EU15. Governments in some countries (Italy, as well as the Netherlands and Spain) departed from the sovereign employer model in the 1980s and 1990s, granting formal bargaining rights to public employees, introducing incentive pay in exchange for reductions in pension benefits, and linking promotion to performance rather than length of service. Other governments (most notably in Germany and Austria, but also in France) resisted this change; while the German government has succeeded in reducing public pension benefits under recent reforms, it has failed to alter legal frameworks governing civil servant pay and employment conditions. Heterogeneity in reform patterns provides a convenient means to examine how public sector bargaining structures enable public employers to moderate wage settlements in line with the preferences of exposed sector wage-setters under monetary union. The disparities in public sector reform paths for three countries, Germany, Italy, and the Netherlands, are highlighted in the next sections to exhibit how their different reform trajectories may have contributed to their varying capabilities in delivering public sector wage moderation under monetary union.

The Confines of Centralized Wage Setting in Germany's Public Sector

Though German public sector industrial relations have not witnessed the erosion of bargaining coverage seen in the private sector, the public sector has not been immune from decentralization pressure. Decentralization has largely been fueled by changes to the organization of employers, to the dismay of the unions. In 2003, the centralized public sector bargaining association (*Tarifgemeinschaft*), where joint collective bargaining between the three levels of German government had been conducted for over forty years, split into two separate bargaining associations (one at the federal and local level and one at the Länder level). The split emerged as a result of the refusal of the Employers' Association of German Länder (TdL) and the Local Government Employers' Association (VKA) to accept the traditional bargaining leadership role of the federal government.[6] The creation of the services union ver.di in 2001, which presides over a significant number of public services collective agreements (Fulton 2013b), though not for civil servants, together with the 2005 conclusion of the public sector (general framework) collective agreement (*Tarifvertrag öffentlicher Dienst, TVöD*) uniting white-collar and blue-collar public sector pay determination, has facilitated some degree of (re)centralization between the federal and local government bargaining levels. Despite this fragmentation, negotiations remain highly coordinated between the three levels of government.

The German public sector constitutes a dual system, with a sovereign employer system for its *Beamte*—career civil servants, who in 2007 represented roughly 40 percent of public employees across all levels of government (Keller 2011)—and a model employer system for blue- and white-collar workers (*Arbeiter* and *Angestellte*). The latter category of public employees is governed by private law, assigning employees formal collective-bargaining status and the right to strike. The government may provide leadership during negotiations, but at no time it is allowed to unilaterally impose conditions on these workers. Within the German Trade Union Confederation (DGB), blue- and white-collar employees are predominantly represented by the ver.di trade union. Ver.di started its first bargaining round in 2001 with an ambitious wage agenda for public services, attempting to compensate for constrained public sector wage growth since reunification, which was persistently below wage growth in other sectors.[7] Despite its organizational strength as DGB's second largest union, ver.di has not managed to close the public/private sector wage gap in recent years.

Organizing *Beamte* is the responsibility of the German Civil Services Union Confederation (*Deutscher Beamtenbund, DBB*), an organization outside the

DGB's umbrella. Though the confederal authority is the only one in Germany to have achieved an increase in membership throughout the 1990s, its members, along with all civil servants, are not formally allowed to collectively bargain or to strike. DBB possesses no formal independent power to negotiate wage settlements or coordinate bargaining with ver.di (Keller 2011, 2339). Before the end of the 1990s, wage agreements concluded by DGB public service affiliates were automatically passed on to *Beamte*. However, since the late 1990s and 2000s, German public employers ended this tradition of employment solidarity between the two categories of public employees. Public employers reduced *Beamte* pay increases below those concluded within white- and blue-collar public sector collective agreements, extended working hours (particularly *Länder* governments), and reduced or in some cases abolished civil servants' bonus payments in 2007 (Keller 2011, 2340, 2344). While state negotiators attempted to enforce the (unilaterally imposed) pay and employment conditions for *Beamte* (whose pay increases were heavily moderated) on non-civil servants employed in the public sector, ver.di's resistance has thwarted such efforts.

German public employers' power advantage lies in their preservation of the public sector's organizational rigidity. Germany has frequently been described as a late-starter with respect to public sector reform (Greiling 2005). However, this perceived shortcoming transformed itself into an asset in public sector pay determination under EMU, with the German state employing two strategies helping to preserve public sector rigidity: restricting performance pay and retaining its wage-setting veto for the *Beamte*. Restrictions in the former thwarted mimicking strategies by ver.di to target (higher) wage settlements in other sectors, although German private employers were also highly effective at imposing wage moderation in the private sector during the 2000s through an embedded pattern bargaining, wage coordination model. German employers' retention of the sovereign employer model for civil servants preserved public employers' capacity to dictate pay conditions for a significant proportion of the public sector labor force.

The German state has not thwarted all attempts to modernize collective bargaining the public sector. However, most recent reforms in public employment—namely, the Civil Service Law Reform of 1997 and the 2005 TVöD general framework—have approached public sector employment and pay reform with caution. Applying solely to *Beamte*, the Civil Service Law Reform was meant to introduce competitiveness into the career civil service by establishing greater flexibility, coupled with a performance-oriented remuneration system.[8] The basic provisions of the act with regard to *pay-setting* did not seriously challenge the status quo, because performance incentives featured more in promotion prospects, where seniority-based career progress was replaced by performance targets. Moreover, the pay-for-performance elements that were introduced were limited to 10 percent of civil servants at any given time.[9] The reform law produced provisions much nearer to the state's objectives to reduce incentive pay in *Beamte salaries*, which, on account of the Maastricht criteria, was under pressure to restrict public budgets. Temporary and probationary periods and measures to support part-time employment for career public servants were introduced, while measures to restrict entitlements and avoid early retirements were enacted with a view to achieve pension cost-savings.[10] Public sector pay dynamics, however, witnessed very little change.

Performance pay was also a subject of debate for the 2005 public sector's "general framework" collective agreement (TVöD), an agreement applying only to Germany's white- and blue-collar federal and local government public employees, not to civil servants. Merging the previously separate blue- and white-collar classifications, it introduced a uniform grading system with fifteen pay grades dependent on education levels and work experience. Hailed as a more transparent and uniform system by not only public employer negotiators but also by ver. di, the agreement also introduced scope for performance pay. This contractual innovation, however, included a maximum ceiling of 8 percent of salary being subject to performance increases (the pilot introduction began with only 1 percent), and its implementation postponed until 2007 (Greiling 2005, 564; Müller and Schmidt 2013).

The German public sector has proved resistant to rapid modernization, due mostly to successive German governments' reticence to introduce widespread reform (Müller and Schmidt 2013). This resistance helped Germany maintain a continuation of sheltered sector wage moderation under EMU by providing public employers the legal and organization mechanisms to uphold Germany's export-centric pattern bargaining system. The wage outputs of these rigid institutions are more than clear—after 1999, Germany along with Austria, which shares very similar public sector bargaining institutions, witnessed the highest degree of public sector wage suppression in EMU. With export sector employers also stifling wage growth, this significant degree of wage suppression helped Germany to persistently undercut its EMU trading partners' inflation and real exchange rates, ultimately strengthening its current account balance from a deficit of 1.3 percent of GDP in 1999 to a surplus of 7.5 percent of GDP in 2007 (EU Commission AMECO Database 2014). Germany's export miracle was not only delivered by wage settlements in its manufacturing sector, but also by the overlooked yet equally important wage moderation in its public sector.

Decentralized Wage Push in Italy

Contrary to Germany, Italy initiated a number of reforms that granted public sector employees greater bargaining power in the 1980s and 1990s. In 1983, the Italian government initiated its first reforms to align public sector wage and nonwage bargaining conditions with those in the private sector. This process de facto curbed the authority of the state and further enhanced a two-tier bargaining model in 1993, giving the bargaining table primacy over unilateral privilege in public sector pay determination (D'Amore 2011). The process of decentralized wage-setting, introduced to enhance bargaining flexibility and increase productivity in the public sector, resulted in wage push and higher wage settlements. Italy's peak bargaining system of coordination added further problems to the presence of sheltered sector wage inflation, as export sector wage-setters also had limited capabilities in mitigating public sector influence within peak-level bargaining.

The 1983 "*legge quadro*" reform was the first reform to align wage bargaining in the public sector with private sector practice. Though the extension of the right to collective bargaining to public sector employees brought bargaining rights closer to those in the private sector, it also generated a regime of double protection as it failed to abolish the sector's special prerogatives (Giugni 1992). This strengthened union power and led to the intensification of disputes, higher wage settlements, and an increasing public/private sector pay gap (EU KLEMS 2010). Italy's state of fiscal distress in the early 1990s, and the urgency to qualify for Maastricht, promoted further pressures for privatization and public sector employment reform, involving not only the off-loading of previously state-owned enterprises, but also the introduction of measures making public sector job conditions, especially public sector pensions (see Levy 1999, 255–256), and wage-setting institutions similar to those in the private sector. Through this process, the legitimacy of collective bargaining was further reinforced as a regulatory tool. The social dialogue of the early 1990s, and the subsequent February 1993 legislative decree (D.Lgs.29/1993) and the July 1993 agreement, created a new labor market environment with important repercussions on wages and employment conditions in both the public and private sectors.

Until 1993, public and private sector employment conditions differed substantially. Public employees had a special employment status ensuring employment security and determining recruitment conditions, mobility, job grading, and pay schemes. The collective and individual bargaining arrangements, as concluded in the legislative decree 29/1993, regulated employment conditions and salaries for roughly 80 percent of public sector employees, although the functions and responsibilities of the remaining 20 percent (e.g., the police and the armed forces, magistrates, prefects, diplomats, and others in public offices) were still determined unilaterally by the state. For all others—approximately 2.8 million employees in 2007 (Bordogna and Neri 2011)—civil law instead of the previous administrative code regulated employment conditions. The long-term effect of the 29/1993 decree, and its subsequent completion through the 1997 Bassanini reform, was not initially apparent in the public sector, given the urgent need to comply with the Maastricht criteria; indeed, the pre-1990 wage gap between the public sector and manufacturing remained relatively stable between the 1993 reform and the introduction of the EMU, only to widen afterward (EU KLEMS 2010).

One of the articles of the legislative decree (article 50 of legislative decree 29/1993) created ARAN, a monopolistic state agency representing employers in national-level collective-bargaining rounds. Its establishment served the purpose of insulating collective bargaining from the political arena, which had been in place since the inception of public sector collective bargaining in 1983. The 1997 Bassanini reform confirmed ARAN's exclusive negotiating competence at national level. The legislative decree 29/1993 established that bargaining over wages and employment conditions would occur at two distinct levels, a national and a decentralized local level. Bargaining at the local level was theoretically subject to the conditions and wage limits set at the national level, and additional wage increases were only allowed within centrally set guidelines. Although local government actors were not allowed to negotiate wage increases in breach of national guidelines, the 1998–2001 national agreements allowed local-level administrations to escape these constraints, provided that certain conditions were satisfied. These exemption conditions, not eliminated in the following bargaining rounds, were widely utilized by decentralized employers, especially in the local government and health sectors. The ensuing regional differentiation in local-level wage drift reflected the differences in the financial conditions of local administrations and local unions' bargaining strength (Bordogna 2002; Dell'Aringa, Lucifora, and Origo 2005).

Following the 1997 Bassanini reform, the Italian public sector job classification system was modified in such a way that national regulations no longer assigned occupational functions to a specific pay-scale grade. Prior to 1993, individual pay increases could only occur when employees were promoted to higher pay grades, with such promotions regulated through public competitions (so-called *vertical career*). This structure reduced the ability of administrations to use promotions as a tool to award additional wage increases (Dell'Aringa, Lucifora, and Origo 2005). The rigidities innate in this system were overcome in the years following the Bassanini reform. Accessibility to higher pay grades through public competition was only retained for progressions in the vertical career system, from a lower to a higher category. However, the new job classification system introduced the possibility of (limited) wage increases within each pay grade that did not require public competition (so-called *horizontal career*). This change saw the number of promotions increasing substantially in the 1998–2001 period and subsequent years. Together with productivity wage increases negotiated at the decentralized firm level, the new job classification system of the Bassanini regulations brought about significant wage drift over the 2000–2007 period, which was particularly marked in the local government and health sectors. Increases in average pay at the local level were mostly due to the fact that numerous workers were promoted without any change in the skill content of their jobs.

The Bassanini reform also changed the rules on the appointment of managers and top state executives. The employment relationship of the latter group, which in 1992–1993 had been regulated under a public law regime, effectively became privatized. The determination of managers' salaries was in a significant part linked to individual negotiations between the top executive and the relevant political authority, typically the relevant minister (Bordogna and Neri, 2011). This development, coupled with a favorable political environment, led to a substantial increase in the wage bill for this employee class: in 2007, salaries of public sector managers, especially of top-level state executives, almost equalled those of their private sector counterparts (Dell'Aringa, Lucifora, and Origo 2005).

The fourth Berlusconi government attempted to address the problematic effects of the 1993 and 1997 privatization efforts through the Brunetta reform of 2008. The reform, however, did not alter the privatized and contractualized nature of the employment relationship of public employees and the two-level decentralized bargaining structure. Addressing the delays deriving from the stalling of bargaining agreements, the Brunetta reform did however restore important powers to the state, reestablishing centralized controls on public sector collective negotiations and their outcomes. The effect of this latest reform on wage developments has not yet become apparent, as the ensuing debt crisis led to a freeze of national-level collective bargaining until 2012, which was then extended to 2014. In addition to these wage freezes, wage increases at local levels of public sector bargaining were also stopped, and wage and salaries of all public sector employees were frozen until the end of 2014.

Since the mid-1990s, the Italian public sector has been subject to rapid modernization and reform, in part as a solution to institutional changes initiated in the 1980s. The July 1993 agreement contractualized the public sector employment relationship, albeit with some exceptions, and created a two-tier bargaining system. These changes increased public sector unions' leverage in wage bargaining, resulting in sheltered sector wage inflation and a growing public/ private wage gap. Had these institutional changes been carried out with adequate safeguards to stop local-level politics from entering the bargaining arena (OECD 2007; Bach and Bordogna 2011), state negotiators may have been able to deliver more moderate pay agreements in Italy's public sector under monetary union. Nonetheless, this case, in contrast to the German one, suggests that the introduction of promotional payments in the absence of strong constraints on public sector bargaining (at both the national and local level) may have offered bargaining actors the opportunity to extract higher wages and better employment conditions.

Dutch National Wage Pacts as a Temporary Solution to Public Sector Wage Drift

The Netherlands provides a convenient shadow case to both the German and Italian experiences. Institutionally, the country's corporatist structures align more closely with Germany; a strong bi/tripartite tradition has ensured the deliverance of persistent wage moderation since the 1982 Wassenaar Agreement. Moreover, domestic politics in both countries have long been geared toward the attainment of low inflation; Dutch and German governments granted their respective national central banks the institutional capacity needed to transition to a low-inflation regime well before governments in other EMU member-states. Despite these similarities, Dutch public sector wage policy in EMU's early years followed a similar trajectory to Italy's. As in Italy, successive Dutch governments modified civil servants' legal bargaining position, moving from unilateral determination of pay conditions by government to an arrangement where formal bargaining rights granted public sector unions the legal capacity to negotiate autonomous agreements with the state. Increased procedural legitimacy made some unions, Abva-Kabo most notably, more ambitious (and successful) in demanding wage increases above that of the manufacturing sector once EMU entry was guaranteed. Yet unlike Italy, the Dutch state could rely on a long tradition of reactive national wage pacts that imposed wage ceilings on all sectors once wage inflation in the public sector threatened to transpire into a national wage-price spiral.

Like Germany and Italy, employment in the Dutch public sector falls within two categories: civil servants and "quasi-public" employment, which encompasses employees working in the state-funded sectors. The former category includes civil servants, teachers, and members of the armed forces and police, while the latter, under the jurisdiction of municipalities, includes healthcare and railway employees.[11] Prior to the 1980s, workers' rights for civil servants were severely limited. In 1903, the Netherlands introduced a ban on strikes in the public sector, and in 1962, government introduced legislation where salaries of public servants were unilaterally determined by Parliament (Visser 1998a, 280). Visser outlines that government's interest in dominating public bargaining was attributed to the public sector wage bill's weight in the federal budget. Due to the growing volume of public employment, pay indexing, and automatic price escalators for the public sector, 60 percent of the annual budget was determined by the outcome of informal annual wage negotiations by the end of the 1970s, and "no government could afford not to be interested in its outcome" (Visser 1998a, 280–281).

Though civil servants did not enjoy the bargaining autonomy of their peers in the private sector, they held a more favorable legal status on nonwage issues, with protection against dismissal and more generous sickness benefits, disability benefits, and pensions. Two significant legal actions were introduced in the 1980s and 1990s that altered this privileged position, bringing public employment rights and conditions in line with those in the private sector: the right to strike, introduced in 1981, and the introduction of formal bargaining rights in 1989.[12] These measures were elements of the Lubbers government's plans to privatize public services (Visser 1998a, 281). Lubbers's intention was to harmonize pay and employment conditions within the public and private sector. These plans, though aimed at reducing public servants' favorable legal status on *nonwage* issues, carried negative feedback effects for wage issues in the late-1990s, when Abva-Kabo union leaders, using Lubbers's previous words, initiated a "catch-up" wage policy with the private sector.[13]

During the politically and economically tremulous period of the early 1980s, public sector unions secured few concessions in legal bargaining status, gaining only the right to strike in 1981. The lifting of the strike ban on public employees was not a core objective of the Van Agt coalition government. Rather, it was the by-product of the Netherlands' signature to the Council of Europe's European Social Charter.[14] Before the austerity reforms in the early 1980s, there was little reason for public sector unions to resort to strike action on pay grounds, as pay was automatically linked to developments in the private sector.[15] Once the public/private pay link was severed in the Lubbers government's austerity measures, however, public unions readily utilized their new legal status, especially during the autumn of 1983, when confrontation with government was at its peak over a proposed 3.5 percent nominal wage cut (Hemerijck 2003). Due to the Netherlands' hard currency policy, and the Lubbers government's commitment to facilitate fiscal adjustment to the new monetary regime, public sector unions were unable to effectively utilize their new strike power for rent capture during the 1980s. The right to strike was practically abandoned by public sector unions after 1984, as public sector militancy buckled and pay fell behind that in the private sector by 10 percent between 1982 and 1990 (Visser 1998a, 281).

Despite the successful delivery of considerable wage growth suppression during the 1980s from public and quasi-public sector employees, the Lubbers government introduced modern management techniques to harmonize public sector employment conditions with those in the private sector. In 1989, the Dutch government introduced the formal right to collectively bargain to all public sector workers. The "Experimentation Protocol," which ran from 1989 to 1991, meant that the government could no longer alter employment or pay conditions of civil servants without the prior approval of trade unions.[16] Government's intention was to use this measure to harmonize generous public sector pensions and dismissal terms with those in the private sector; however, to make inroads into both areas, concessions were delivered on bargaining rights. Not formally outlined in law, this bargaining experiment applied only to civil servants employed in central levels of government; it was later introduced in the "semi-public" municipalities in the 1990s.[17] The implications of the reform for pay were significant. Parliament could no longer cap the resources available for public employees' pay increases. Moreover, contrary to previous practice, government could not restrict increases in future public sector pay-bills in its budgetary proposals.[18] Under the auspices of the Maastricht criteria, government secured a temporary exemption from the dissolution of federal control over public pay increases via agenda-setting within the budget. Lubbers expressed his opinion that a 3 percent ceiling should be established in the 1992 budgetary review in order to bring the deficit within the 3 percent criteria, and all major union confederations consented to his request.[19]

Visser (1998a) outlines that Lubbers's privatization efforts had been widely successful in public/private sector employment harmonization; civil servants lost most of their special privileges with respect to pensions and dismissal protection, as government intended. Such improvements, however, were not witnessed in wage policy. By the late 1990s, wage growth in the public and quasi-public services sectors had caught up with that in manufacturing. In autumn 1998, with Dutch entry to monetary union guaranteed and both the Maastricht and monetary threat rendered obsolete, civil servants' unions claimed that wage trends in the market sector would serve as a (lower-bound) benchmark for wage negotiations.[20] Enhanced public sector bargaining rights, though reducing the privileged nonwage status of civil servants during the 1980s and 1990s when a hard currency policy and the Maastricht criteria stifled inflationary wage demands, created perverse wage effects under EMU. Public sector unions utilized their formal bargaining power and the government "work harmonization" campaign to pursue wage catch-up with the private sector.

Decentralization efforts within the public sector further threatened government's bargaining position under EMU. Public sector decentralization was not an isolated process from the establishment of formal bargaining rights. It was pursued by government for identical reasons: to introduce incentive structures to public employees, bringing pay and conditions in the public sector in line with those in the private sector. After the announcement of formal bargaining rights to the public sector in 1988, a five-year process began where bargaining was decentralized from the central level to separate sectoral bargaining jurisdictions, which included the central government, local government, police, education, defense, and health (Visser 1998a, 281). Throughout the 1990s, variable pay elements were introduced into several public and quasi-public sectors, yet they not did not necessarily produce the intended effect of enhancing worker productivity. A report by the Dutch auditing firm KPMG in 2002 found that roughly 40 percent of public organizations surveyed had introduced performance-related pay, although its report concluded that variable pay did not lead to enhanced performance across all organizations.[21]

After the early 1990s, further decentralization efforts within the public sector ceased, with the exception of the health sector, where bargaining was further devolved to subsectors after a failed sector-level agreement in 1999.[22] After 1998, hospital employees pursued separate negotiations with employers, and nurses soon followed. It is not coincidental that the public sector wage-price spiral of the late 1990s originated from the healthcare sector. Decentralized bargaining created a perverse system of pattern bargaining coordination, where subsectors with stable labor supplies mimicked those with acute labor shortages, once the urgency of Maastricht was removed.

Enhanced bargaining autonomy offered Dutch public sector unions' greater capacity to coordinate inflationary wage demands in EMU's early years. Government was able to reimpose wage moderation via *national corporatist institutions*, state-led wage pacts, where nationwide wage freezes were exchanged for welfare reform concessions (see chapter 4). Unlike the Italian government, which lacked similar national corporatist structures, the Dutch could resort to national-level wage pacts as a reactive measure to correct public sector wage inflation in 2002. Yet before its big-bang public sector reforms in the late 1980s, Dutch public employers were able to pursue a more proactive approach in thwarting public sector wage inflation via *public sector specific* institutions, as those in place in Germany. Prior to 1989, Dutch public sector unions could, and did, point to the unilateral nature of pay determination in the public sector to justify low settlements to their members. After 1989, however, unions could no longer blame government for the imposition of unfavorable outcomes. With formal bargaining status, public sector unions were held directly accountable to their rank-and-file for final settlements. Maastricht provided a convenient institutional constraint to temporarily evade the wage-inflationary repercussions of government's public/private employment harmonization initiatives. Once membership was guaranteed, the wage push consequences associated with public sector unions' enhanced legal bargaining power and incentive pay structures were allowed to play out.

The experience of Germany, Italy, and the Netherlands highlight how rigid public sector bargaining structures enabled governments to uphold an export-centric wage bargaining model under monetary union. The introduction of flexible and individualized pay bargaining in the state sector presented hidden complications for reformist-minded governments. While the Italian and Dutch governments introduced these measures with the intention of reducing (non-wage) public sector employment costs, public sector unions, which were forced to accept prolonged wage moderation under the ERM and Maastricht regimes, took advantage of their new legal bargaining status in wage negotiations under monetary union. In Germany as in Denmark, where public sector reform in 2007 recentralized tax revenue collection into the hands of the federal government, the state retained the (legal) rigidity of public employees' bargaining rights. While some decentralization efforts were made, they were limited in scope. Limited bargaining rights and highly centralized pay negotiations granted the German state considerable authority over wage decisions and helped sheltered sector employers deliver significant wage suppression, which contributed to Germany's low-inflation, competitive "success."

The Italian experience under EMU presents a contrast to that of Germany, and even that of the Netherlands, which was able to rely on national wage-pacts to quell growing wage-price spirals stemming from the public sector. Public sector decentralization and employment reforms impeded the Italian state's capacity to deliver the degree of wage moderation seen in Germany. Wage excess was *not* rife in Italy—average annual inflation in Italy under the pre-crisis EMU year was only 2.3 percent, the lowest of all EMU's peripheral economies (EU Commission AMECO Database 2014). Italy's "competitiveness" problem, rather, stemmed from the fact that it was trading with countries like Germany, where rigid public sector wage structures granted the state considerable authority to exert *persistent* and *excessive* public sector wage suppression.

Italy's EMU experience mirrors that of Spain's which, along with Ireland, is the focus of the next chapter. Spain, like Italy, undertook similar measures toward public sector decentralization, granting further managerial and expenditure powers to Spanish regions in the late 1990s and early 2000s. While Spanish peak-level union confederations were strongly committed to wage moderation under EMU, recommending modest pay increases despite significant declines in unemployment, bargaining fragmentation (especially at the regional level), extensive wage indexation coverage, and the devolution of public sector employment relations to regional governments inhibited social partners and the state from delivering these commitments. In Ireland, meanwhile, public sector unions engaged in a considerable, organized wage push during the 2000s. Chapter 6 dissects the political and institutional features of wage-setting regimes that favor sheltered sector interests. Using a least-likely case design, I highlight that the common denominator behind Spain's and Ireland's competitive decline was that both countries lacked a coherent export sector (or state) actor that could deliver encompassing wage moderation.

6

SHELTERED SECTOR DOMINANCE UNDER A COMMON CURRENCY

Irrational Exuberance in Ireland and Fragmentation in Spain

Spain's and Ireland's exposure to the sovereign debt crisis in Europe provides a stark empirical contrast to predictions of the fiscal hypothesis. Aside from Finland, both countries were the only EMU members that consistently produced average annual government surpluses between 1999 and 2007. Moreover, both realized impressive declines in unemployment since the beginning of the 1990s, while average unemployment in the EU15 stayed more or less stagnant. Ireland witnessed a reduction in unemployment from 13.4 percent in 1990 to 4.7 percent in 2007; Spain witnessed a similar dramatic reduction from 15.5 percent in 1990 to 8.2 percent in 2007 (EU Commission AMECO Database 2014). Their GDP growth performances were equally impressive. Though the EU15 witnessed a 43 percent expansion in real GDP between the early 1990s and 2007, Ireland witnessed a startling 179 percent growth expansion, and Spain a 68 percent increase in real GDP (EU Commission AMECO Database 2014). On the basis of their healthy fiscal and economic performance alone, Ireland and Spain should have been most resilient to the economic calamity that the 2008 global financial crisis brought to Europe's doorstep.

If one considers warnings from the competitiveness hypothesis, however, the performance of both countries raised numerous red flags. Of EMU's initial entrants, Ireland and Spain witnessed the largest deteriorations in their real exchange rates between 1999 and 2007, buoyed in part by their high-inflation performances. Both countries also witnessed sharp deteriorations in their current account balances and were heavily exposed to external borrowing during the pre-crisis EMU period. Both countries entered EMU with relatively healthy external balances (Ireland's current account was in surplus, and Spain's current account deficit was roughly 2.5 percent of GDP). Yet by the 2008 financial crisis, Ireland and Spain had amassed significant current account deficits (5.5 percent in Ireland and 10 percent in Spain) that far exceeded Italy's (EU Commission AMECO Database 2014).

Many attribute Ireland's and Spain's exposure to the European debt crisis to their significant overextension in private borrowing, caused by private domestic demand booms, particularly in real estate and construction (Burda 2013; E. Jones 2014; E. Jones 2015; Lane 2012). This overextension of borrowing was further fueled by the availability of cheap credit amid interest rate convergence during the process of European integration. This demand-boom argument, however, suffers from two major caveats in its generalizability. First, like the fiscal argument, it does not travel well to other cases. The Netherlands also witnessed the significant expansion of its GDP, driven in part by its impressive decline in unemployment during the 1990s, yet the Netherlands largely avoided over-extension of external borrowing, despite the Eurozone's low interest rates. Like-wise, Italy lacked a domestic demand boom and was crippled by high unemploy-ment and low growth (Italy's real GDP expansion between 1990 and 2007 was half that of the EU15's), and yet despite this was exposed to speculative crisis.

The second caveat of this domestic demand-boom argument is that it fails to explain why domestic demand booms were sustained in Ireland and Spain, but not elsewhere. As highlighted in previous chapters, the Netherlands provides an important contrast. In the midst of a domestic demand boom and the inflation-ary outcomes it produced, the Dutch government was proactive in the early 2000s and convinced social partners to adopt wage freezes in exchange for welfare reform concessions in order to combat wage-price spirals. Social partners and the state in Spain and Ireland failed to initiate the same response. This may not be particularly surprising in Spain, which lacks the microfoundations of a cohesive, export-oriented wage bargaining system (Pérez 2000; Hancké and Rhodes 2005). Admittedly, Spanish unions strongly *endorsed* wage moderation within their national wage guidelines in the 2000s but were relatively powerless to im-plement it, given the highly fragmented nature of collective bargaining and the prominence of wage indexation clauses in collective agreements. Spain's wage drift under EMU was by no means excessive compared to wage developments in the 1980s and early 1990s. It was "excessive," however, compared to the (signifi-cantly) depressed benchmark of German wage moderation after 1999.

The lack of *Irish* wage moderation under EMU is surprising, because Irish social partners, notably unions in the public sector, helped restructure national wage bargaining around the export sector in the 1987 Programme for National Recovery (PNR). PNR aligned the small country with a wage-moderating, export-growth model aimed at improving the competitiveness of the dynamic multinational corporation (MNC) sector (Baccaro and Simoni 2007). By the late 1990s, instead of conforming to their historic wage-setting arrangements, wage push was widespread in the Irish public sector. Driven by electorally motivated public sector pay rises, average nominal compensation per worker in Ireland's sheltered, nonmarket sector grew by 72 percent between 1999 and 2007, in contrast to the 47 percent growth in Ireland's manufacturing sector in the same period (EU KLEMS 2010).

In this chapter, using a most-different case comparison of Ireland and Spain, I explain why both of these countries, despite their different institutional, political, and economic characteristics, suffered similar declines in real exchange rate competitiveness. The common feature that united the Irish and Spanish experience in the 2000s was the lack of a cohesive, exposed sector collective bargaining actor that could facilitate wage moderation nationwide. Though public sector unions and the Irish state helped to secure Ireland's export-oriented PNR in bad economic times, they were unwilling to maintain it once the Celtic tiger growth phenomenon was in full swing.[1] Ireland's MNC sector benefited significantly from the PNR, yet it was largely uninvolved in the creation of Irish tripartite agreements given the fact that these firms, particularly those of U.S.-origin, were nonunionized. Consequently, when public sector interests reoriented Ireland toward considerable wage-price spirals, MNCs were unable to exert any influence within the Irish Congress of Trade Unions (ICTU).

In Spain, by contrast, the Unión General de Trabajadores (UGT) and Confederación Sindical de Comisiones Obreras (CCOO), the country's two primary union confederations, aligned with employers and government in their support for wage moderation, not only for the sake of fulfilling the Maastricht criteria, but also to enhance Spanish price competitiveness under monetary union.[2] Despite these commitments, collective bargaining in Spain was so fragmented and poorly articulated, especially along regional and provincial lines within sectors, that it was impossible for UGT and CCOO, let alone exposed sector unions within these confederations, to deliver on these commitments (the organization of Spanish employers is also heavily fragmented). Though Spain witnessed the promising emergence of sectoral coordination at the national level with 1998's first comprehensive national metalworking agreement, this agreement stipulated that bargaining on wages would remain devolved to the provincial level. During the 2000s, national, regional, and company agreements continued to articulate different wage and employment negotiation guidelines.[3]

Similar fragmentation occurred within the public sector, where the Spanish government, like that in Italy, further devolved agenda-setting powers in local pay bargaining to regional governments during the late 1990s and early 2000s. These decentralization trends were further exacerbated due to the shift in Spanish public sector employment away from the central government to regional and provincial governments.[4] Despite Spain's impressive strides in recentralizing wage setting in the late 1990s, by 2009, national-sectoral agreements applied to only 28 percent of Spanish employees covered by collective bargaining (Aguilera, Peralta, and Párraga 2012, 4). Coupled with a heavy incidence of wage revision clauses (in 2009, only 29 percent of workers in Spain were *not* subject to wage indexation, compared to 64 percent in the Eurozone and 94 percent in Italy), fragmentation in Spanish collective bargaining severely impeded the capacity of exposed sector wage-setters and the state to deliver wage moderation in the 2000s (Bank of Spain 2009). After entry into EMU, wages in Spain's public sector, construction sector (Spain's prominent *private*, sheltered sector), and even its manufacturing sector consistently overshot national wage guidelines, leading to inflationary wage drift (see figure 6.1).

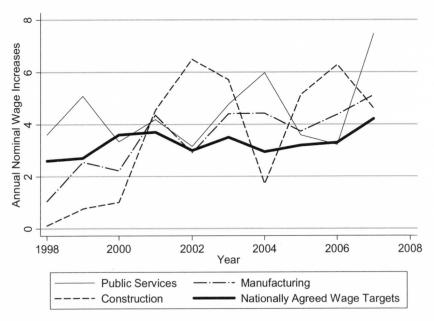

FIGURE 6.1. Spanish nominal wage increases, by sector, in relation to nationally agreed pay targets (1998–2007)

Source: EU KLEMS (2010). Nationally agreed wage targets from EIRO 1998, 1999, 2000, 2001, 2002, 2003, 2004, and 2009 Annual Reviews for Spain.

Economic and Institutional Diversity and the Paradox of a Common Fate

The diverse economic, political, and institutional characteristics of Ireland and Spain suggest that both of these countries should have shared different fortunes once they entered EMU. Both economies possess different sectoral comparative advantages, which were promoted by different government macroeconomic and industrial restructuring strategies. Ireland's economy is strongly oriented toward international multinational corporations. Ireland's high-skilled labor force, low corporate tax rate, tax incentives to foreign firms to establish production facilities in the country, strategic location within the single market, and the presence of English as the national language made the country an attractive destination for (American) MNCs. By the end of the 1990s, employment in MNCs accounted for a third of the Irish industrial labor force; these companies accounted for over 50 percent of Irish manufacturing output and 70 percent of the country's industrial exports (Gunnigle and McGuire 2001, 45).

Given the significant economic weight of this sector and its potential to contribute to Ireland's economic success (between 1985 and 1998, MNCs increased their gross output in Ireland by 383 percent and employment by 51 percent, compared to 87 percent output and 15 percent employment increases for domestic industrial firms), Ireland's government and social partners, through the 1987 PNR, sharply oriented national wage-setting toward an export-led growth model centered around wage moderation in the dynamic foreign sector (Baccaro and Simoni 2007, 432). Employers in the foreign sector agreed to set wage increases on par with wage and productivity developments within the country's more sluggish domestic sectors, which in turn led to significant wage moderation in the multinational sector, given its high productivity increases (Baccaro and Simoni 2007). Despite this change in wage-setting strategies in the multinational sector, however, *employees* from MNCs were largely uninvolved in social partnership dialogue due to their low unionization rates.

Spain, in contrast, undertook industrial restructuring in the 1980s that significantly weakened its manufacturing sector. In his first and second terms in office during the 1980s, Socialist Prime Minister Felipe González restructured multiple sectors, but focused largely on the unprofitable mining, iron, and steel industries. The plans of the center-left socialist government (Spanish Socialist Workers' Party, or PSOE) included reducing by a third the 280,000 labor force in these sectors; by 1989, the workforce had been reduced by 84,000 (Hamann 2012, 113). At the same time, González oriented Spain's economy toward its existing specializations in tourism, property development, and construction (expansion in home-ownership was strongly emphasized). During the widespread privatization of public services within the decade, the González government ensured that banking, construction, and state-owned utility companies were protected from the selling of state assets; banking and construction would later become industrial champions of successive governments in the 1990s (López and Rodríguez 2011, 6). Spain's shift toward a domestic-based growth model, where services and construction emerged as the country's major industrial specializations, not only reduced the weight of manufacturing in national output, but also, through declining employment, reduced manufacturing's proportional representation within UGT and CCOO.

This shift away from manufacturing to nontradable sectors had important implications for Spanish wage policy in the late 1980s and early 1990s. The downgraded role of the (exposed) manufacturing sector allowed UGT's and CCOO's sheltered and public sector affiliates to establish wage standards, and growth in the consumer price index of nontradable services reflected this power dynamic. Between 1985 and 1992, the nontradable price index exceeded that of the tradable sector by 60 percent, compared to the 10 percent price wedge that emerged within Germany (Pérez 2000, 449–450). Wage inflation within Spain's sheltered sector also indirectly affected the competitiveness of Spanish manufacturers, given the heavy use of wage indexation clauses in collective agreements. If wage excess in the sheltered sector placed upward pressures on inflation, this would automatically influence wage settlements in manufacturing retroactively.

Ireland and Spain also differ in their collective-bargaining structure and coordination. Trade union density is higher in Ireland. Between 1999 and 2007, roughly 35 percent of the labor force was unionized, compared to 15 percent in Spain. Due to extension clauses where provincial and sectoral agreements are applied to unionized and nonunionized workers alike, however, collective-bargaining coverage in Spain during the pre-crisis EMU years—80 percent of the labor force—was almost double that of Ireland's 43 percent (Visser 2011). In Ireland, no framework exists for the legal extension of wage settlements to nonunionized workers. This feature of Irish industrial relations is an intended result of successive Irish governments' foreign and direct investment (FDI) recruitment strategies: in order to attract foreign MNCs, the Irish government placed no legal requirement for the extension of collectively negotiated wage settlements on foreign firms, making it easy for MNCs to set employment and wage terms separately of Irish union and employer confederations (Regan 2012; Regan 2014). As a result of this sectoral bifurcation, amplified by the voluntary nature of Irish wage-setting (the ICTU has no coercive power to force its affiliates to comply with nationally agreed provisions), divisions between public and private sector industrial relations are particularly acute: in 2005, union density was 85 percent in the public sector, but only 20 percent in the domestic private sector and 11 percent in the foreign-owned private sector.[5]

Despite its low bargaining coverage, Irish wage-setting has been highly coordinated since the 1987 PNR. Hardiman (2002) highlights that coordinated wage bargaining in Ireland was a top-down, elite-driven process, where the ICTU and the Irish Business and Economic Confederation (IBEC) realized the gains of wage moderation for an export-driven economy, although Baccaro and Simoni (2007) outline that democratic voting on national agreements within the ICTU provided it with the legitimacy needed to steer nationwide wage coordination. Since the 1987 PNR agreement, Irish social partners have consistently negotiated three-year national wage agreements (although during the 2000s, this consistency was lost). For the most part, private and public employers involved in these agreements adhered to their terms; however, as I will explain shortly, this was not true of the public sector in the late 1990s and 2000s.

Part of Ireland's success with wage coordination can be attributed to the fact that Irish trade unions do not exhibit strong partisan bias within social partnership. Though Ireland's centrist Fine Gael/Labour government actively excluded trade unions from policy making during its rein in the 1980s, most Irish trade unions worked with whichever government was in office since the 1987 PNR (Grumbrell-McCormick and Hyman 2013, 145). National governments, regardless of their political leanings, provided and supported institutional mechanisms for social partnership, including the tripartite National Economic and Social Council. "Shared understandings" between Irish unions, employers, and the state aligned to the idea that cooperative and communicative dialogue was the best way to secure wage moderation (Regan 2012, 480).

In contrast, relations between trade unions and PSOE in Spain were heavily strained after the 1988 general strike, and industrial conflict in the late 1980s and early 1990s reflected these union/leftist government tensions. Spanish bargaining fragmentation can be attributed not only to the historical traditions of collective bargaining under the Franco regime, but also to the primacy of provincial and regional-level bargaining. Prior to Franco's death, the state's labor ordinances unilaterally determined working conditions for the labor force and trade unions were illegal. These industry-level labor ordinances, however, were less adhered to than company agreements, where established "works committees" provided some additional bargaining space for workers' representation (Hamann 2012, 29). Trade unions and collective bargaining were legalized in the democratic transition. Yet though Spanish trade unions, employers, and, at times, the state successfully concluded national incomes policies in the early 1980s, PSOE's controversial introduction in 1984 of labor market reforms that liberalized fixed contracts and significantly increased the prominence of temporary contracts, led to a breakdown in bipartite and tripartite bargaining (Royo 2006, 974).[6] In the absence of sectoral and national interconfederal agreements, regions and provinces became the nexus of Spanish collective bargaining, leading to limited articulation, high fragmentation, repetition, and overlap of the content and scope of collective agreements at different levels of bargaining (Molina Romo 2005, 11, 15).

Spain made significant strides in rectifying the fragmented nature of its collective-bargaining system in the 1990s. In 1992, the Economic and Social Council (CES) was established to provide a tripartite forum for unions, employers, and government to engage in social dialogue about the state of the economy (Hamann and Martinez Lucio 2003, 63). In 1997, the Interconfederal Agreement on Collective Bargaining (*acuerdos interconfederales sobre negociación colectiva*, or AINC) and the Interconfederal Agreement on Bargaining Coverage Gaps (*acuerdos interconfederales sobre cobertura de vacíos*, or AICV) rationalized and improved collective-bargaining articulation by increasing the power and autonomy of the sectoral confederations vis-à-vis national confederations, producing a more hierarchical bargaining model (Molina Romo 2005, 18–19). In line with the AINC, the metalworking sector signed its first collective-bargaining agreement in March 1998 that rationalized and standardized the basic norms and procedures for Spain's entire metalworking sector.[7]

Though many scholars of Spanish labor market politics laud these events as leading to the (needed) centralization and coordination of Spain's collective-bargaining system (Pérez 2000; Hancké and Rhodes 2005; Royo 2006), their impact on shifting the primacy of collective bargaining from the regional to the national-sectoral level was limited. CES provided a new forum for tripartite exchange, yet the Council did not have the capacity to make binding decisions (Hamann and Martinez Lucio 2003, 63). Likewise, though AINC enabled national-sectoral agreements to establish thresholds for wage increases, these wage guidelines served as minima for lower regional and provincial level wage negotiations (Molina Romo 2005, 19; Jaumotte 2011). In 2000, national-sectoral agreements applied to 28.8 percent of Spanish workers covered by collective bargaining; by 2009, this figure declined slightly to 27.7 percent (Aguilera, Peralta, and Párraga 2012, 4).[8]

Finally, Ireland and Spain committed to a hard currency policy at different points in time; consequently, the impact of European monetary integration in the 1990s on nominal interest rates was markedly different for both countries. Ireland and Spain were late converts to the Exchange Rate Mechanism (ERM), yet Ireland made the transition to a hard peg first in 1987 with the conclusion of the PNR. Spain, in contrast, entered the ERM in 1989 with a wider fluctuation band of ±6 percent (Ungerer et al. 1990). Due to the lack of coordinated wage moderation, the Bank of Spain initiated three consecutive peseta devaluations in 1992 and 1993, and Spanish adjustment toward a hard currency policy, facilitated through organized wage moderation, did not begin in earnest until 1994 (Hamann 2012, 109). Spain's late transition to a non-accommodating monetary regime meant that social partners had to deliver significant wage moderation if the country was to fulfill the Maastricht criteria in a short period of time. Spanish social partners were successful in this endeavor—Spain witnessed some of the highest annual reductions in real unit labor costs of all EMU candidate countries during the mid-1990s. Between its entry into the ERM in 1989 and 1993, Spanish real wage growth exceeded productivity growth by 0.74 percent per annum; between 1994 and 1998, however, Spanish real wage growth under-shot productivity growth by over 3 percent *per annum* (EU Commission AMECO Database, 2014). Though both countries successfully reoriented their collective-bargaining systems in order to commit to a low-inflation monetary regime, Ireland's earlier transition produced a less dramatic reduction in nominal interest rates during the 1990s. Between 1990 and 1999, Ireland's long-term nominal interest rate declined by 5.4 percentage points, while Spain's declined by 10 percentage points, suggesting that Ireland *should have* been less prone to the cheap borrowing binge that befell Spain (EU Commission AMECO Database 2014).

In light of these differences, Ireland shared Spain's fate in the resurgence of public sector wage inflation and declines in real exchange rate competitiveness after EMU entry. What is even more remarkable is that the public sector wage push in Ireland far exceeded that in Spain during the pre-crisis EMU era. After outlining the monetary transition of Ireland and Spain in greater detail, I will highlight that the crucial similarity that led both countries to a similar fate after 1999 was the absence of a strong export-sector check on collective bargaining. In Ireland, this check was removed when unions and government engaged in wage, tax, and regulatory policies that oriented the Irish economy away from the multinational sector and toward its domestic sector. In Spain, this check was removed with the lapsing of the Maastricht criteria, the return to a fragmented bargaining environment, and unions' success in restoring wage indexation clauses in order to compensate for real wage declines in the 1990s. Though collective bargaining in the public sector was restrained by annual budgetary limits, increased regional fragmentation, brought about by Spain's 1998 Civil Service Statute and 2003 State Budget, granted regional and local governments greater maneuvering room to deviate from pay increases that were legislated for central government employees.

Birds of Different Feathers Flocking Together: Spanish and Irish Commitments to the EMS

Both Ireland and Spain undertook attempts to commit to a hard currency regime in the early 1980s, yet were unsuccessful in making the shift due to the fragmented and confrontational nature of their collective-bargaining systems. In Spain, four national incomes policies were negotiated in the early 1980s, whose terms largely revolved around wages (Hamann and Martinez Lucio 2003; Royo 2006, 982). However, PSOE's controversial 1984 labor market reform introducing temporary contracts, and the government's industrial restructuring plan that led to the closure of large manufacturing firms increased conflict between unions and their traditional center-left PSOE ally.[9] Consequently, incomes policies were absent after 1984, and bargaining was further devolved to the regional and provincial level, where fragmentation inhibited the collective exertion of wage restraint. Fragmentation was further exacerbated by the government's industrial restructuring reforms, which reduced the size of Spain's manufacturing sector and consequently its wage-moderating influence in Spanish industrial relations.[10]

During the 1980s, the González government attempted to address inflation by adopting a restrictive monetary policy stance similar to that established by the ERM's "core" Deutsch mark bloc. However, Spain lacked the cohesive labor market structures needed to produce nationwide wage restraint that was required for adjustment to a low-inflation regime. Reverting back to the sequential bargaining game framework (see chapter 2), employers in Spain's sheltered sector did not possess the capacity to thwart a monetarist threat like their counterparts in the ERM's (export-favoring) corporatist economies, because their organized representation was nowhere near as encompassing. What ensued was a classic Olsonian collective action problem: Spanish sheltered sector employers, *individually*, were too small to incite a response from a monetarist central bank, but in *collectively* permitting wage indexation and higher wage increases, they continued to fuel Spain's high-inflation rate. Employers were unable to control labor costs in such a fragmented bargaining environment. Spain's restrictive monetary stance failed to deliver wage-restraint while simultaneously increasing unemployment and interest rates. Though the government formally committed itself to the ERM in 1989, albeit with a wider fluctuation band, it continued to initiate peseta devaluations in the early 1990s (Pérez 2000, 449; Hamann 2012, 109).

Spain's watershed year came in 1994, after the explosive general strike against government's labor market reforms. In the early 1990s, the PSOE government, desperate to deliver wage moderation, attempted to tie wage increases to productivity increases but was largely unsuccessful (Pérez 2000, 443). In both 1991 and 1992, real wage growth exceeded labor productivity growth by 4 percent per annum, compared to the 1980s, where labor productivity growth exceeded real wage growth by 4 percent per annum on average (EU Commission AMECO Database 2014). With a keen eye on fulfilling the Maastricht criteria, government pushed through unilateral, comprehensive labor market reforms in 1994. This reform removed restrictions on labor mobility, formalized productivity-linked pay increases at the company level, granted further autonomy of collective bargaining to social partners by withdrawing the last remnants of Spain's old labor ordinances (which unions believed would throw Spain in a deregulatory spiral), lowered dismissal costs, and granted employers an opt-out clause of conditions negotiated at higher bargaining levels (Pérez 2000, 443; Molina Romo 2005, 17; Royo 2006, 985).

Unions immediately staged a general strike and threatened to escalate industrial conflict. However, the Spanish government launched an effective media campaign, convincing the public that such reforms were needed in order to join EMU (Molina Romo 2005, 17). Spanish unions were cornered and, thanks in part to leadership changes and the sidelining of more radical factions within CCOO, adopted a pragmatic approach to bipartism (Hamann and Martinez Lucio 2003, 63). The result was a "shadow" pact between employers and unions on wage policy; the latter agreed to deliver wage moderation while the former agreed to limit the application of some of the most controversial clauses of the 1994 reform. While Spanish industrial relations experts disagree on the instigator of this pact—Royo (2006) outlines that it was facilitated by the more practical reorientation strategies of unions, while Pérez (2000) claims the shift was facilitated by employers who could no longer afford the high labor costs that resulted from escalated industrial conflict—the outcome was a structural shift in Spanish wage policy. Between 1994 and 1998, labor productivity in Spain outgrew real wages by 15 percent, and crucial to this success was union support for the reduction of wage indexation clauses and a freeze on public sector employment and compensation from 1995 to 1998 (Hancké and Rhodes 2005, 159).

Spanish bipartism transformed into tripartism in 1997 with the conclusion of the AINC and AICV under Jóse Aznar's center-right People's Party (PP).[11] In return for agreeing to reduce dismissal costs, unions were not only granted further autonomy within collective bargaining, but also a more centralized bargaining structure that emphasized national-sectoral agreements over provincial-level agreements (wage negotiations remained bipartite between unions and employers). Social partners' first commitments to recentralization came in 1998, which marked the first comprehensive national-sectoral collective agreement between the Confederation of Metal Employer Organizations (CONFEMETAL), the UGT, and CCOO covering the manufacturing sector.[12] Further regional consolidation of manufacturing collective bargaining occurred within Catalonia in May 2000, when metalworking employers in Catalonia's four provinces agreed to establish collective bargaining at the regional (Catalonian) rather than provincial level.[13] These new developments were acclaimed as a shift away from Spain's historically fragmented and confrontational bargaining structure toward more comprehensive system of incomes policies/social pacts (Pérez 2000; Rhodes 2001; Royo 2006).

Before the 1987 PNR, Ireland shared Spain's fragmented system of collective bargaining. Garret FitzGerald's Fine Gael/Labour coalition government (1981–1982 and again in 1983–1987) actively promoted the decentralization of Irish wage-setting (Culpepper and Regan 2014, 733). Rather than reflecting the parsimony after the 1987 pact, Irish industrial relations during the 1980s were highly confrontational. Labor unions used their strength at the firm level to secure generous wage settlements and engaged in widespread strike activity when these wage demands were not met: 400,000 working days were lost due to strikes in Ireland between 1980 and 1990, although much of this occurred before 1987 (Culpepper and Regan 2014, 733–734).

Irish unions' engagement in wage push had serious consequences for Irish competitiveness. Between 1980 and 1986, the Irish real exchange rate appreciated by 13 percent, the third highest increase among the then-current EMU12, behind Italy and Finland. Greece in contrast witnessed a real exchange rate appreciation of only 4 percent during this period, while the United Kingdom, Ireland's largest trading partner, witnessed a real exchange rate depreciation of 9 percent (EU Commission AMECO Database 2014). Yet while Irish unions were successful in securing generous wage increases for their members (between 1981 and 1987, nominal earnings of manual workers increased by 101 percent), these wage increases did not translate into higher after-tax disposable income (Hardiman 2002, 9). Because Ireland suffered from an acute fiscal crisis in the early 1980s, FitzGerald's government increased income taxes to tackle the deficit, which ultimately led to a decline in *after-tax* real income by 7 percent between 1981 and 1987 (Hardiman 2002, 9).

By early 1987, Irish social partnership was at a low point. Irish unemployment was over 16 percent, the fiscal deficit was over 10 percent of national income, and the nominal interest rate was above 11 percent (EU Commission AMECO Database 2014). Ireland's political landscape was also plagued with uncertainty. In January, the Labour Party withdrew from its coalition with Fine Gael due to its opposition to FitzGerald's budgetary proposals; this opposition was fueled by trade union protests against retrenchment, which made fiscal adjustment a salient political issue (Culpepper and Regan 2014, 733). The 1987 elections brought a minority Fianna Fáil minority government, which lacked the political muscle to introduce needed reforms on its own.

Yet this low point also aligned the interests of the ICTU, IBEC, and government to seek compromise. Organized labor was at an impasse, realizing that its wage strategies were impeding economic recovery. ICTU was also cognizant of the impending defeat of British trade unions, and knew that if they pursued their previous course of action, there was a good possibility that they would share a similar fate (Hardiman 2002; Grumbrell-McCormick and Hyman 2013, 121–122). High nominal wage increases placed domestic employers under considerable cost-strain, and the appreciating Irish pound put export-oriented firms at a competitive disadvantage. The new Fianna Fáil minority government also found itself in a precarious position, as ICTU had the capacity to derail its weak electoral mandate (Culpepper and Regan 2014, 734). Social partnership was a clear Pareto improvement for all involved. The result of such compromise was the Programme for National Recovery, spanning from 1987 to 1990, in which government exchanged personal income tax cuts for wage moderation from unions. Employers and government benefited from wage restraint, which steered the export-driven economy toward recovery; in addition to realizing gains from lower taxes, unions gained influence in (fiscal) policymaking.

The PNR has been acclaimed as a crucial turning point for Irish industrial relations. Wage moderation made it possible for Ireland to credibly commit to a hard-currency stance within the ERM, placing the country on a more stable footing once the Maastricht criteria for EMU membership were introduced. What is perhaps most surprising about the 1987 pact, and those concluded subsequently, is the fact that its conclusion resulted from the endorsement of major public sector and services unions within the ICTU. Defying the logic of the sequential game put forward in chapter 2, craft-based unions in the ICTU were strongly opposed to the PNR, and unions representing the preferences of MNC were completely absent. Rather, Ireland's public sector unions played the pivotal role in the success of 1987 agreement. When the pact was put to a vote within the ICTU for membership approval, it was approved only because members of the ICTU's two general unions and the major public sector union voted overwhelmingly in its favor (Baccaro and Simoni 2007, 443).

Public sector trade union support for the PNR may be due to the uniqueness of PNR's wage adjustment along sectoral lines. Contrary to those initiated in the Netherlands and Denmark, wage adjustment within the PNR was not facilitated by lower-than-average wage settlements in the public sector. Rather, adjustment focused more exclusively around Ireland's MNC sector. Before 1987, the more generous pay increases in the foreign sector served as benchmarks for domestic pay bargaining, leading to sheltered sector wage inflation. PNR reversed this, selecting productivity-linked pay in the domestic sector as the wage target for MNCs (Baccaro and Simoni 2007). Because productivity in Ireland's domestic public and private sectors was far lower than that in its MNCs, tying wage growth in the former to those in the latter produced unprecedented levels of (foreign sector) wage moderation. Productivity gains in the foreign sector during the late 1980s and 1990s were explosive (productivity increased by 203 percent in the foreign sector between 1985 and 1998, compared to only 40 percent in Ireland's private domestic sector), but during the same period real hourly wages in the foreign sector grew by only 41 percent compared to 45 percent in the domestic sector (Baccaro and Simoni 2007, 438). As long the sluggish private and public domestic sector established wage settlements that were not too far afield from their productivity developments, more intense wage moderation in the foreign sector would compensate for sheltered sector wage inflation. Due to the fact that this wage shift required more moderate pay settlements in the MNC sector, and because Ireland's tripartite pacts established predictability in cost developments in the domestic sector, MNC employers were more than happy to accommodate the PNR and Irish social partnership more generally (Hardiman 2003).

Irish social partnership continued throughout the 1990s with regular three-year incomes policies. The Programme for Economic and Social Progress (1991–1993) established a cumulative nominal wage increase of 10.75 percent over three years in both the public and private sector in exchange for income tax reductions equating to roughly 400 million pounds for the pact's duration (Hardiman 2002, 19). The 1994–1996 Programme for Competitiveness and Work marked the first tripartite pact that established different pay targets for the public and private sectors. Private sector pay increased by 8 percent over thirty-nine months, while the 8 percent pay increase in the public sector spanned over forty-two months—during the first five months of the agreement, the public sector observed a pay pause (Hardiman 2002, 19). During the 1990s, MNCs upheld their end of the bargain and obeyed the moderate pay guidelines established within Ireland's national agreements. However, once Ireland's growth miracle was in full swing, sectoral demarcations within Irish social partnership became apparent. By 1997, when Irish entry into EMU appeared certain, ICTU found it increasingly difficult to reconcile the wage demands of exposed and sheltered sector unions. As Hardiman outlines, "the expectations consensus (of Irish social partnership) began to unravel" (Hardiman 2002, 13).

The Re-emergence of Sheltered Sector Dominance in Wage-Setting under EMU

By 1999, Ireland and Spain had achieved EMU entry requirements. Given the revival of corporatism in both countries, scholars were optimistic that such developments would continue under EMU. However, Spain and Ireland succumbed to rising inflation and the most significant losses in real exchange rate competitiveness in the first decade of the euro.[14] These processes were driven by similar political characteristics. Spain and Ireland lacked a cohesive export-oriented actor that could organize wage moderation across the entire economy in general, and in sheltered sectors in particular. In Spain, this absence stemmed from a combination of a weak manufacturing sector and the highly fragmented nature of its collective-bargaining system, due to the failure of centralizing *wage* bargaining at higher (national-sectoral) levels after the 1997 AINC and AICV agreements. In Ireland, the lack of the export-sector check stemmed from the nonunionization of the dynamic MNC sector and the prominence of the public sector within Irish social partnership.

This absence of an export-sector break on wage bargaining was further fueled by both governments' prioritization of the real estate and construction sectors and the wealth effects on private consumption that followed construction-friendly policies. In Spain, the 1998 Land Act quickened procedures for obtaining building permits and the Aznar government made large tracks of land available for development (López and Rodríguez 2011). Both Anzar's PP and Zapatero's PSOE governments encouraged policies that led to rises in property values. Regional governments reinforced these policies by providing development loans and construction permits. These policies had significant impacts on domestic consumption and, with it, nominal wage growth. The Spanish "wealth effect" led to an *annual* average increase of 7 percent in private consumption between 2000 and 2007, compared to a 4.9 percent annual increase in the United Kingdom; by 2007, private home-ownership stood at 87 percent (López and Rodríguez 2011, 8–9).

Ireland's Fianna Fáil government aggressively expanded tax incentives to the building industry during the 2000s. By the late 2000s, taxation revenue loss that resulted from benefits and credits aimed at the construction sector amounted to over €3 billion, and total Irish tax relief directed at home-ownership was three times the European average (Regan 2012, 483; Dellepiane and Hardiman 2010, 480). These policies had devastating effects for the Irish economy. Ireland, along with Spain, witnessed the most pronounced housing bubble within the OECD during the 2000s: between 2000 and 2007, Irish and Spanish nominal housing prices grew by 105 percent and 140 percent, respectively (OECD 2012). With rising housing prices and income tax reductions, Ireland's public revenue stream became increasingly dependent on property taxes, making the implosion of its housing bubble particularly damaging to its fiscal balances.

Real estate prices also had knock-on effects on wage settlements in both countries during the 2000s, as asset bubbles fueled Irish and Spanish public sector wage push. Sheltered sector wage push was an *intentional* strategy of the ICTU's public sector affiliates, while in Spain, sheltered sector wage push was the result of a fragmented bargaining environment where wage indexation clauses were the norm (both UGT and CCOO strongly endorsed wage moderation throughout the 2000s). But despite the different organizational forces that led to sheltered sector wage push, the common absence of a veto player from the export sector produced the same inflation outcome. By 2011, the European Central Bank (ECB) had singled out Ireland and Spain for their disproportionate public/private sector wage gaps among Eurozone economies, with Ireland witnessing a rise in this gap from 14 percent to 26 percent between 2003 and 2006 alone (Giordano et al. 2011).

Squaring Recentralization Ambitions with Practical Disorder: Reality of Bargaining Fragmentation in Spain

Spain undertook noteworthy steps toward the recentralization of its collective-bargaining system in the 1990s. Yet these efforts were largely symbolic and did little to change the fragmented nature of Spanish collective bargaining. The terms of the 1998 comprehensive manufacturing sector agreement provides insight as to why national sectoral agreements failed to remove the primacy of regional and provincial bargaining. While the types of employment contracts, occupational grading, minimum standards, and geographical mobility were to be negotiated exclusively at the national level, the criteria for wage structures, pay increases, and working hours within the manufacturing sector were *negotiated* at the national level, but their subsequent *development* was left to lower levels of bargaining.[15] This lack of *wage* centralization in the manufacturing sector was due to employers' refusal to upload wage issues to the new national-sectoral bargaining space. Consequently, regional differences in pay bargaining continued to persist in manufacturing (bargaining conflict was particularly acute in the Basque country during the 2000s).[16] By 2008, wage growth and wage structures for 90 percent of workers in the manufacturing sector (covered by any type of collective agreement) continued to be determined by provincial agreements, while the remaining 10 percent were covered by company agreements.[17] In regards to deeper coordination within the Catalonia metalworking sector, employers also refused to include the subject of wages and working hours within their discussions about the creation of a regional agreement, which was finally introduced in 2009.[18]

Fragmentation in the public sector too was on the rise in the late 1990s and 2000s. Like Germany, Spain has two classes of public employees: civil servants (*funcionarios públicos*), whose contractual and pay conditions are not concluded through formal collective bargaining but are regulated by state legislation, and the *personal laboral*, whose working conditions are concluded through collective bargaining (Garcia-Perez and Jimeno 2007). The latter group of employees is free to collectively bargain with their employers, but pay increases have to comply with state budgets, which are subject to approval and review by Parliament (Molina 2014, 32). The state's rigid control over civil servant pay, and its imposition of budgetary caps on non-civil servant pay, would indicate that the Spanish government should be capable of delivering wage moderation for public employees more uniformly than employers in Spain's fragmented manufacturing sector. However, several decentralization processes during the 1990s and 2000s weakened this capacity.

First, the Spanish government implemented wide-sweeping decentralization that allotted regional and local governments a greater share of employees and more maneuvering room to determine the terms and conditions of their contracts. During the Franco regime, the central (government) administration controlled and regulated all public services. By the 2000s, most of these services were devolved to regional and local governments. These changes are also visible in public sector employment trends: between 1985 and 1999, the share of total public employees working for the central government decreased from 40 percent to 26 percent.[19] Regional governments gained increased autonomy to conclude differentiated collective agreements with their respective employees. The 1998 Basic Statute of the Civil Service granted regional administrations greater freedom to regulate the working conditions of their employees, providing them the foundation to "customize" regulation.[20] More important for pay settlements, the 2003 budget guaranteed further administrative deregulation granting the responsibility of pay determination and the management of public services to regional governments.[21] These wider decentralization trends have been cited as contributing to rising public sector pay gaps between regions within Spain. Garcia-Perez and Jimeno (2007) note that Spain's regional public wage differentials can be explained largely by the actions of regional governments and local corporations.

Second, the collective bargaining rights of Spain's civil servants, like their counterparts in Italy and the Netherlands, were subject to greater "privatization" during the 1980s and 1990s. The first break in legislation of the state's unilateral regulation of public sector came in 1984, when civil servants were granted formal collective bargaining rights (these rights came into effect in 1987 under

Law 9/1987).[22] However, Law 9/1987's impact on civil servant collective bargaining was limited because agreements had to be submitted to the central government following a series of regulatory steps through Parliament before negotiated terms came into effect.[23] In 1994, the Law on Staff Representation Bodies in the Public Administration (*Ley sobre Órganos de Representación del Personal al Servicio de las Administraciones Públicas*) established channels for public employees' participation in pay bargaining. The most expansive extension of civil servant bargaining rights, however, came with the 1998 Basic Statute of the Civil Service, which mandated that the central administration was bound to comply with the agreements it negotiated with civil servant/public sector unions.[24] This increased recognition of bargaining rights curtailed the Spanish government's capacity to impose wage freezes on civil servants. In 1997, Aznar's minority government rescinded his predecessor's 1995–1997 wage agreement for civil servants and non-civil servant public employees (which had granted wage increases in line with the retail price index) and imposed a wage freeze in order to comply with the Maastricht fiscal criteria. However, Spanish civil servant unions appealed to Spain's National Court about the legality of this wage freeze, and in 2001, the court ruled in favor of the trade unions, mandating that the government make back-payments to public employees amounting to 500 billion Spanish pesetas (roughly €3 billion).[25]

These decentralization trends substantially decreased unilateral state intervention in Spanish public sector wage bargaining.[26] Despite this increased liberalization of collective-bargaining rights in the public sector, however, Spain did not witness public sector union wage "militancy" within its major trade union confederations after EMU entry, like Ireland and the Netherlands. UGT and CCOO voiced their continued commitment to wage moderation under EMU and recommended low nominal wage targets during the 2000s that never reached 4 percent and in some years were below increases in the retail price index (see figure 6.1). UGT and CCOO continually suggested that their affiliates shoot for wage targets that accounted for inflation plus increases in productivity—the 2002 Intersectoral Agreement, for example, did not establish a fixed figure for pay increases, but rather recommended affiliates to use predicted inflation (2 percent) and productivity increases (calculated at that time as 1.1 percent) as a target.[27] For an economy that had witnessed over 10 percent reduction in its unemployment rate between 1995 and 2005, these benchmarks were quite modest, especially when considering the explosive wage-price spirals that were occurring in Ireland during the same period.

In light of this continued commitment to wage moderation, why did Spain produce one of the highest inflation rates of EMU's original entrants and the associated real exchange deteriorations that resulted from it? The answer lies in the influence of wage indexation clauses on *actual* Spanish wage growth. Despite the low benchmarks established by UGT and CCOO, wage growth in Spain's public, manufacturing and construction sectors continually overshot these targets (see figure 6.1). This was due to the fact that Spanish unions were effective at reimposing wage indexation clauses in collective agreements where they had been temporarily abandoned in the run up to Maastricht.

After EMU entry had been secured, unions immediately demanded the reintroduction of wage revision clauses: by June 1999, the proportion of workers affected by wage revision clauses was 61 percent, and by 2005, roughly 70 percent of workers benefited from wage revision clauses, 35 percent of which allowed for payments to be backdated.[28] These wage revision clauses also applied to the minimum wage. In December 2004, Zapatero's new PSOE government agreed with the unions to apply a wage guarantee clause to the minimum wage that would adjust it upwards in the event of higher-than-predicted inflation increases.[29] Wage revision clauses not only allowed more generous pay settlements in Spain's sheltered sectors to influence those in manufacturing, but more importantly, allowed price shocks in commodities and the sharp increases in oil prices in the mid-2000s to impact (upward) wage adjustment. Jaumotte (2011) outlines that wage indexation reinforced a wage-price spiral in Spain during the 2000s: while these clauses corrected agreements for higher-than-anticipated inflation, wages were not adjusted downwards if predicted inflation exceeded actual inflation. Wage revision clauses disproportionally impacted the sheltered public sector more than manufacturing and construction, whose wages were partially suppressed due to the high incidence of temporary contracts (in 2000, 35 percent of the private sector was covered by temporary contracts, compared to 19 percent in the public sector). In construction, wage growth was further suppressed due to vast inflows of low-wage, unskilled migrants into the (precarious) Spanish construction labor market. Between 1998 and 2007, the wage gap between the public sector and manufacturing grew from 17 percent to 25 percent, and the gap between public and construction sector wages grew from 33 percent to 47 percent (EU KLEMS 2010).

In many respects, Spain is one of EMU's most tragic cases. Despite commitments to wage moderation throughout the 2000s, social partners were unable to deliver. This failure did not result from union pay militancy either at the national level or in the public sector, but rather to the deeply fragmented nature of Spanish collective bargaining and the prominence of wage revision contracts that were meant to preserve purchasing power: the abolition of *scala mobile* in Italy, by contrast, meant that by the mid-2000s, only 6 percent of Italian workers' contracts were linked to inflation (Bank of Spain 2009). Contrary to its corporatist northern neighbors, Spain simply did not have a cohesive wage-setter from the export sector that could dictate its preferences for wage moderation at the sectoral or provincial level. Likewise, in surrendering its unilateral authority to dictate the pay increases of civil servants and decentralizing pay-setting and income determination to regional levels during the 1990s and 2000s, the state also lost this coordination capacity in the public sector. Like Ireland, the absence of a state or export-sector check in collective bargaining destined Spain to a higher-than-EU-average inflation trajectory. Unlike Spain, however, Ireland's (more extensive) wage inflation during the 2000s was largely the result of *deliberate* wage strategies undertaken by unions, in addition to permissive public sector wage policies undertaken by the government for electoral purposes.

From Feast to Bonanza: Wage Inflation in Ireland's Sheltered Sector

To suggest that Ireland had a problem with wage inflation in general, and public sector wage push in particular, during the 2000s would be an understatement. The country's explosive wage growth phenomenon after 1999 has been thoroughly dissected within recent Irish corporatist literature (see Hardiman 2010; Regan 2012; Culpepper and Regan 2014; and Regan 2014 for excellent accounts). Ireland found itself in a proliferating wage-price spiral during the 2000s which far exceeded that of any of EMU's original entrants, including Greece. Between 1999 and 2007, the public services/manufacturing pay gap grew from 28 percent to 50 percent, and between 2002 and 2003 alone, this wage gap grew by over 12 percent (see figure 6.2). As a point of reference, the 10 percent wage gap that emerged between the manufacturing and public sector in the Netherlands during the 1980s, when the Lubbers coalition government imposed severe nominal wage adjustments on the latter, took almost a *decade* to materialize.

Ireland's expansive public sector wage growth cannot be attributed to its economic activity alone. Of EMU's three "employment miracle" economies (Ireland, the Netherlands, and Spain), only Ireland witnessed such an extreme rise in (public sector) wage *growth*: between its entry into EMU and 2007, growth in nominal public sector wages in Ireland was 70 percent higher than that in Spain and more than double that in the Netherlands (EU KLEMS 2010). These dynamics are also reflective in different levels of nominal sectoral wage *restraint* (i.e., wage growth in excess of changes in sectoral value-added productivity). While nominal wage growth in manufacturing persistently undercut the sector's value-added productivity developments during the 2000s, nominal wage growth in Ireland's public services significantly outstripped productivity developments, in some years by over 10 percent, and was far higher than Spanish public sector wage inflation (see figure 6.3).

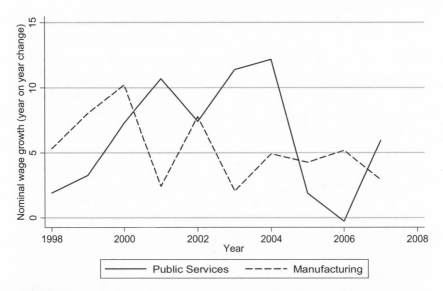

FIGURE 6.2.   Irish nominal wage increases by sector (1998–2007)

Source: EU KLEMS (2010).

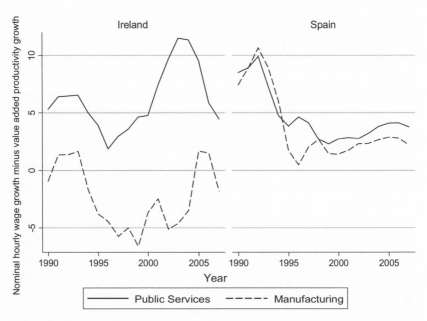

FIGURE 6.3.   Nominal wage restraint, by sector, for Ireland and Spain, three-year moving averages (1990–2007)

Source: EU KLEMS (2010).

The return of public sector wage push in Ireland closely mirrored Dutch public sector developments in the late 1990s. Pressures arose first in the healthcare sector in 1997 and created a knock-on effect in other public services subsectors. In Ireland, the catalyst was the 1997 nursing union's dispute. In February of that year, four trade unions representing 26,000 nurses threatened industrial action over the pursuit of a major overhaul in their pay structure. This call to strike action was revoked when Ireland's health service managers provided a £85 million package (a significant rise from their original £20 million offer), which increased nurses' pay by 6.5 percent to 11.5 percent, depending on where nurses were located in the pay scale.[30] These increases were in addition to the Partnership 2000 (P2000) national wage agreement, which provided a 9.25 percent increase in wages across Ireland from 1997 to 1999. Such wage developments quickly influenced wage demands within other public services. Citing the nurses' dispute payment, 3,700 paramedics engaged in industrial action for two weeks in April 1997 over increases in pay. Ireland's Labour Court recommended that the paramedics be paid an additional 12.5 percent on top of P2000's 9.25 percent wage increase, and this proposal was immediately accepted by the Irish government in early May.[31]

By August 1998, similar pay concessions were made to police unions. Prime Minister Bertie Ahern outlined that additional "catch-up" payments in the public sector needed to be made before the expiry of P2000 in March 2000.[32] An interim pay rise of 9 percent in addition to P2000 was provided to 10,500 policing staff.[33] Given the spread of additional payments to the third public services subsector within eighteen months, concerns that other leading public sector unions would attempt to emulate this pay deal, and that government would cater to them in order to "buy" industrial peace, became prominent within the IBEC and ICTU. By 1999, there was concern that public sector wage relations could unravel the fabric of Irish social partnership. In October 1999, nurses again went on strike over pay and secured wage increases of 26 percent on top of agreed basic pay rises over a two-year period, well ahead of the 5.5 percent to 14 percent increases secured by other public services.[34] Middle-ranking civil servants and teachers, who had a direct pay relationship with the nurses, were waiting in the wings for their chance to secure additional pay concessions from government. This heightened pay militancy was even criticized by the Services Industrial Professional and Technical Union (SIPTU), ICTU's largest union. Des Geraghty, SIPTU president, told the ICTU that its public sector affiliates should no longer demand special pay increases, because to fall victim to further sectionalism would mean that "we (the ICTU) will descend into the worst form of dog-eat-dog capitalism, where the strong will succeed and the poor will go to the wall."[35]

By the time Ireland entered the single currency, clear sectoral tensions about the priority of wage moderation were present. Though public sector unions were pivotal supporters of social partnership and wage restraint during hard economic times, they were less enthusiastic about its success in Ireland's boom years and immediately thereafter. In 1999, a survey of firm managers and trade union officials in the private sector, conducted by the independent Irish Productivity Centre, revealed that the majority of respondents perceived wage moderation to be the most important issue facing the Irish economy, and 71 percent of them perceived that pay bargaining and partnership at the national level was important for Irish competitiveness.[36] As public sector affiliates secured significant wage increases above P2000's suggested targets, roughly 88 percent of the 1,222 recorded private sector pay settlements in Ireland had adhered to P2000's conditions.[37]

Possible continuation of special pay revisions in Ireland's subsequent national agreement, Programme for Participation and Fairness (PPF) covering 2000 to 2003, surfaced immediately after its conclusion. The original agreement, which provided a 15 percent cumulative pay increase over thirty-three months, also included a one-off, special 3 percent pay award for 60 percent of Ireland's public sector, in order to restore parity between other public sector employees and nurses and prison officers who had secured more generous payments under P2000.[38] With the sharp rise in inflation in 2000, SIPTU and Ireland's largest public sector union, the Irish Municipal, Public and Civil Trade Union (IMPACT), sought additional pay increases to compensate for these developments (Hardiman 2002, 11). In December, PPF was "saved" by an extra 2 percent wage increase slated for 2001, a 1 percent lump sum increase in 2000, and government's promise of major cuts in income taxation.[39] More pivotally for public sector wages, social partners agreed to establish the Public Service Benchmarking Body that would examine pay differentials between the private and public sector.[40] The conclusions from this review board, released in July 2002, would have significant implications for public sector wage push in the mid-2000s.

As PPF was being finalized, Ireland's three main teaching unions broke ranks with the ICTU and called for a 30 percent pay award, 12 percent higher than PPF's (revised) 18 percent pay increase.[41] Civil servants joined the pay militancy trend, and in 2001, per the recommendations of the Buckley Review Body, received pay increases of 7.4 percent above those already delivered in PPF (heads of government departments, including the prime minister, received pay increases of up to *33 percent* in addition to PPF's thirty-three-month pay awards).[42] The most emphatic expansion in public sector pay, however, came in July 2002, with the findings of the Public Service Benchmarking Body. This board recommended that to compensate for private and public sector wage differentials, public sector pay should be increased by an additional 8.9 percent (in January 2008, the Public Service Benchmarking Body acknowledged that this recommendation was incorrect and caused average public sector earnings to outstrip average private sector pay by 15 percent).[43] The recommendation added €1.1 billion to government's public sector pay bill, and while Prime Minister Ahern claimed that the settlement would add a "horrendous cost" to Irish public accounts, the 2003 state budget made provisions for €565 million for the first-phase payment of the 8.9 percent recommendation (the remaining installment was paid by the end of 2005).[44] Though these payments placed considerable strain on Ireland's fiscal expenditures, Ireland's property tax revenues, buoyed by the sharp increases in housing prices, hid the impact of the public sector wage push on fiscal balances. Sensing the instability that resulted from Ireland's widespread income tax cuts and growing public sector wage bill, the European Commission, in February 2001, reprimanded Ireland under article 121(4) of the Broad Economic Policy Guidelines. However, Ireland's finance minister, Charlie McCreevy, lambasted the Commission's targeting of small nations in fiscal surplus, and after finding itself isolated by the OECD's and IMF's reluctance to criticize Ireland's fiscal stance, the Commission abandoned its disciplinary warning in late 2001 (Hodson 2011, 81–82).

Generous public sector pay settlements that were being awarded with little complaint from government did not spill over into the private sector. By April 2001, it was estimated that up to 75 percent of private sector pay deals adhered to the terms of PPF.[45] While private sector affiliates in ICTU expressed unease about public sector benchmarking, their awareness of job losses in the private sector made them reluctant to join in the pay bonanza gripping the public sector. In the MNC sector, PPF's guidelines remained largely unenforced. In 2003, Intel Ireland, the subsidiary of the U.S. tech firm, introduced a yearlong pay freeze for its 3,200 workforce in order to reduce labor costs and expressed little intent to implement Ireland's next national agreement, Sustaining Progress (2003–2005), which provided a 7 percent pay increase over eighteen months.[46] As Ireland's social partners began negotiations on the *second stage* of Sustaining Progress in early 2004, IBEC was adamant against excessive pay increases, arguing that pay increases in the agreement had already been frontloaded and that increasing labor costs contributed to the doubling of redundancies since 2000.[47] Yet though employers and foreign MNCs were highly critical of the wage push that was gripping Ireland in the 2000s, they had little ability to correct it. ICTU was overrun with its public sector affiliates' pay demands and the Fianna Fáil government continued to cater to these demands in order to buy industrial peace and boost the party's electability. After Ireland's significant benchmarking exercise, a further round of "special pay" increases were made to civil servants: in 2005, the Higher Review Body on Remuneration awarded 3,000 top civil servants a 7.5 percent pay increase on top of those awarded in Sustaining Progress, and in

2006, Ireland's Towards 2016 national agreement provided a 10 percent pay increase over twenty-seven months.[48] Though the Public Service Benchmarking Body outlined in its second January 2008 report that benchmarking had led to a significant expansion in the public/private sector pay gap, government continued to award catch-up pay extensions to medical consultants in the healthcare sector in exchange for public sector reforms in May 2008, and a 20 percent pay increase for lower-paid employees at the Central Bank of Ireland and the Financial Services Authority in July of the same year.[49]

It is not entirely surprising that Ireland succumbed to such significant public sector wage push in the late 1990s and 2000s. Irish social partnership in the late 1980s, though led by the public sector, was founded on an environment of economic stagnation. Public sector commitments to national wage moderation collapsed once economic prosperity returned and the need to comply with monetary constraints was lost. Ireland's dynamic MNC sector, whose competitiveness was impacted by high Irish inflation, was absent from the bargaining table and had little influence or capacity to steer Ireland back toward wage restraint. The Irish state, like its Spanish counterpart, lacked the organizational capacity and, unlike the Spanish government, the political will to stop the public sector wage bubble. Irish civil servants enjoyed a more privileged status than non-civil service public employees, but they were not legally restricted from collective bargaining like their counterparts in Germany. Hence the state could not unilaterally impose pay settlements on these workers at will. Yet even if the state had the capacity to do so, based on its actions in the 2000s, it is not entirely clear that the government would have exerted such restraint. Permissive public sector wage policies, along with generous tax credits and income tax cuts, bought Fianna Fáil electoral points and sustained its long reign in government. Once the seriousness of Ireland's crisis had materialized, the Irish press and public had adopted strong anti-union attitudes. Trade unions were perceived as a public sector interest group that set Ireland on course for crisis and were labeled as "public sector cartels" in the mainstream Irish press (Culpepper and Regan 2014, 737).

Comparing the experiences of Denmark, Germany, Ireland, Italy, the Netherlands, and Spain before and after the introduction of EMU offers a helpful qualitative configuration of cases to establish necessary and sufficient conditions for low inflation and price competitiveness. Germany demonstrates that employers' preservation of cohesive bargaining in the public sector, in addition to limiting civil servants' bargaining rights, helps to maintain wage moderation in the absence of a non-accommodating monetary authority at the national level. Likewise, though the Dutch lacked cohesive sectoral institutions that could keep sheltered sectors in check, they could fall back on national wage pacts to rein in inflation and restore national competitiveness.

These bargaining institutions were not present in Ireland, Italy, Spain, or Denmark, all of which possess more inflation-prone peak bargaining and "soft pact" coordination systems. Yet, as outlined in chapter 4, Denmark remained successful at keeping inflation low by retaining its inflation-averse *national* central bank. Because Denmark's opt-out left this institution intact, Danish authorities continued to rely on a national-level, hard monetary constraint that required the implementation of public sector moderation. As a result of limiting sheltered sector wage growth, Denmark, like Germany and the Netherlands after its national wage pacts, upheld a low-inflation rate after 1999. Denmark's low-inflation performance assisted the small Scandinavian state in producing healthy current account surpluses during the 2000s, when Denmark had an average current account surplus of 2.7 percent of GDP between 1999 and 2007 (EU Commission AMECO Database 2014).

Ireland, Italy, and Spain lacked both of these institutional attributes once they entered monetary union. All three countries had impressive records of reducing inflation and public deficits in the 1990s; these reductions were largely facilitated by the political incentives to join a hard currency regime in general and EMU in particular. These events unified coordination of these countries' fragmented collective-bargaining systems, promoting celebrated revivals in corporatism. With EMU membership achieved, however, wage moderation disappeared from the Irish, Italian, and Spanish macroeconomic landscape, given either the lack of bargaining articulation in the public (and private) sector (in the case of Italy and Spain) or the agency capture of national wage-setting by public sector interests (Ireland). The reemergence of (relative) public sector inflation, which drove a rise in these countries' inflation and real exchange rates, was the logical consequence of the removal of national-level, inflation-averse central banks and the Maastricht criteria. In rendering all of Ireland's, Italy's, and Spain's institutional checks against wage inflation obsolete, European Monetary Union placed these three countries in a position where competitive decline was inevitable. The rise in current account deficits and the reliance on external borrowing to finance them was the result of these countries' poor inflation performance relative to their corporatist trading partners.

EMU, THE POLITICS OF WAGE INFLATION, AND CRISIS

Implications for Current Debates and Policy

It took very little time for a full-scale economic crisis to reveal the fissures of Europe's incomplete monetary union. Default risk, once unthinkable, became a reality and required urgent address. At the time of this writing (late 2015), five EMU member states (Cyprus, Greece, Ireland, Portugal, and Spain) have required assistance from jointly negotiated EU and IMF bailout packages. Eurozone leaders, including a reluctant Germany, agreed on EMU's first bailout package (for Greece) on May 2, 2010. It was agreed that the EU15 would provide €80 billion in funds to the small country spread over three years, while the IMF would contribute an additional €30 billion over the same time horizon (BBC News 2010). In response to the Greek crisis, and in efforts to avoid contagion of the debt crisis to other European economies, the Council of the European Union established the €440 billion European Financial Stability Facility (EFSF) in order to provide temporary financial assistance to Eurozone governments under financial duress. Just six months after the EFSF's creation, a second EMU member-state, Ireland, requested €85 billion in assistance (Brown, Chaffin, and Barber 2010). With the consolidation of the EFSF and the European Financial Stability Mechanism into a wider and more permanent centralized borrowing facility, the European Stability Mechanism (ESM), Europe's leaders have abandoned preconceived notions of how the governance of the single currency should operate.

Europe's sovereign debt crisis taught us much about what we correctly knew, as well as what we failed to appreciate, about the adverse economic consequences that result when merging diverse labor markets into a single currency.

When EMU was introduced, there was considerable attention given to the fact that the Eurozone was an incomplete monetary union, and that incomplete monetary unions that lack appropriate macroeconomic adjustment mechanisms are likely to fare poorly in the event of asymmetrical economic shocks (Bayoumi and Eichengreen 1992; Bean 1992; De Grauwe 1999, 2014). Labor markets in general, and wage-setting systems in particular, were regarded as crucial policy domains where economic adjustment would need to happen in the event of heterogeneous economic shocks across EMU's member-states (Eichengreen 1993; Bertola and Boeri 2002). Eight years into the crisis, predictions about the burden of adjustment lying within national labor markets have proved largely correct. Despite the creation of a centralized bailout facility, fiscal union continues to remain aspirational. EMU's northern economies remain reluctant to enter into a financial arrangement that would involve permanent income transfers to struggling peripheral economies. With the ESM acting largely as a financial Band-Aid, the burden of adjustment continues to lie within national labor markets.

Yet the current crisis has also taught us about what we failed to appreciate about adjustment mechanisms between countries with diverse national institutions in the European Monetary Union. At the launch of the euro currency, economists predicted that *flexible, decentralized* labor markets would be the most valuable asset of nation-states in weathering diverse economic shocks under a one-size-fits-all monetary policy (Bean 1998; Soltwedel, Dohse, and Krieger-Boden 1999; Calmfors 2001; Sibert and Sutherland 2000). The call for greater labor market reforms and the decentralization of wage-setting was the European Commission's main policy recommendation for combating unemployment in the 2000s.[1] Looking at the trajectories of EMU's member-states during the current crisis, however, one realizes that it is countries not with decentralized and flexible labor markets but those with centralized labor market institutions and powerful union confederations that have fared best. More rigid labor markets with highly coordinated wage-setting appear to have presented participating (EMU North) member-states with a more optimal comparative institutional advantage under the Eurozone's crisis-riddled single currency.

Why have rigid labor markets proven so successful under monetary union? I have argued that the crux of their success relies on how they promoted the continuation of sectoral labor market politics that are conducive to producing (severe) wage moderation under monetary union. Prior to EMU, candidate countries operated under a more even playing field in regards to their inflation performance. Peripheral countries that lacked a domestic political tradition that favored low inflation, and the wage-setting institutions that accompanied these politics, adopted monetary institutions and conditionality rules that enabled them to mimic the economic performance of their export-oriented neighbors.

Peripheral countries made dramatic strides in wage and inflation adjustment, defying their conflict-prone wage-setting traditions, and the ultimate effect of inflation-averse national central banks and the Maastricht criteria was the imposition of common low-inflation standards on diverse political economies. Convergence ensued, and the periphery's domestic demand-oriented economies and the core's export-led economies coexisted with minimal external divergence between them.

EMU removed these common rules, creating an uneven playing field for its member-states' inflation performance. (Sheltered sector) employers and governments in peripheral economies no longer were exposed to constraints that enabled them to mimic their northern neighbors. It would be untrue to say that wage-setting in the EMU South returned to (pre-Maastricht) business as usual. Peripheral economies' inflation records improved tremendously since the early 1990s. This absolute improvement, however, was irrelevant for the periphery's external deficits within a common currency. What truly mattered in Europe's monetary union, where the real exchange rate between participants was solely a function of inflation, was *relative* price performance. Countries that possessed labor market institutions that could deliver persistent wage moderation realized persistently competitive real exchange rates. The tragedy of the periphery's debt crisis did not stem from its fiscal performance. It also did not stem solely from the periphery's exposure to international capital flows. Northern economies too were exposed to cheap and more plentiful capital under monetary union, and those that realized domestic demand booms in the 2000s (the Netherlands) did not suffer similar fates as their southern neighbors witnessing similar developments (Ireland and Spain). Rather, the periphery's plight stemmed from its (labor market) institutional incapacity to match the wage moderation and inflation performance of its EMU trading partners and its incapacity to counteract domestic demand booms with collectively exerted wage restraint (as seen in the Netherlands in the early 2000s).

What does the economic success of the North and the failures of the South teach us about the sustainability of a currency union between members with diverse national systems? One important lesson we have learned from the first decade and a half of the single currency is that EMU introduced a low-inflation biased institutional design that favored labor markets that are prone to wage moderation. At the aggregate level, EMU's inflationary bias is clearly depicted in the European Central Bank's strict 2 percent inflation mandate. What is less obvious, however, is how EMU's removal of important adjustment mechanisms—mechanisms that not only helped to deliver inflation convergence among member-states, but also helped to compensate for inflation's direct effect on the real exchange rate—established an institutional design that rendered EMU's low-inflation prone corporatist economies and high-inflation prone noncorporatist economies incompatible. In this chapter, I explain EMU's institutional bias toward the competitive performance of its low-inflation economies, how this bias has contributed to the gaping imbalances between the EMU North and South after the launch of the common currency, and what policy options are available, which are currently being overlooked, that can help rectify it.

Economic Integration and the Compatibility of Diverse National Systems

Two competing theories offer explanations to whether diverse national systems can coexist under common pressures of globalization. Neoliberal arguments stipulate that trade's enhancement of product market competition and capital mobility renders the sustainability of inflexible labor markets (and expensive welfare states) impossible (see OECD 1994; Nickell 1997; and Siebert 1997 for a general overview). The broader neoliberal argument explains that centralized wage-setting and powerful unions make wages inflexible to price shocks. As a result, wages are artificially higher than what the market would dictate, if they are not already too high due to opportunistic behavior by rent-seeking unions trying to secure generous wage settlements for their members. These high wages impose costs onto firms that are increasingly exposed to competition from third-world countries where labor costs are comparatively marginal. Higher labor costs make firms less competitive in global markets, ultimately leading to low output and employment. For countries to enhance the competitive position of their national firms, leaders must liberalize labor markets, diminish the power of unions, and dismantle centralized wage-setting.

A second line of institutional literature, starting first within the corporatism debate (Cameron 1984; Katzenstein 1985; Bruno and Sachs 1985; Calmfors and Driffill 1988; and Soskice 1990) and expanding more recently into the "varieties of capitalism" literature (Hall and Soskice 2001), outlines how institutional diversity can coexist within a globalized international system. Rigid labor markets are not destined to produce inefficiencies in the presence of trade competition. If collective wage-setters encompass a significant proportion of the labor force, they can use highly centralized and coordinated wage bargaining institutions to overcome collective action problems that result when individual wage-setters simultaneously demand higher wages. These encompassing, centralized wage-setting institutions have the potential to keep nominal unit labor costs below what would otherwise be dictated by the market, producing cost advantages to firms and enabling these firms to compete with those stemming from a liberalized and decentralized capitalist system. Rigid collective-bargaining structures also have the potential to deliver unique national comparative advantages in high value-added goods, as centralized unions and employer associations can safeguard the acquisition of industry-specific skills that enhance product quality (Hall and Soskice 2001).

Over time, the neoliberal argument has lost empirical ground in the institutional convergence/divergence debate. Europe's labor markets continue to exhibit institutional heterogeneity amid globalization, and these differences have led to "diverse responses to common challenges" (Scharpf and Schmidt 2000). Others have outlined that national diversity of the EU's member-states may better explain the pattern of economic integration in Europe, rather than European integration dictating the survival of specific types of national capitalist systems (E. Jones 2003b). Yet in the first decade and a half of European Monetary Union, which one could argue is a more intense form of globalization that not only requires the integration of trade and capital markets but also the unity of currencies, there is a clear demarcation of which capitalist systems have best weathered the economic storm. Europe's northern, corporatist economies, including the former sick man of Europe, Germany, have emerged from the global economic crisis on a more advantageous economic footing. Unemployment is lower, growth prospects are more optimistic, especially in manufacturing, and the large current account deficits and external borrowing balances that pushed Europe's peripheral economies into the abyss after 2008 have been conspicuously absent in these centralized and rigid national systems.

The institutional disarray of Europe's "mixed-market economies" (Greece, Italy, Portugal, and Spain) is not a novel concept and has been highlighted as a key factor behind this region's poor economic performance (Heckman 2000; Sapir 2006). These countries have long experiences with high inflation and unemployment (although Spain made considerable inroads into reducing unemployment in the early and mid-2000s); perhaps it should not be particularly surprising that these economies were picked off as EMU's weaker links in capital's flight to quality.[2] Yet what is surprising about the gaping external deficits of Europe's mixed-market economies is that they are only a recent phenomenon. Peripheral Europe's conflict-prone economic institutions did not thrust them into the significant current account and external lending imbalances prior to the establishment of the single currency that they witnessed in the 2000s. Current account and external lending balances were largely synchronous between the EMU North and South in the 1980s and 1990s (see figure 1.1), and when examining individual national performance, there was a significant reversal of fortunes between the 1990s and 2000s for many of EMU's southern and northern economies (see figure 7.1). Between the 1990s and 2000s, Greece, Portugal, and Spain witnessed

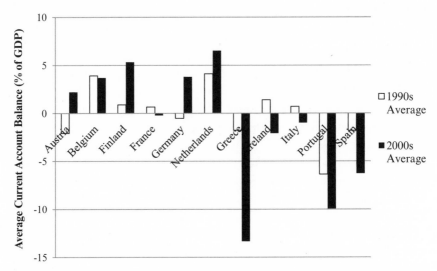

FIGURE 7.1.   Current account balances for the EMU11 (1990s and 2000s decade averages)

Source: EU Commission AMECO Database (2014).

considerable increases in their current account deficits; Ireland and Italy switched from surplus countries to deficit countries; Austria and Germany switched from deficit to surplus countries; and Finland and the Netherlands recorded considerable gains in their current account surpluses.

If EMU's diverse capitalist systems were able to coexist in their external trade and lending performance within an economically integrated Europe, this compatibility certainly is predicated on timing. The growth of external imbalances between EMU's corporatist and noncorporatist economic systems is conspicuously tied to the existence of monetary union. This may not be entirely coincidental, when one conceptualizes how EMU introduced an inflation bias within the real exchange rate, which had significant implications for trade and external borrowing performance between national systems with different inflation rates. EMU not only removed important institutions, described in previous chapters, that enabled peripheral Europe to converge toward corporatist Europe in its inflation and real exchange rate performance. EMU also removed an important economic adjustment mechanism—the nominal exchange rate—that could compensate for inflation's negative impact on the real exchange rate when peripheral Europe lacked national inflation-averse central banks and the Maastricht convergence criteria prior to 1992. In rendering the real exchange rate purely as a function of relative inflation between its member-states, in addition to removing pivotal institutions that assisted Europe's mixed-market economies to produce low inflation, monetary union established an environment that advantaged its corporatist economic models, helping to spare them from speculative crisis.

EMU's Low-Inflation Bias: Placing Current External Imbalances in Historical Perspective

To understand how monetary union created a low-inflation bias in the external economic relations of its participants, it is helpful to dissect how EMU altered political dynamics within its member-states' real exchange rates. Outside of monetary union, two worlds of monetary regimes exist: hard currency regimes, where either central bank mandates focus predominantly on the delivery of low inflation or national monetary authorities shadow an inflation-averse anchor currency, and soft currency regimes, where central banks accommodate inflation. Both regimes delivered contained current and capital account balances between EMU's corporatist and mixed-market economy member-states during the 1980s and 1990s. This was due to the fact that these currency regimes delivered adjustments in the real exchange rate (the nominal exchange rate multiplied by the ratio of a country's price level to that of its foreign competitors), ensuring that neither of Europe's national systems would enjoy persistently competitive real exchange rates over time.

The main emphasis of this book has highlighted how the transition to a hard currency regime under the ERM and Maastricht delivered wage moderation within all of EMU's current member-states, including those with conflictual, inflation-prone labor market institutions, and led to inflation convergence across diverse national systems. E(M)U member-states shifted toward a hard currency regime for one of three reasons: 1) their central banks had a strict inflation mandate, as in the case of Germany; 2) their political leaders made a credible commitment to a restrictive fixed exchange rate system where sizable devaluations against a (low inflation) anchor currency were not permitted—Austria, Belgium, France, and the Netherlands during the early or mid-1980s are examples; and/or 3) their political leaders made a credible commitment to fulfilling the Maastricht nominal criteria for EMU entry in the 1990s (which applies to all EMU candidate countries between 1992 and 1998). Wages played an important role in inflation adjustment. If wage growth was too high, it would place upward pressures on prices, defeating a low-inflation monetary policy. National central banks with low-inflation goals had to counteract inflationary wage growth with monetary contraction, placing low-inflation objectives onto wage-setters in sectors where the unemployment consequences associated with inflationary wage bills was not severe. ERM's and Maastricht's hard currency regime transformed Europe's diverse national labor market systems into inflation equals. Convergence in inflation, coupled with a fixed nominal exchange rate under the Exchange Rate Mechanism, facilitated convergence in the real exchange rate of both EMU's corporatist and noncorporatist economies. The transition to a hard currency regime limited external trade and lending imbalances between the EU's different capitalist systems, and in the case of Italy, turned what were previously economically dysfunctional national systems into consistent net exporters.[3]

The mass adoption of a hard currency regime by EMU member-states led to impressive inflation convergence in the 1990s. Before the 1992 ERM currency crisis, however, there was a clear distinction between countries upholding a hard and a soft currency regime; European countries were not the inflation equals in the 1980s that they would become under the Maastricht period. E(M)U's low-inflation performers in the 1980s adopted a credible commitment to a monetarist position early in the ERM regime. Austria, Germany, and the Netherlands entered ERM with an inflation-averse monetary regime in place, and Belgium and France made the switch from a soft to hard exchange rate peg, permitting only a +/−2.25 percent fluctuation band around the European Currency Union (ECU) by the mid-1980s (McNamara 2005). Italy, however, failed to exit its more generous +/−6 percent ERM fluctuation band until 1990, and when Spain and Portugal entered the ERM in 1989 and 1992, respectively, they too adopted the more flexible +/−6 percent band (Ungerer et al 1990).[4] This latter group of countries with more permissive currency pegs witnessed much higher inflation rates as central banks were not politically required to aggressively target and enforce low inflation in order to adhere to a restrictive fixed exchange rate regime (see table 7.1). Despite significant differences in inflation performances between the Eurozone core and periphery in the 1980s, however, external imbalances between these two country groups remained contained in this time period.

The Eurozone core produced far lower national inflation than the periphery in the 1980s as compared with the 1990s and 2000s. Nevertheless, these gaping inflation differentials did not transpire to significant imbalances in the real exchange rate. The adjustment mechanism that facilitated current account and net external lending convergence between the hard currency core and the soft currency periphery in the 1980s was variation in the *nominal* exchange rate. If the nominal exchange rate is permitted to fluctuate more widely, high-inflation currencies lose their nominal value vis-à-vis low-inflation currencies via depreciation/

TABLE 7.1. Inflation and exchange rate (real and nominal) movements (1980s decade average)

	AVERAGE ANNUAL CHANGE IN INFLATION	AVERAGE ANNUAL CHANGE IN THE NOMINAL EXCHANGE RATE	AVERAGE ANNUAL CHANGE IN THE REAL EXCHANGE RATE
Austria	3.84%	2.41%	0.52%
Belgium	4.90%	−0.56%	−1.96%
Finland*	7.32%	1.43%	3.39%
France	7.38%	−1.69%	−1.24%
Germany	2.90%	2.89%	−0.67%
The Netherlands	3.00%	1.84%	−2.00%
Eurozone "Core"	4.39%	1.60%	−0.33%
Greece	19.50%	−11.67%	0.79%
Ireland	9.34%	−1.33%	−0.17%
Italy	11.20%	−2.41%	2.96%
Portugal	17.35%	−8.83%	0.01%
Spain	10.26%	−2.34%	−0.08%
Eurozone "Periphery"	14.58%	−6.31%	0.70%

SOURCE: EU Commission AMECO Database (2014).
* Despite the fact that Finland possesses the functional corporatist institutions outlined in chapters 2 and 3, which limited high inflation to some extent in the 1980s, its late transition to a hard currency regime was more aligned with that of the Eurozone periphery.

devaluation. Such nominal exchange rate depreciations/devaluations, which were notably present in the periphery during the 1980s (see table 7.1), significantly blunted the impact of the periphery's higher inflation rates on its real exchange rates. Consequently, the periphery's high-inflation performance did *not* lead to the significant deterioration of external balances prior to mass inflation convergence in the 1990s because devalued/depreciated nominal exchange rates narrowed gaps in real exchange rate movements between the EMU North and South. During the 1980s, growth in the average *real* exchange rate of the Eurozone core economies was 1 percent lower per year than it was in the periphery. During the 1990s, this per-year growth differential shrunk to 0.65 percent. During the pre-crisis 2000s, however, the gaps in annual real exchange movements grew to 1.6 percent per year in favor of the Eurozone's core economies (EU Commission AMECO Database 2014).

Europe's monetary union changed its participants' real exchange rate adjustment calculus so that high-inflation prone countries were presented with a persistent competitive disadvantage. During the 1980s, the EMU periphery, which lacked cohesive corporatist institutions that produced low inflation, could find competitive solace in nominal exchange rate depreciations/devaluations. These nominal exchange rate movements ensured that real exchange rate dynamics would not significantly differ between Europe's low-inflation prone corporatist economies and high-inflation prone noncorporatist economies. Though the periphery lost the nominal exchange rate as an adjustment tool in the 1990s, Maastricht's requirement of a firm commitment to low-inflation and a stable nominal exchange rate granted these countries inflation-averse, national central banks that could target national wage developments and penalize inflationary wage settlements. These national central banks promoted further real exchange rate convergence through the delivery of low inflation in otherwise inflation-prone noncorporatist economies. The single currency removed *both* inflation-averse national central banks and Maastricht's entry criteria that delivered inflation and real exchange rate convergence, *as well as* nominal exchange rates. Countries that could persistently produce low inflation relative to their trading partners realized persistently advantageous real exchange rates. Despite its strict price stability mandate, the European Central Bank (ECB) could do little to address inflation problems in peripheral economies, as long as the core's inflation developments realigned the aggregate Eurozone inflation rate at or below its 2 percent target. The lack of institutional and economic adjustment mechanisms between high- and low-inflation economies set the stage for the corporatist core's persistent accrual of current account surpluses and net external lending balances, which ultimately had destabilizing effects.

The institutional literature championing the mutual coexistence of diverse capitalist institutions amid globalization was conditionally correct. Although Europe's labor market institutions have come under strain from processes of decentralization and reform, increased trade flows and capital mobility have not completely dismantled these embedded structures. However, if economic integration is conceptualized more narrowly, such as the unification of national economies into a common currency, the sustainability of diverse capitalist systems that differ in their inflation performance becomes more circumspect. EMU's national systems remain unable to confront a common debt crisis with diverse institutional responses. Rather, EMU's corporatist economies have emerged as the national champions, while its noncorporatist member-states suffer persistent economic decline, made worse by the lack of adjustment mechanisms at their disposal and the austere policy demands of the European Commission. The success of Europe's low-inflation prone models of capitalism should not be entirely surprising. EMU created a regime that persistently rewarded low-inflation performers in their external balances, and these healthy current account and net lending surpluses helped to spare them from speculative crisis. The good news for Europe is that there are means to rectify this inflation bias problem that is inherent in EMU's institutional design. The bad news for Europe is that these means have been ignored in favor of other policy responses that have targeted the debt crisis's red herrings.

Solutions for EMU's Current Crisis

Early Policy Responses: Compensating for Previous Fiscal Monitoring Mishaps

As the sovereign debt crisis revealed the inherent weaknesses of the single currency, the EU has proposed and implemented an abundance of policy responses to mend these cracks in the system. After the establishment of significant financial resource pools (the EFSF, which later became the ESM) to assist member-states on the verge of default, EMU's creditor nations, pushed strongest by Germany, demanded stricter and more efficient fiscal rules to make EMU's future less susceptible to the spillovers of excessive public spending. The deficiencies in the Stability and Growth Pact's preventive arm (convergence toward balanced budgets in the medium-term) and corrective arm (the 3 percent annual deficit rule) were targeted first in efforts to strengthen the enforcement of responsible public borrowing. Introduced in late 2011, the EU "six pack" implemented five regulations and one directive aimed at strengthening budgetary surveillance, enhanced the enforcement of the excessive deficit procedure, introduced requirements for member-states' budgetary frameworks, and established two new regulations directed at the prevention and correction of general macroeconomic imbalances (EU ECFIN 2013b). Enforcing the new "six pack" under a period of severe economic duress, however, proved futile. With the exception of Italy, which complied with the deficit rule, in 2012 all of EMU's crisis-ridden peripheral economies realized fiscal deficits that were more than double (and in the case of Spain more than triple) the 3 percent benchmark, due in most part to the vicious cycle of negative GDP growth and low tax revenues that bailout austerity conditionality helped fuel. Some of EMU's core economies also proved incapable of living up to the fiscally prudent image that they publicly demanded from their struggling southern neighbors; Belgium, France, and the Netherlands produced fiscal deficits in excess of 4 percent in 2012, further demonstrating the difficulties of adhering to fiscal rules during recession (EU Commission AMECO Database 2014).

Admitting that "the global economic and financial crises exposed shortcomings in economic governance and budgetary surveillance at the EU level," the European Commission, further pressured by Germany, introduced the Fiscal Compact and "two pack" in 2013 to reinforce the "six pack" regulations (EU

Commission 2013). Dressed as a budgetary "coordination" tool between Euro-area member-states, these two initiatives significantly increased the scope of the European Commission's involvement in EMU member-states' sovereign determination of their fiscal budgets. The Fiscal Compact required Eurozone countries to incorporate a balanced budget rule into national law that stipulated that annual structural deficits were not to exceed 0.5 percent of GDP (EU ECFIN 2013c). Countries undergoing severe economic downturns would be exempt from compliance, but those that failed to comply in more favorable economic conditions would be subjugated to disciplinary action by the European Court of Justice and fines worth 0.1 percent of GDP.

The "two pack," passed in May of the same year, further reinforced the Fiscal Compact's budgetary rules. Regulation 473/2013 of article 136 of the Treaty on the Functioning of the European Union (TFEU) intensified the depth and frequency of the monitoring process for countries involved in the Excessive Deficit Procedure (EDP) or the Excessive Imbalance Procedure (EIP). Regulation 472/2013 of article 136 of the TFEU provided the Commission greater oversight over budgetary procedures within Eurozone countries that were not undergoing EDP or EIP. While not given a formal veto over national budgets, the Commission was granted the right to assess national draft budgetary proposals before they were discussed and ratified in national parliaments. If national budgets of Eurozone member-states appeared to compromise the Fiscal Compact's objectives, the Commission possessed the power to issue stern warnings, leaving a paper trail for the implementation of corrective fines should these budgets ultimately lead to fiscal noncompliance.

Renewed attempts at effective fiscal surveillance have occupied the majority of EU legislative efforts to uphold the resilience of monetary union. The creation of this new framework of fiscal management is unlikely to address the source of Europe's debt crisis or to alleviate its new low/no growth equilibrium. Assuming that more effective fiscal rules even *could* safeguard the single currency, it is doubtful whether EMU's member-states would consistently follow them if fiscal surveillance reform episodes under EMU's early years are anything to go by. The new "six pack," Fiscal Compact, and "two pack" suffer from the same credibility problems that followed Stability and Growth Pact's (SGP) enforcement, and such credibility problems are highly dependent on the cyclical reversal of fortunes of EMU's large member-states. It is easy for a hawkish Germany to demand and receive greater fiscal surveillance at the EU level when its fiscal position is healthy and countries relying on its financial assistance through EU stability facilities are operating in deficit. Yet Germany's true commitment to this new macroeconomic governance framework will be measured once these rules apply to its own fiscal transgressions. At the onset of EMU, Germany barked a similar fiscal tone as it does now. Once its deficits persistently breached the SGP's limits in the early 2000s, Germany undertook steps not to enhance the enforcement of EMU's fiscal rules, but pushed for their relaxation.

Credibility problems aside, the revival of European fiscal regulation is also problematic because fiscal excess was not the foundation of Europe's current crisis. In ignoring the underlying causes behind the growth of external imbalances between the North and South, policies directed as fiscal prudence have not only failed in safeguarding the stability of the single currency, but have worsened crisis exposure within its struggling member-states. In their misguided efforts to restore sustainable fiscal balances, the European Commission's austerity measures have led to severe reductions in public investment and social safety nets that affect the most vulnerable and initiated measures that have caused significant reductions in wages, in some countries by more than 30 percent. These initiatives have caused a collapse in demand and a surge in unemployment rates, which have pushed peripheral economies into either double-dip recessions if not prolonged depression. More tragically, the IMF and even some of the Europe Commission's own economic departments have publicly accepted the obvious fact that the EU's austerity efforts have made fiscal records in the European periphery worse due to their devastating effects on income growth (Stiglitz et al. 2014).

The failure of EMU's new fiscal framework in rectifying the crisis has highlighted the need for new forms of European integration. Because the crisis was triggered by a financial shock and the resulting contagion that followed in its wake, the creation of a banking union to manage failing and destabilizing financial institutions was initiated as a further backstop to uphold the euro. Eurobonds, common European debt instruments not native to national issuers, are also under serious discussion to prevent the disruptive effects of flight to quality within EMU's borders. Yet these supply-side solutions to the crisis, admittedly much better initiatives than the troika's (the European Commission, the European Central Bank and the IMF) current path of austerity, still evade the divergence problem of the rise in external imbalances between EMU's member-states that precipitated speculative crisis in the South. Both EMU's core and peripheral economies were exposed to the creation of large multinational banks through mergers and acquisitions as well as increased financial liberalization that saturated markets with a plethora of borrowing instruments in the 1990s and 2000s. However, these common credit shocks did not equally expose EMU member-states to sovereign debt crisis after 2008. Creating a framework to wind down failing banks will certainly help to isolate the effects of contagion, but it does not address the fundamental inflation bias in EMU's institutional design that gave rise to the EMU South's greater propensity to run current account and external net lending deficits vis-à-vis its northern neighbors.

The Forgotten Role of Supranational Wage-Setting

Wage-setting remains one policy realm that has been conspicuously absent from the Commission's recent attempts to manage the crisis. EMU's institutional predecessors indirectly coordinated wage-setting within member-states by advancing a low-inflation ideal within individual candidate countries. These institutions delivered inflation convergence, and it was anticipated that such inflation convergence would continue in their absence. EMU's early years demonstrated that in producing divergence in income growth, diverse wage-setting institutions can also produce divergence in countries' accumulation of external debt and the overextension of external consumption. Divergence in external trade and lending imbalances had serious implications for the sustainability of a single currency without a system of fiscal transfers between regions. EMU's diverse national labor market institutions could not achieve convergence in an economic union when left to their own accord. Some type of coordination mechanism or common low-inflation rule within member-states is required to limit the scale of external imbalances between these systems.

It is too late to revert back to a system of national central banks upholding common inflation rules. The coordination of wage growth at the EU level, however, is a possible way forward to correct the inflation bias innate in EMU's institutional design. Supranational wage coordination is not an innovative concept to European monetary integration; the idea has been promoted by members of national trade union movements since the single currency became functional. Near the launch of the euro, trade union leaders within candidate countries were conscientious about a "race to the bottom" in wage costs. Cross-border collective bargaining was perceived as one useful policy avenue that could avoid this outcome (Crouch 2000; Marginson and Traxler 2005). In 1999, the European Trade Union Confederation (ETUC) established a committee for the coordination of collective bargaining across E(M)U member states. ETUC's objectives for cross-border collective bargaining were to provide a coordination mechanism in wage-setting that would parallel macroeconomic policy coordination within the ECB and Broad Economic Policy Guidelines and specifically avoid wage divergence within Europe in the effort to promote "upward convergence" in living standards (Eurofound 2009a).

Despite the ETUC's prophetic aim to limit wage growth divergence under EMU, most coordination efforts at the EU level have been piecemeal and unsuccessful, targeting regions or sectors where wage divergence was not a significant problem. In 1998, the Doorn group was created to initiate cross-border coordination of collective bargaining across major sectoral unions, including those in public services; the group's founding declaration even comprised a common wage formula for its members (Eichhorst, Kendzia, and Vandeweghe 2011). Yet the Doorn group encompassed union confederations in the Benelux countries and Germany only, all low-inflation performers due to the presence of cohesive wage coordination institutions that limited wage growth in nontradable sectors. By the September 2000 meeting in Luxembourg, it became apparent that collective action problems could hamper coordination efforts even among EMU's low-inflation prone corporatist economies; Belgium was the only country whose wage developments were on par with the formula stipulated in the Doorn Declaration, while wage growth in Germany was significantly below target (Eurofound 2009b).

More inclusive inroads involving wage coordination between both EMU core and peripheral economies were undertaken within the manufacturing sector under the leadership of the European Metalworkers' Federation (EMF). Like the Doorn Declaration, the EMF expressed its desire in 1998 to establish a European coordination rule where collective agreements across the EU's manufacturing sectors would offset inflation and account for labor's contribution to national productivity growth.[5] The EMF has been more successful at cross-border wage coordination than the Doorn group—it has engaged the participation of European employer associations (the Council of European Employers of Metal, Engineering, and Technology-Based Industries) and created a durable supranational venue for collective dialogue that received the endorsement of the European Commission (Eichhorst, Kendzia, and Vandeweghe 2011). Yet like the Doorn group, the EMF's initiatives largely target (exposed) sectors whose wage developments would likely converge, due to market pressures, without its attempts at supranational wage coordination. After 1999, EMU's manufacturing sectors conformed to moderated wage growth as employers and unions within these sectors were subject to the common constraint of international competition.

The coordination of wage developments in *nontradable* sectors across EMU's diverse national systems remains a pivotal objective that has evaded recent efforts at supranational wage coordination. I have argued here that wage dynamics in nontradable sectors drove inflation divergence between EMU's corporatist and noncorporatist member-states. Delivering an effective coordination mechanism that drives convergence in sheltered sector wage growth, therefore, is far more vital in correcting EMU's inflation bias than the establishment of coordination rules in Europe's more uniform manufacturing sectors. Had nontradable sectors produced similar levels of wage growth across countries, the conformity of wage dynamics in EMU's manufacturing sectors to a competitive rule may have ensured the continuation of inflation convergence after 1999 and, with it, the containment of real exchange rates and external balances. Once EMU

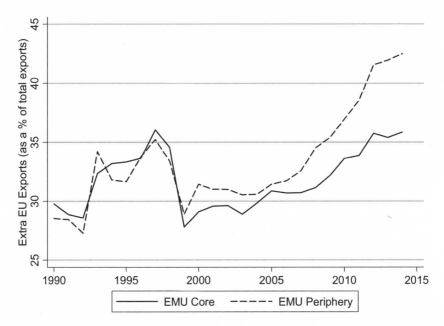

FIGURE 7.2. Extra-EU exports as a proportion of total exports (1990–2014)

Note: EMU core includes Austria, Belgium, Finland, France, Germany, and the Netherlands. EMU periphery includes Greece, Ireland, Italy, Portugal, and Spain.
Source: EU Commission AMECO Database (2014).

recovers from the crisis, the successful implementation of a common wage norm within EMU's sheltered sectors would help break the institutional advantages of its corporatist economies by continually realigning inflation developments across diverse national labor markets.

In EMU's current condition, however, the restoration of economic growth may require a divergence trajectory *opposite* to that witnessed under EMU's pre-crisis years—promotion of inflation and demand stimulus in the North to alleviate the South's collapse in incomes. Though not doing so intentionally, the European Commission is supranationally managing income divergences between EMU's corporatist and noncorporatist economies via its significant reductions of incomes in peripheral economies, which have produced deflationary effects in noncorporatist economic systems. In addition to unleashing economic devastation on bailed-out states, this supranational income management has been heavily one-sided. EMU's noncorporatist countries have pursued painful austerity measures that reduced inflation, yet no attempt has been made to correct the excessive levels of wage moderation in the corporatist North, which are equally responsible for Europe's crisis, via income expansion. EU political leaders, driven strongly by the political weight of Germany, have placed the full burden of inflation adjustment on "high" inflation economies, enabling EMU's low-inflation performers to escape from their responsibilities in symmetrical adjustment.

The result has not only been the establishment of an asymmetrical, low-growth equilibrium in Europe, where the collapse of import demand in periphery economies has corrected its current account imbalances while export-led economies continue to pursue low-inflation strategies to sustain their current account surpluses. More problematic to the European Union's original goals of promoting peace through trade dependence, EMU's current path of adjustment may also be driving its member-states more economically distant from each other. Export composition data highlights an exponentially rising trend in *extra-EU* exports as a proportion of total exports in both the core and periphery since the onset of the debt crisis (see figure 7.2). The South no longer provides the North with robust import demand, and the continuation of wage moderation in the North has limited southern firms' entry into their domestic markets.

The Politics of Inflation and the Sustainability of EMU: Silver Linings on the Horizon?

Austerity politics in EMU's northern economies have prohibited an effective and comprehensive European response to resolving its current path of asymmetrical crisis adjustment. Perceiving the virtues of their low-inflation performances and healthy current account and external lending surpluses, politicians in Germany and her northern satellites expressed strong reluctance to pursue the United States' demand-expansion path in the early days of the crisis. EMU core political leaders quickly pointed out that prudent management of income growth was one crucial factor that spared their economies from the periphery's fate. Income policies initiatives that would cause their economies to converge in their wage performance with the pre-crisis "irresponsible" wage trends witnessed in the South were initially ruled out. Additionally, (German) employers' organizations refuted the need to promote solidaristic wage adjustment to assist the periphery with economic recovery; in early 2013, Peer-Michael Dick, the managing director of the Metalworking and Engineering Employers' Federation in Germany, indicated that "it makes no sense at all economically, the notion that we have to pay higher wages so that southern Europe can get back on its feet" (Böll and Tietz 2013).

Early crisis policy rhetoric from the European Commission was also largely unhelpful in negotiating symmetrical adjustment from EMU's northern member-states. In addition to its austerity drive, the Commission established the 2011 Macroeconomic Imbalance Procedure (MiP), a warning system aimed at discouraging the accumulation of untenable external balances. The MiP was heavily skewed toward correcting current account and borrowing deficits rather than extreme surpluses. The MiP's classification of a "sustainable" (three-year average) current account balance is one that lies between a 6 percent surplus and a 4 percent deficit. The higher allowable threshold for surplus countries, however, provides them with greater leniency in disciplinary action than deficit countries, despite the fact that sizable current account surpluses may well cause 4 percent (or more) current account deficits elsewhere. Though fiscal austerity has proved the wrong direction forward for Europe, deficit targets in the EU's fiscal framework does not pose the same asymmetrical adjustment problem as deficit targets for external balances. National fiscal performance is *not* relative— countries can run fiscal deficits or surpluses regardless of the fiscal positions of their trading partners, and countries' capacities to address fiscal imbalances is largely, but not completely, independent of the actions of their neighbors. External deficits, however, *are* relative—a country's accumulation of a current account deficit, or capital account surplus, is purely dependent on its trading partner's accumulation of current account surpluses. Countries' capacity to rectify their external deficit not only depends on their own actions, but also the "wage dumping" actions of their neighbors.

Within the early years of the crisis, the EU in general and its northern corporatist economies in particular were routinely criticized for a lack of leadership and political capacity to manage economic recovery in the Euro-area. After seven years of stagnation and previous actions' lack of success, however, there are signs that political dialogue may be shifting in favor of symmetrical adjustment via the promotion of wage growth in the North. In mid-2013, László Andor, the European Union Social Affairs Commissioner, called on EMU's creditor countries, particularly Germany, to "spend more" and for Europe to shift away from austerity and the consolidation of national budgets toward demand stimulus (*Der Spiegel* 2013). In its March 2014 Macroeconomic Imbalances report of Germany, the European Commission admitted that "the size and persistence of the current account surplus in Germany deserves close attention" and that action was needed "to reduce the risk of adverse effects on the functioning of the (German) domestic economy and of the euro area . . . given the size of the German economy" (European Commission 2014, 3).

Germany is also witnessing a shift in national dialogue toward the promotion of pay increases. In the run up to the 2013 German federal elections, the Social Democratic Party made the establishment of a statutory pay floor a central campaign issue and was successful in eliciting a national minimum wage as a concession from Merkel's Christian Democrats during the formation of a grand coalition government. While deeply critical of it at first, German business leaders have warmed to the new 2014 minimum wage law (Thomas and Dauer 2014). Germany has also witnessed a cross-sectoral coalition among its trade unions to push for higher wages. Both the major services union ver.di and the metalworkers' union IG Metall aggressively focused on substantial wage increases for the 2013 bargaining round. This is not the first time German trade unions have advocated for significant increases in pay against a backdrop of prolonged wage moderation, but it is the first time during the crisis that once-reluctant economic interests are sympathizing with these tones. Members of the German Council of Economic Experts have acknowledged that German wages have a necessary role to play in EMU's adjustment process while even Finance Minister Wolfgang Schäuble agreed with the principle of notable wage increases, arguing that such developments would "also contribute to eliminating imbalances within Europe" (Böll and Tietz 2013). Growing sympathies toward German inflation have also arisen from a most unlikely source. In July 2014, the Bundesbank, famed for its hardline approach to inflation, made an unprecedented public shift in its incomes policy stance, backing German trade unions' campaigns for significant wage increases (C. Jones 2014).

Though it is too soon to determine whether recent political rhetoric will materialize into tangible economic outputs, especially in light of the hard-line stance Germany has taken toward Greece during the negotiation of its third (2015) bailout, the transformation away from previous austerity tones is a promising step in the right direction. Germany has long been Europe's reluctant hegemon, but its export model has revealed its dependence on robust income growth within its trading partners. Political leaders and policymakers in EMU's northern corporatist economies exhibited subtle degrees of schadenfreude toward the "dysfunctional" periphery's early exposure to crisis, yet seven years of prolonged stagnation and the collapse of import demand in the EMU South has highlighted the fact that the North's economic success also depends on that of Europe's non-corporatist economies. This eventual realization of interdependency may be the political shift needed to initiate symmetrical adjustment that is desperately needed in monetary union. EMU's design is, and will remain, biased toward persistent low-inflation performers. However, one silver lining the current crisis may have delivered to EMU's political leaders is the realization that the single currency's long-term success depends on effectively coordinating the idiosyncrasies between its diverse national systems.

Appendix I

EXPOSED AND SHELTERED SECTORS AND THE MEANING OF WAGE MODERATION

Nominal unit labor cost growth is frequently used as a proxy for wage moderation (Visser 1998a; Traxler and Kittel 2000; Pichelmann 2001), yet this indicator suffers from a "kitchen sink" problem. In its reduced form, nominal unit labor costs capture labor's share in GDP, which can change due to other variables, most notably those that influence the accumulation of capital (e.g., capital substitution and the price of capital). Selecting this as a measurement for wage restraint therefore is problematic for two reasons: one, it does not isolate for wage excess above productivity that is attributed to *only* labor, and two, endogeneity problems arise because firms may decide to substitute and move away from labor toward capital if unit labor cost growth is persistently high.

Blanchard's wages in efficiency units, or WEU (Blanchard and Wolfers 2000; Blanchard and Philippon 2003; Blanchard 2006), partially overcomes these caveats. Blanchard's WEU is equal to the (log) change in the real product wage minus the (log) change in labor's contribution to total factor productivity—in other words, it captures the degree to which wage growth overshoots or undershoots labor productivity growth. Blanchard controls for changes in capital substitution/accumulation in his productivity measurement. Labor's contribution to productivity growth is defined as the ratio of total factor productivity (the Solow residual) to labor's share in GDP. If the efficiency wage unit is positive—real wage growth exceeds productivity—wage inflation exists. If the efficiency wage unit is negative—productivity exceeds real wage growth—wage restraint is present.

Blanchard's WEU have been employed in recent empirical scholarship on wage inflation (Estevão 2005; Simoni 2007; Baccaro and Simoni 2010). I also employ it here to measure aggregate wage restraint given its advantages in separating out labor's share in total factor productivity. Though national WEUs provide a focal point for wage developments at the national level, they do not measure sectoral wage moderation, which is the primary phenomenon of interest in this book. Ideally, the construction of sectoral wage moderation/inflation would merely involve applying sectoral data to Blanchard's WEUs. One major problem with this, however, is the absence of *sectoral-level* total factor productivity data—the Solow residual at the sectoral level has not been computed for a major cross-national database. The EU KLEMS Growth and Productivity Accounts Database (EU KLEMS 2010) is one of the few databases that provide consistent data on gross value added per hour worked by sector for the EU27 and several major OECD economies.[1] Gross value added per hour worked is used in place of the weighted Solow residual for the productivity measure in computing sectoral wage moderation. Sectoral wage moderation/inflation is calculated by taking the difference in sectoral real hourly wage growth and growth in sectoral gross value added per hour worked.

EU KLEMS explicitly notes some methodological limitations regarding productivity data for several nonmarket services sectors (including public administration and defense, healthcare and social work, and education, which I select as proxies for the sheltered sector). Though the EU KLEMS Database does not differentiate between private and public provision within a given nonmarket industry, it does acknowledge that national statistical agencies differ in their estimation of public sector output and productivity. Some countries make assumptions on improvements in labor productivity in the public sector, revolving around residuals in national labor productivity that are not absorbed by all other sectors within the economy (Timmer et al. 2007, 47–48). Consequently, the creators of the database urge caution in the interpretation of productivity data for nonmarket services.[2] To overcome this productivity reporting bias, sectoral wage gaps in isolation of productivity developments are also utilized to gauge sectoral wage bifurcation, serving as one of the primary dependent variables in the empirical panel analysis in chapter 3. Leaving aside technicalities regarding the measurement of productivity in (nonmarket) services sectors, the core sectoral convergence/divergence phenomenon before/after the introduction of EMU continues to hold in sectoral wage gap data.

In regards to the selection of exposed and sheltered sector proxies, most work, both empirical and theoretical, that focuses on sector cleavages in wage-setting identifies the manufacturing sector as a proxy for the exposed sector and general services as a proxy for the sheltered sector (Crouch 1990; Johnston and Hancké 2009; Herman 2009; Traxler and Brandl 2010). Recent empirical evidence supports assumptions of the reduced price markup capabilities of manufacturing sector firms, given their exposure to trade (Druant et al. 2009). Services sectors are identified as relatively sheltered from trade given the presence of a joint production trap; both the consumer and producer must be in the same geographical location in order for the service to take place, unlike goods-based sectors, where production and consumption can be geographically de-linked (Herman 2009).[3] Despite these general classifications, some empirical work on the volume of gross output that is traded by sector has identified "tradable" services. De Gregorio, Giovannini, and Wolf (1994) surveyed the export share (of total production) for several sectors among fourteen OECD countries and outlined that the (service-based) transportation sector possessed higher export shares than agriculture and paper products. Allard-Prigent, Guilmeau, and Quinet (2000), who provide a more detailed breakdown of service sector tradability using French data, add financial services to the list of tradable services sector, finding that over 20 percent of production in this sector was traded between 1990 and 1997. Services sectors identified as having low exposure to trade, in terms of the proportion of production that was exported or imported, include wholesale and retail trade, business services,[4] and nonmarket services such as public administration and defense, health services, and education (Allard-Prigent, Guilmeau, and Quinet 2000).

In line with the empirics that describe trade exposure by sector, I select the manufacturing sector (ISIC category D) as the proxy for the exposed sector, while a composite, weighted according to employment share, of public administration[5] and defense (ISIC category L), education (ISIC category M), and health and social work (ISIC category N) serves as a proxy for the sheltered sector. While the selection of these sectors, which predominate the highly sheltered and union-organized public sector, may exaggerate the sheltered sector proxy's lack of competitiveness, making it a purer fit to the theory outlined in chapter 2, similar empirical results found in figures 1.2 and 1.3, and the panel regression analysis in chapter 3, emerge if private-sheltered sector composites—wholesale and retail trade sector (ISIC category G) and the real estate, renting, and business services sector (ISIC category K)—are used to proxy the sheltered sector (Johnston 2011). Both the manufacturing and sheltered services composite constitute notable employment shares in the national economy for all economies studied, averaging (in combination) 43 percent of total employment in the EMU10 in 2007 (EU KLEMS 2010).

VARIABLE MEASUREMENT AND DATA SOURCES

DEPENDENT VARIABLES	MEASUREMENT	SOURCE
Differences in sectoral hourly wage growth	The difference in the following values: 1) the log change of the sum of compensation of employees within the public administration and defense (ISIC category L), education (ISIC category M), and health and social work (ISIC category N) sectors divided by the sum of total hours worked within these sectors, and 2) the log change of the sum of compensation of employees within manufacturing (ISIC category D) divided by the sum of total hours worked within manufacturing. Hourly wages are then deflated according to the consumer price index.	Compensation of employees and number of hours worked by sector taken from the EU KLEMS database. Consumer price index data taken from the OECD Main Economic Indicators.
Export share growth	Year-on-year percentage change in the export share (exports/GDP).	European Commission AMECO Database.

INDEPENDENT VARIABLES	MEASUREMENT	SOURCE
(Weighted) central bank non-accommodation index	Based on Iversen's (1999a) index. Index is the average of Cukierman's (1992) central bank independence index and (normalized) 4-year moving averages of the nominal effective exchange rate. Variable is then weighted according to the proportion of employees working in the public sector (ISIC categories L, M, and N) to the entire economy over which the central bank presides.	Central bank independence data taken from Cukierman (1992) and Polillo and Gullién (2005). Nominal effective exchange rate data taken from the European Commission AMECO Database. Public sector and total economy employment taken from EU KLEMS.

(continued)

INDEPENDENT VARIABLES	MEASUREMENT	SOURCE
Maastricht dummy	Assumes the value of 1 for years 1992–1998 for the following countries: Austria, Belgium, Finland, France, Germany, Ireland, Italy, the Netherlands, Portugal, and Spain. 0 if otherwise.	NA
EMU dummy	Assumes the value of 1 for years 1999–2007 for the following countries: Austria, Belgium, Finland, France, Germany, Ireland, Italy, the Netherlands, Portugal, and Spain. 0 if otherwise.	NA
Differences in sectoral productivity growth	The difference in the following values: 1) the log change of the (employee weighted) average of gross value added per hour worked for the public administration and defense (ISIC category L), education (ISIC category M), and health and social work (ISIC category N) sectors, and 2) the log change in gross value added per hour worked for the manufacturing sector (ISIC category D).	EU KLEMS database.
Differences in sectoral employment growth	The difference in the following values: 1) the log change of the number of employees working within the public administration and defense (ISIC category L), education (ISIC category M), and health and social work (ISIC category N) sectors, and 2) the log change of the number of employees working within the manufacturing sector (ISIC category D).	EU KLEMS database.
Net public lending	Net public lending divided by GDP.	European Commission AMECO Database. Sweden and Australia's more complete deficit data was obtained from the OECD.
Partisanship	Right-party legislative seats as a percentage of total legislative seats. In election years, party seats are weighted according to tenure.	Swank's (2006) comparative parties dataset
Wage bargaining centralization	Based on Iversen's (1999a) centralization index. Ranges from 0 (no centralization among unions) to 1 (monopoly centralization among unions).	Visser (2011).

INDEPENDENT VARIABLES	MEASUREMENT	SOURCE
Export-favoring wage coordination regime	A dummy variable embodying the value of 1 if a country has one of the following coordination regimes at time t: pattern bargaining, state-imposed coordination, and state-led wage pacts. 0 if otherwise.	Traxler, Blaschke, and Kittel (2001); Brandl (2012); Visser (2011); various articles from the European Industrial Relations Observatory.
Relative sectoral union density	Ratio of the membership of the three largest public-sector affiliates to the three largest exposed-sector affiliates within a country's largest union confederation.	Traxler and Brandl (2010).
Total factor productivity growth	The percentage change in total factor productivity growth (from the previous year).	European Commission AMECO Database.
Terms of trade shocks	The percentage change in the terms of trade (from the previous year).	European Commission AMECO Database.
Real exchange rate shocks	The percentage change in the real exchange rate (from the previous year).	European Commission AMECO Database.
Social benefits	Social benefits other than social transfers in kind as a percentage of GDP.	European Commission AMECO Database.
Sheltered sector employment share	The number of employees within the public administration and defense (ISIC category L), education (ISIC category M), and health and social work (ISIC category N) sectors as a proportion of the total labor force.	EU KLEMS Database.

Notes

1. INCOMPLETE MONETARY UNION AND EUROPE'S CURRENT CRISIS

1. Throughout this book, the terms "peripheral" and "southern" economies will be used interchangeably to describe the group of countries (Greece, Ireland, Italy, Portugal, and Spain) that have been exposed to market speculation amid the European sovereign debt crisis. Likewise, the terms "core" and "northern" economies will be used interchangeably to describe the group of countries (Austria, Belgium, Finland, France, Germany, and the Netherlands) that have emerged relatively unscathed from speculative pressure amid the current crisis.

2. Germany may be one possible exception to national inflation targeting under monetary union, because its large economy could influence EMU's average inflation rate.

3. Throughout this book, the terms "exposed" and "sheltered" are used interchangeably with the terms "tradables" and "nontradables," respectively, in defining a sector's exposure to trade.

4. The EMU10 are Austria, Belgium, Finland, France, Germany, Ireland, Italy, the Netherlands, Portugal, and Spain. Luxembourg is omitted from this analysis given its size. While including Greece was highly preferred, despite its later entry date, sectoral wage and productivity data were not as consistent and widely available; Greece is therefore excluded from presentations of sectoral data (available aggregate data are, however, included in the presentation of national statistics). Given qualitative and quantitative accounts of Greece's wage and inflation adjustment under Maastricht (Pagoulatos 2000) and the country's inflationary trajectory under EMU (Kouretas and Vlamis 2010; Featherstone 2011; Gibson, Hall, and Tavlas 2012; Christopoulou and Monastiriotis 2014a), it is likely that Greece's sectoral data would conform to trends exhibited by EMU's other southern economies.

5. While northern EMU economies have been more successful at expanding their non-EU export market shares than southern economies, given the specialization of the former in high value-added goods, trade between both groups of countries predominated within the EU during EMU's pre-crisis era.

6. In the 2000s, trade with EMU's northern economies was quite substantial for the EMU South, although less so for Ireland. In 2005, imports from Austria, Belgium, Finland, France, Germany, and the Netherlands accounted for 40 percent of Italy's and Spain's total imports, 30 percent of Greece's and Portugal's imports, and 20 percent of Ireland's imports (IMF 2008a).

7. Gaulier, Taglioni, and Vicard (2012) acknowledge that the appreciation in the periphery's unit labor costs can be largely attributed to price developments in their sheltered sectors.

2. FROM ORDER TO DISORDER

1. The terms "inflation-averse" and "non-accommodating" are used interchangeably to define central banks' increased commitments to upholding low inflation.

2. High wage settlements are defined as those where awarded nominal wage growth exceeds the sum of productivity and inflation. Low wage settlements are defined as those where awarded nominal wage growth is less than the sum of productivity and inflation.

3. The Netherlands provides a case in point. In September 1982, the Christian Democratic Party campaigned on introducing civil servant pay freezes *before* the general election; see EIRR 105 (October 1982), "Focus on job creation," p. 4.

4. Services constitute a significant proportion of the sheltered sector, because they are more difficult to trade in lieu of the "joint production" trap, where both the producer and consumer have to be in close physical proximity of each other in order for production to take place (Herman 2009). Additionally, services have also been identified as low-productivity sectors, relative to goods, because quantity gains are difficult without significantly impeding on quality (Baumol and Bowen 1965). Taking these facts together, sheltered sectors are often identified as "low productivity" sectors compared to goods-based export sectors, given the high prevalence of services within them.

5. Notable exceptions include Germany, the Netherlands, and in the late-1970s, Austria.

6. The original EMS participants included Belgium, Denmark, France, Germany, Ireland, Italy, Luxembourg, and the Netherlands, while Austria was a de facto member through its unilateral fixed exchange rate arrangement with the German mark.

7. Walsh (1999) claims that Italian monetary adjustment began in 1988, although Weber (1991) doubts whether Italy moved away from its soft currency policy during the 1980s.

8. EIRR 98 (March 1982), "Pay indexation modified," p. 4; EIRR 120 (January 1984), "Reduced working time in the public sector," p. 3.

9. EIRR 75 (May 1980), "Government seeks further wage controls," p. 5.

10. EIRR 103 (August 1982), "Pay bargaining and pay restraint," pp. 18–19.

11. EIRR 108 (January 1983), "Incomes policy and pay bargaining," pp. 13–14.

12. EIRR 120 (January 1984), "Public service dispute ends," p. 5.

13. EIRR 136 (May 1985), "Government imposes two-year pay settlement," pp. 11–12.

14. Though Mitterrand originally wanted to withdraw the franc from the ERM to protect French industry from import competition, the threat of Prime Minister Pierre Mauroy's resignation if France left the ERM, and Finance Minister Jacques Delors's warnings of the severe economic costs to France for abandoning the exchange rate arrangement, caused him to reluctantly commit in the mid-1980s (Walsh 2000, 64–65).

15. The British pound had a brief history with the European Monetary System, entering the ERM in October 1990 and exiting in 1992 (McNamara 2005, 146). Since then, the country has made no attempts to reenter a fixed exchange rate arrangement with the Deutsche mark, ECU, or euro.

16. While a 60 percent debt rule also existed, this criterion was loosened for a number of EMU candidate countries. The 3 percent deficit criteria, however, remained a prerequisite to join monetary union.

17. EIRR 277 (February 1997), "EU social partners consider the impact of EMU," pp. 19–21.

18. Ibid.

19. EIRR 279 (April 1997), "Collectively agreed pay rose by 2.4% in 1996," p. 4.

20. EIRR 289 (February 1998), "New taxation bill provokes disputes," p. 7; EIRR 290 (March 1998), "Controversial taxation bill passed," p. 8.

21. While Germany's sheltered sector composite constituted roughly 25 percent of the German labor force, it constituted only 8 percent of the Eurozone's collective labor force, the largest employment share of all Eurozone economies. For small member-states, the sheltered sector employment weight in the central bank's reaction function (i.e., its weight in the total labor force over which the central bank has authority) declined from roughly 15 percent to 30 percent under the EMS/Maastricht period to less than 1 percent under the EMU period.

22. EIRO (8 October 2012), "Pay developments 2011." All EIRO articles can be accessed from the online database of the European Foundation for the Improvement of Living and Working Conditions (https://www.eurofound.europa.eu/observatories/eurwork).

3. MONETARY REGIMES, WAGE BARGAINING, AND THE CURRENT ACCOUNT CRISIS IN THE EMU SOUTH

1. These countries include ten EMU participants—Austria, Belgium, Finland, France, Germany, Ireland, Italy, the Netherlands, Portugal, and Spain—and seven nonparticipants: Australia, Canada, Denmark, Japan, Sweden, the United Kingdom, and the United States.

2. In his construction of central bank non-accommodation, Iversen uses the average of three indices—Bade and Parkin (1982); Grilli, Masciandaro, and Tabellini (1991); and Cukierman (1992)—to gauge operational central bank independence.

3. Ideally, sectoral trade union density would be included as a control; however, sectoral data on union density is scant at worst and patchy at best. Visser (1991) presents data on union membership by ISIC sector classification, yet the dataset is limited to five individual years, the last of which is 1988.

4. Likelihood ratio tests for the baseline model (model I, table 3.2) was highly significant (140.9, p-value=0.000) indicating a high likelihood of panel heteroskedasticity. Additionally, the F-statistic from the Wooldridge test for autocorrelation within panels was 9.659 (p-value=0.007) for model I in table 3.1, indicating a significant likelihood of first-order correlation. Plümper, Troeger, and Manow (2005) report that a Prais-Winsten transformation neither fails autocorrelation tests nor shows spherical distribution of errors, yet manages to absorb less time-series dynamics than a dependent lag. Results were not impacted by alternative means of controlling for autocorrelation.

5. Time dummies were omitted to avoid multicollinearity problems with the Maastricht and EMU dummies, as well as the weighted monetary threat variable.

6. A panel-specific Prais-Winsten transformation and panel corrected standard errors were also incorporated into the models discussed next, because similar to those described previously, there was sufficient evidence that panel heteroskedasticity and first-order autocorrelation were present. Time dummies are included in the models to control for unobserved time effects.

7. Results in table 3.3 are not impacted by the use of random effects, and the significance and sign of the beta coefficients on sectoral wage growth differences remain unaffected.

8. Given that all countries within the sample are developed and possess limited capital controls, it is fair to assume that this condition would hold.

9. Interaction terms between differences in sectoral wage growth and an EMU dummy were also examined for the models in table 3.3, but the product term emerged as insignificant while results for the differences sectoral wage growth remained unchanged. This is likely due to collinearity. Results in table 3.2 outlines a clear link between monetary union and the rise in sheltered sector wages, indicating that these variables are not independent of each other.

4. NATIONAL CENTRAL BANKS AND INFLATION CONVERGENCE

1. In 2002, sector-wide collective agreements covered roughly 72 percent of the Dutch labor force while company-level agreements covered only 12 percent; see EIRO (21 November 2002), "Debate over viability of collective bargaining system." In Denmark, there have been repeated attempts to create sectoral bargaining cartels during the 1990s, although some general unions (the General Workers' Union, SiD, and the Union

of Commercial and Clerical Employees, HK) continue to organize across more narrow sectoral lines (Scheuer 1998).

2. EIRO (28 July 2001), "Controversy over wage moderation."

3. EIRR 300 (January 1999), "Flexible pay gains prominence," p. 9.

4. EIRO (28 July 1997), "Public sector faces prospect of implementing pay bargaining reform."

5. Despite high rates of growth and job creation elsewhere, Dutch *manufacturing* experienced job losses throughout this period (Auer 2000, 13).

6. EIRR 343 (August 2002), "Labour market bottlenecks," p. 4.

7. EIRO (28 July 2001), "Controversy over wage moderation"; EIRR 325 (February 2001), "Concern over wage demands," p. 9.

8. Ibid.

9. More detailed funding rules have since been agreed on between the Ministry of Finance and the Nationalbank in November 2006 (Danmarks Nationalbank 2007, section 1.1.4).

10. Weber (1991) declared Germany and the Netherlands a de facto monetary union after the Netherlands' last and minor devaluation of 2 percent in 1983.

11. EIRR 75 (May 1980), "Government seeks further wage controls," p. 5.

12. EIRR 105 (October 1982), "Focus on job creation," p. 4.

13. Ibid.

14. EIRR 108 (January 1983), "Incomes policy and pay bargaining," pp. 13–14.

15. EIRR 119 (December 1983), "Public service dispute latest," p. 5.

16. EIRR 139 (August 1985), "ILO Advises Government on Indexation," p. 4.

17. EIRR 233 (June 1993), "Public sector industrial relations in the 1990s," pp. 14–15.

18. EIRR 136 (May 1985), "Government imposes two-year pay settlement," pp. 11–12.

19. EIRR 137 (June 1985), "Union protest to ILO," p. 3.

20. The Danish General Workers' Union (SiD), which represented 25 percent of LO's membership in 1985, was against any break in a centralized wage policy, as it would marginalize its power within LO (Iversen 1996, 419).

21. By December 1992, the union members of the Dutch Social Economic Council (SER) U-turned on the issue, proclaiming that government's reform was necessary amid a worsening economy and the necessity to fulfill the Maastricht criteria. EIRR 220 (May 1992), "Policy on incomes under discussion," p. 9; EIRR 227 (December 1992), "SER against pay/benefits link," p. 9.

22. EIRR 221 (June 1992), "Central talks proposed," p. 9.

23. Ibid.

24. EIRR 224 (September 1992), "FNV puts employment above pay," p. 10.

25. EIRR 226 (November 1992), "SER opinion to pave way for central deal?" p. 9.

26. Ibid; EIRR 227 (December 1992), "Central agreement provides for pay pause," p. 9.

27. EIRR 233 (June 1993), "Budget proposals lead to protest," p. 10.

28. EIRR 233 (June 1993), "Public sector dispute," pp. 10–11.

29. EIRR 236 (September 1993), "Solidarity Pact or Statutory Pay Freeze," p. 11.

30. EIRR 239 (December 1993), "Central Agreement on Pay Moderation," pp. 10–11.

31. EIRR 246 (July 1994), "Bargaining Round-Up," p. 10.

32. EIRR 261 (October 1995), "New agreement for civil servants reached," pp. 8–9.

33. EIRR 264 (January 1996), "Public sector bargaining update," p. 10.

34. Rasmussen himself was an economist for LO before entering politics.

35. EIRR 230 (March 1993), "Bargaining breakthrough for state sector employees," p. 6; EIRR 232 (May 1993), "Bargaining round completed," p. 5.

36. Ibid.

37. EIRR 262 (November 1995), "The Danish 1995 collective bargaining round in focus," pp. 24–27.

38. According to statistics from the Confederation of Danish Employers (DA), the average pay increase for blue-collar workers for the third quarter of 1993 was 1.7 percent, with 11 percent of them receiving no change in pay during the four-month period. The comparative statistic for white-collar workers was 0.9 percent, while 29 percent of this group had no change in pay. EIRR 244 (May 1994), "Pay increases down," p. 5.

39. Such shortages were partially the result of a long-term leave scheme, introduced by government to alleviate unemployment. EIRR 253 (February 1995), "Bargaining underway," p. 6.

40. EIRR 256 (May 1995), "Bargaining round over," p. 6.

41. EIRR 258 (July 1995), "Nurses back at work," p. 5; EIRR 262 (November 1995), "The Danish 1995 collective bargaining round in focus," pp. 24–27.

42. EIRR 277 (February 1997), "Collective bargaining round begins," p. 4.

43. EIRR 279 (April 1997), "Public sector bargaining ends," p. 5.

44. Ibid; EIRO (28 February 1997), "Two-year collective agreement for Government employees"; EIRO (28 May 1997), "The 1997 Danish collective bargaining round completed."

45. EIRO (28 July 1997), "Public sector faces prospect of implementing pay bargaining reform."

46. EIRO (28 August 1997), "The Danish model under threat?"

47. EIRO (28 April 1998), "1998 bargaining round ends in major conflict."

48. EIRR 293 (June 1998), "General strike ends," p. 5.

49. EIRO (28 August 1997), "Dutch unions to end policy of wage restraint?"; EIRR 277 (February 1997), Trade unions flex their muscles in wage negotiations," p. 11.

50. Trade union confederations in the Netherlands can only suggest pay limits for its affiliates. EIRR 293 (June 1998), "Agreement in healthcare sector," pp. 10–11.

51. EIRO (28 May 1998), "Bargaining parties in healthcare reach agreement"; EIRO (28 April 1998), "Arbitration by Prime Minister in Healthcare bargaining dispute."

52. EIRR 305 (June 1999): "Negotiations for hospital workers," p. 9; EIRR 305 (July 1999): "Agreement in hospitals," p. 10.

53. EIRR 330 (July 2001), "New report shows increase in wage inflation," p. 9.

54. EIRO (28 June 2001), "Strikes in healthcare and docks while rail agreement is rejected"; EIRO (19 April 2002), "Annual review for the Netherlands."

55. EIRO (28 July 2001), "Controversy over wage moderation."

56. EIRR 288 (January 1998), "Unions demand higher sector pay rises," p. 10; EIRR 297 (October 1998), "In brief," p. 10.

57. EIRR 308 (September 1999), "Unions abandon pay moderation," pp. 9–10; EIRR 311 (December 1999), "Confusion over pay demands," p. 9; EIRR 312 (January 2000), "FNV abandons pay moderation," pp. 9–10.

58. EIRR 318 (July 2000), "FNV demands 4 percent in 2001", p. 10; EIRO (28 December 2000), "FNV seeks 4 percent wage increase in 2001."

59. EIRR 325 (February 2001): "Concern over wage demands," p. 10; EIRO (28 January 2001): "2001 bargaining round likely to be difficult."

60. EIRO (28 April 2001), "Tight labour market and inflation drive collective bargaining outcomes"; EIRO (28 July 2001), "Controversy over wage moderation."

61. EIRO (28 April 2001), "Tight labour market and inflation drive collective bargaining outcomes."

62. EIRO (28 July 2001), "Controversy over wage moderation."

63. EIRR 334 (November 2001), "FNV 4 percent demand condemned as 'irresponsible,'" p. 9; EIRO (5 December 2001), "Unions aim to take moderate approach in bargaining."

64. Balkenende's first coalition, with the populist Pim Fortuyn List (LFP) party and the Liberals (VVD), collapsed in November 2002 because of internal conflicts within LFP. Elections in January 2003 brought the return of Christian Democratic Party (CDA) to government, with the VVD and the Democraten 66.

65. EIRO (9 December 2002), "Social partners and Government reach a 'social agreement' for 2003."

66. EIRO (29 October 2003), "Pay freeze agreed for 2004–2005."

67. Ibid.

68. EIRR 359 (December 2003), "Wage freeze agreed," pp. 16–17; EIRO (29 October 2003), "Pay freeze agreed for 2004–2005."

69. Ibid.

70. EIRO (27 November 2006), "Government pushes for wage moderation despite union demands for wage increases"; EIRO (13 June 2007), "Industrial relations developments 2006—the Netherlands."

71. EIRO (18 June 2007), "New collective agreements for civil servants and towage workers signed following strike action."

72. EIRR 303 (April 1999), "Bargaining round concluded," pp. 4–5; EIRO (28 March 1999), "New pay settlements take decentralised approach."

73. Ibid.

74. EIRR 306 (July 1999), "Government intervenes in nursing dispute," p. 4; EIRR 306 (July 1999), "Teachers accept new working time deal," pp. 4–5.

75. EIRO (7 January 2002), "New government challenges trade union movement."

76. Arbejdsmarkedsstyrelsen. "Undersøgelse af flaskehalse på det danske arbejdsmarked 2001," Hovedrapport, Copenhagen, April 2001.

77. EIRR 337 (February 2002), "Settlement for state employees," p. 4; EIRO (24 April 2002), "Three year agreement concluded in central government sector."

78. EIRO (11 March 2002), "Deadlock in municipal/county bargaining."

79. EIRR 339 (April 2002), "Bargaining in municipal sector," pp. 4–5; EIRO (8 May 2002), "Agreement concluded for municipal/county sector."

80. EIRR 341 (June 2002), "Local and regional municipality accords accepted," p. 3.

81. EIRO (9 December 2003), "Health unions to leave municipal bargaining unit."

82. Ibid.

83. EIRO (16 March 2005), "New agreement concluded in local public sector"; EIRO (1 April 2005), "New agreement concluded for employees in the state sector."

84. EIRO (25 April 2005), "New agreement signed for healthcare staff."

85. Ibid.

86. Ibid.

87. EIRO (16 October 2006), "Wage increases moderate despite economic boom"; EIRO (13 June 2007), "Industrial relations developments 2006—Denmark."

88. Ibid.

89. EIRO (14 January 2008): "Public sector unions anticipate conflict in wage bargaining round."

90. Ibid; EIRO (22 May 2007), "New industry agreement market by innovatory elements"; EIRO (4 June 2007), "Social partners sign new three-year agreement in manufacturing."

91. EIRO (14 January 2008), "Public sector unions anticipate conflict in wage bargaining round."

92. Ibid.

93. EIRO (29 September 2008), "Longest strike in public sector ends with pay settlement."

5. STRENGTH IN RIGIDITY

1. Here, the terms "public sector liberalization," "public sector pay decentralization," and "new public management" are used interchangeably.

2. EIRO (28 December 2000), "2000 Annual Review for Italy."

3. EIRO (28 December 2000), "Agreement signed for ministry employees."

4. Given the government's unilateral privileges in pay determination, DBB possesses no formal independent power to negotiate wage settlements in the public sector or coordinate bargaining with unions under the DGB umbrella, most notably the encompassing German services sector union ver.di (Keller 2011, 2339).

5. Under the Calmfors-Driffill hypothesis, countries with intermediately centralized collective bargaining exhibit the highest levels of inflation and unemployment, because unions are large enough to command generous wage increases for their members, but too small to internalize their rent-seeking actions. In decentralized bargaining regimes, unions are too weak to command generous pay settlements, and hence inflation and unemployment are relatively low. Similarly, in highly centralized regimes, because unions are so encompassing that their wage-setting actions influence inflation, ultimately reducing real wages, they internalize their actions and establish moderate wage settlements, producing low, stable inflation.

6. EIRO (10 June 2003), "Public sector employers' bargaining association collapses."

7. EIRO (28 April 2001), "Unified Service Sector Union (ver.di) created."

8. EIRO (28 July 1997), "Civil service law reform comes into force on 1 July 1997."

9. Ibid.

10. Ibid.

11. EIRR 221 (June 1992), "New industrial relations in the public sector," pp. 21–23.

12. Ibid.

13. EIRO (28 August 1997), "Dutch unions to end policy of wage restraint?"; EIRR 277 (February 1997): Trade unions flex their muscles in wage negotiations," p. 11.

14. EIRR 221 (June 1992), "New industrial relations in the public sector," pp. 21–23.

15. Ibid.

16. Ibid; EIRO (28 April 1999), "Civil service industrial relations moves towards market sector model."

17. EIRO (28 April 1999), "Civil service industrial relations moves towards market sector model."

18. EIRR 219 (April 1992), "Bargaining developments in the public sector," p. 9.

19. Ibid.

20. Ibid.

21. EIRO (13 March 2002), "Variable Pay under Debate."

22. EIRO (28 May 1999), "Industry-wide collective agreements under increasing pressure."

6. SHELTERED SECTOR DOMINANCE UNDER A COMMON CURRENCY

1. This abandonment of a wage-moderation-driven export model by the Irish government is perhaps best embodied by Fianna Fáil's Finance Minister Charlie McCreevy's pro-cyclical motto, "When I have it, I spend it" (Dellepiane and Hardiman 2010, 482).

2. EIRO (28 December 1997), "Unions set agendas for collective bargaining in 1998"; EIRO (20 July 2005), "2004 Annual Review for Spain"; EIRO (13 January 2005), "Social partners debate bargaining framework for 2005."

3. EIRO (28 May 1998), "Spain's first sectoral agreement on the structure of collective bargaining."

4. EIRO (28 February 2001), "The institutional framework of public sector industrial relations."

5. EIRO (22 April 2005), "Irish industrial relations system no longer voluntarist."

6. To ensure that unions were committed to a smooth democratic transition process, the Spanish government passed the 1980 Workers' Statute, which not only introduced formal collective bargaining, but also maintained the strong employment protection rules from the Franco regime and increased the generosity of unemployment insurance (Bentolila, Dolado, and Jimeno 2012). Spain's rigid employment protection laws, some argued, exacerbated its unemployment problem. In order to rectify this situation, the PSOE government unilaterally implemented the 1984 labor market reform, in which temporary contracts were liberalized and dismissal costs associated with these contracts were significantly reduced. This reform led to an explosion in low-wage temporary contracts—by 1990, temporary contracts accounted for 30 percent of total salaried employment in Spain—and the marked dualization of Spain's labor market (Dolado, García, Serrano, and Jimeno 2002).

7. EIRO (28 May 1998), "Spain's first sectoral agreement on the structure of collective bargaining."

8. EIRO (19 April 2002), "2001 Annual Review for Spain."

9. PSOE and union relations hit a low point after the 1988 general strike. UGT refused to support PSOE in the 1989 election, and PSOE removed the requirement that its party members be registered members of a trade union (Hamann and Martinez Lucio 2003, 65).

10. The relative bargaining strength of UGT's and CCOO's affiliates was further highlighted in the aftermath of Spain's 1988 general strike: the González Socialist government, among other things, increased wages for public sector workers to compensate for the 1988 deviation in targeted inflation and signed an agreement with unions in the 1990s that established further bargaining rights for the public sector (Royo 2006, 986).

11. While several scholars have outlined that the 1997 agreement highlighted the new cross-party nature of Spanish tripartitism (Pérez 2000, notes that this was a feature of the PP learning from PSOE's mistakes), Hamann (2012) is more skeptical of this shift due to the fact that Aznar was presiding over a minority government and therefore needed union cooperation to gain legitimacy and fulfill the Maastricht criteria (Hamann 2012, 179).

12. EIRO (28 May 1998), "Spain's first sectoral agreement on the structure of collective bargaining."

13. EIRO (28 July 2000), "Prospects of framework regional agreement for metalworking in Catalonia."

14. Additionally, though the inclusion of Spain's unions in policymaking was revitalized in the 1997 pact, by 2001, conflictual relations between government and unions were back: as employers and unions failed to make progress on the negotiations of collective bargaining, Anzar's government, which then enjoyed a majority in the Spanish Parliament, unilaterally imposed its structural labor market reforms.

15. EIRO (28 May 1998), "Spain's first sectoral agreement on the structure of collective bargaining."

16. EIRO (23 December 2010), "Representativeness of the European social partner organizations: Metal sector—Spain."

17. Ibid.

18. EIRO (28 July 2000), "Prospects of framework regional agreement for metalworking in Catalonia." https://www.interempresas.net/MetalWorking/Articles/32957-Establishing-the-Observatory-of-the-industry-of-the-Metal-of-Catalonia.html.

19. EIRO (28 February 2001), "The institutional framework of public sector industrial relations."

20. EIRO (28 March 1998), "Basic statute of the civil service agreed."

21. EIRO (26 November 2002), "2003 state budget approved."

22. EIRO (28 February 2001), "The institutional framework of public sector industrial relations."

23. EIRO (28 October 2000), "Disagreement over civil service pay and conditions."

24. Ibid.; EIRO (28 March 1998), "Basic statute of the civil service agreed."

25. EIRO (28 February 2001), "National court rules against freezing of civil servants pay."

26. State intervention in public sector bargaining returned with a vengeance during Spain's debt crisis. In 2010, the unilaterally imposed Royal Decree 8/2010 reduced nominal public sector wages by 5 percent, with high salaried public employees witnessing reductions by 15 percent; see EIRO (26 June 2014), "Spain: Industrial relations in central public administration—Recent trends and features."

27. EIRO (19 April 2002), "2001 annual review for Spain."

28. EIRO (28 December 1999), "1999 annual review for Spain"; EIRO (1 September 2006), "Increase in collective bargaining during 2005."

29. EIRO (16 February 2005), "Minimum wage agreement introduces guarantee clause."

30. EIRO (28 February 1997), "National nurses strike averted as pay offer is accepted."

31. EIRO (28 May 1997), "Labour court plays key role in public pay dispute."

32. EIRO (28 August 1998), "Prime Minister seeks to dampen pay pressures in the wake of police deal."

33. Ibid.

34. EIRO (28 December 1999), "Nurses deal clears way for talks on new national agreement."

35. Ibid.

36. EIRO (28 January 2000), "Survey finds strong support for pay moderations and social partnership."

37. EIRO (28 May 1999), "Pay issues come into focus as private sector remains stable."

38. EIRO (28 March 2000), "Irish social partners endorse new national agreement."

39. EIRO (28 December 2000), "Giveaway budget and extra pay increase save national partnership."

40. EIRO (28 March 2000), "Irish social partners endorse new national agreement."

41. EIRO (28 May 2000), "Teachers and government on collision course over pay."

42. EIRO (28 March 2001), "Politicians and top civil servants awarded up the 33 percent."

43. EIRO (9 July 2002), "Benchmarking body recommends public sector pay awards"; EIRO (19 February 2010), "Ireland 2008 EIRO annual review."

44. EIRO (9 July 2002), "Benchmarking body recommends public sector pay awards"; EIRO (24 March 2003), "2002 annual review for Ireland."

45. EIRO (28 June 2001), "Adherence to national pay deal high but failing."

46. EIRO (12 March 2003), "Intel implements pay freeze."

47. EIRO (1 June 2004), "Parties set out priorities for national pay talks."

48. EIRO (11 August 2005), "Top people get 7.5 percent interim award"; EIRO (6 September 2006), "Social partners agree to new national partnership agreement."

49. EIRO (19 February 2010), "Ireland 2008 EIRO annual review"; EIRO (9 July 2008), "Hospital consultants agree to change work practice in return for increase in pay"; EIRO (17 July 2008), "Benchmarking report urges pay rise for lower paid grades in banking."

7. EMU, THE POLITICS OF WAGE INFLATION, AND CRISIS

1. The EU Directorate General for Economic and Financial Affairs' Labor Market Reform Database monitors the success and speed of labor market reforms in nine different areas for its member-states, praising countries that introduce intensive structural reforms more rapidly (EU ECFIN 2013a).

2. Ireland does not fit into this mixed-market economy typology, although it also does not persistently conform to the export-driven growth models of the corporatist EMU North. After 1987, Ireland used centralized and coordinated wage bargaining to reorient its more liberalized economy toward an export-driven model (see Baccaro and Simoni 2007). However, as outlined in chapter 6, the commitment to an export-driven economic model was lost in the late 1990s, when Ireland's banking, construction, and public sector overtook the economic prominence of its multinational corporate sector in domestic politics. The Irish government pursued pro-cyclical fiscal policies that drove the economy to a bubble-prone, domestic demand-led growth model, placing heavy pressures on inflation that resulted in the significant decline of the country's current account balance (Regan 2014).

3. Italy produced current account deficits for ten of the twelve years it operated under a soft currency policy in the ERM (1979–1991). Once the country made a firm commitment to achieving low inflation in order to qualify for EMU membership in 1992, it produced current account surpluses in six of the seven years under the Maastricht regime (EU Commission AMECO Database 2014).

4. Greece failed to make a credible transition to a hard currency regime until 1994 (Tavlas and Papaspyrou n.d.).

5. EIRO (28 December 1998), "European Metalworkers' Federation adopts European Coordination rule for national bargaining."

APPENDIX I

1. OECD's Structural Analysis (STAN) industrial database also proxies sectoral labor productivity using a value-added approach, although it is not used in this analysis because EU KLEMS provides more complete sectoral data for the countries and time period examined. Also, unlike OECD's STAN database, EU KLEMS acknowledges changes in the composition of factor inputs over time in sectoral productivity measurements, correcting STAN's weighting biases (Timmer et al. 2007, 2).

2. An added conceptual complication exists for public sector productivity in that for some subsectors (i.e., policing and defense) increased output (i.e., the issue of more fines or the pursuit of warfare) for a given labor force may not be reflective of higher productivity but rather ineffective management or perverse incentives. Focus on sectoral wage dynamics, alongside sectoral WEU dynamics, within countries over time, partially avoids this problem.

3. This does not completely shield services from trade. Herman (2009) further outlines that some sectors, notably financial services but also healthcare, have bridged this geographical problem with reduced transportation costs for consumers or through the use of communicative technology.

4. Business services include consumer credit reporting agencies, services to office buildings (such as cleaning and maintenance), computer services, and security services.

5. Public administration includes the administration of social security, taxation, monetary policy, public spending programs, and national regulatory bodies, as well as government representatives and employees of the courts.

References

Afonso, António, and Pedro M. Gomes. 2014. "Interactions between private and public sector wages." *Journal of Macroeconomics* 39: 97–112.

Aguilera, Jesús Cruces, Ignacio Álvarez Peralta, and Francisco José Trillo Párraga. 2012. "Collectively agreed wages in Spain." Working Paper for the European Trade Union Institute's European Policy Conference. 29 November. Brussels, Belgium.

Alesina, Alberto, Silvia Ardagna, and Vincenzo Galasso. 2008. "The Euro and Structural Reforms." National Bureau of Economic Research Working Paper No. 14479. New York: NBER. http://www.nber.org/papers/w14479.

Allard-Prigent, Céline, Hélène Guilmeau, and Alain Quinet. 2000. "The Real Exchange Rate as the Relative Price of Nontradables in Terms of Tradables: Theoretical Investigation and Empirical Study on French Data." *Série des documents de travail*, No. G-2000/02, INSEE, Paris.

Allington, Nigel F. B., Paul Kattuman, and Florian A. Waldmann. 2005. "One Market, One Money, One Price? Price Dispersion in the European Union." *International Journal of Central Banking* (October): 73–115.

Andersen, Hans Thor. 2008. "The emerging Danish government reform—centralised de-centralisation." *Urban Research and Practice* 1 (1): 3–17.

Arghyrou, Michael G., and John D. Tsoukalas. 2011. "The Greek Debt Crisis: Likely Causes, Mechanics, and Outcomes." *The World Economy* 34 (2): 173–191.

Auer, Peter. 2000. *Employment Revival in Europe: Labour Market Success in Austria, Denmark, Ireland, and the Netherlands.* Geneva: International Labour Organization.

Baccaro, Lucio. 2002. "The construction of 'democratic' corporatism in Italy." *Politics & Society* 30 (2): 327–357.

———. 2003. "What Is Alive and What Is Dead in the Theory of Corporatism." *British Journal of Industrial Relations* 41 (4): 683–706.

Baccaro, Lucio, and Marco Simoni. 2007. "Centralized Wage Bargaining and the 'Celtic Tiger' Phenomenon." *Industrial Relations* 46 (3): 426–455.

———. 2010. "Organizational Determinants of Wage Moderation." *World Politics* 62 (4): 594–635.

Bach, Stephen, and Lorenzo Bordogna. 2011. "Varieties of new public management or alternative models? The reform of public service employment relations in industrialized democracies." *International Journal of Human Resource Management* 22 (11): 2281–2294.

Backus, David, and John Driffill. 1985. "Inflation and Reputation." *American Economic Review* 75 (3): 530–538.

Bade, Robin, and Michael Parkin. 1982. "Central Bank Laws and Inflation—A Comparative Analysis." University of Western Ontario Working Paper.

Balassa, Bela. 1964. "The purchasing power parity doctrine: A reappraisal." *Journal of Political Economy* 72: 584–596.

Bank of Spain. 2009. "El Funcionamiento del Mercado de Trabajo y el Aumento del Paro en Espana." *Boletin Economico* (Julio-Augosto): 95–115.

Baskaran, Thushyanthan, and Zohal Hessami. 2012. "Monetary integration, soft budget constraints, and the EMU sovereign debt crisis." American Political Science Association 2012 Annual Meeting Paper.

Baumol, William, and William Bowen. 1965. "On the Performing Arts: The Anatomy of Their Economic Problems." *American Economic Review* 55 (1): 495–502.

Bayoumi, Tamim, and Barry Eichengreen. 1992. "Shocking Aspects of European Monetary Integration." National Bureau of Economic Research Working Paper No. 92–187. New York: NBER.

Bean, Charles. 1992. "Economic and Monetary Union in Europe." *Journal of Economic Perspectives* 6 (4): 31–52.

——. 1998. "The Interaction of Aggregate Demand Policies and Labor Market Reform." *Swedish Economic Policy Review* 5 (2): 353–382.

Bean, Charles, Richard Layard, and Stephen Nickell. 1986. "The Rise in Unemployment: A Multi-Country Study." *Economica* 53: SIS–22.

Beck, Nathaniel, and Jonathan Katz. 1995. "What to Do (and Not to Do) with Time-Series Cross-Section Data." *American Political Science Review* 89 (3): 634–648.

Becker, Uwe. 2005. "An example of competitive corporatism?: The Dutch political economy 1983–2004 in critical examination." *Journal of European Public Policy* 12 (6): 1078–1102.

Belke, Ansgar Hubertus, and Christian Dreger. 2011. "Current Account Imbalances in the Euro Area: Catching Up or Competitiveness?" *Ruhr Economic Papers* No. 241.

Bentolila, Samuel. 2008. "Lift the Ban on Spanish Labour Reform," VoxEU.org, 28 November. http://www.voxeu.org/article/lift-ban-spanish-labour-reform.

Bentolila, Samuel, Juan Dolado, and Juan Jimeno. 2012. "Reforming an insider-outsider labor market: the Spanish experience." *IZA Journal of European Labor Studies* 1 (4): 1–29.

Bernanke, Ben. 2009. "Financial Reform to Address Systemic Risk." Speech at the Council on Foreign Relations, Washington, DC, 10 March. http://www.federalreserve.gov/newsevents/speech/bernanke20090310a.htm.

Bertola, Giuseppe, and Tito Boeri. 2002. "EMU labour markets two years on: microeconomic tensions and institutional evolution." In *EMU and Economic Policy in Europe: The Challenge of the Early Years*, edited by Marco Buti and Andre Sapir, 249–280. Northampton, MA: Edward Elgar Publishers.

Bibow, Jörg. 2012. "The Euro Debt Crisis and Germany's Euro Trilemma." Levy Economics Institute of Bard College. No. 721. Annandale-On-Hudson, New York.

Blanchard, Olivier. 2006. "European Unemployment: The Evolution of Facts and Ideas." *Economic Policy* 21: 5–59.

Blanchard, Olivier, and Thomas Philippon. 2003. "The Decline of Rents and the Rise and Fall of European Unemployment." Unpublished manuscript, Massachusetts Institute of Technology.

Blanchard, Olivier, and Justin Wolfers. 2000. "The Role of Shocks and Institutions in the Rise of European Unemployment: The Aggregate Evidence." *Economic Journal* 110 (462): 1–33.

Böll, Sven, and Janko Tietz. 2013. "Possible Boost for EU Economy: Germany Gears Up for Big Pay Hikes." *Der Spiegel*, 8 January. http://www.spiegel.de/international/germany/german-trade-unions-demanding-big-pay-increases-after-years-of-restraint-a-876268.html.

Bordogna, Lorenzo. 2002. *Contrattazione integrativa e gestione del personale nelle pubbliche amministrazioni*. Milan: Franco Angeli.

——. 2008. "Moral Hazard, Transaction Costs, and the Reform of Public Service Employment Relations." *European Journal of Industrial Relations* 14 (4): 381–400.

Bordogna, Lorenzo, and Stefano Neri. 2011. "Convergence towards an NPM programme or different models? Public service employment relations in Italy and France." *International Journal of Human Resource Management* 22 (11): 2311–2330.

Borghans, Lex, and Ben Kriechel. 2007. "Wage Structure and Labour Mobility in the Netherlands: 1999–2003." National Bureau of Economic Research Working Paper No. 13210. New York: NBER.

Brandl, Bernd. 2012. "Successful Wage Concertation: The Economic Effects of Wage Pacts and their Alternatives." *British Journal of Industrial Relations* 50 (3): 482–501.

British Broadcasting Corporation (BBC) News. 2010. "German parliamentary vote backs Greece bail-out funding." 7 May. http://news.bbc.co.uk/1/hi/8666860.stm.

Brown, John, Joshua Chaffin, and Tony Barber. 2010. "Eurozone signs up to Irish rescue." *Financial Times*, 22 November.

Brown, William, and Janet Walsh. 1991. "Pay Determination in Britain in the 1980s: The Anatomy of Decentralization." *Oxford Review of Economic Policy* 7 (1): 44–59.

Bruno, Michael, and Jeffrey Sachs. 1985. *The Economics of Worldwide Stagflation.* Cambridge, MA: Harvard University Press.

Buiter, Willem, and Ebrahim Rahbari. 2010. "Greece and the fiscal crisis in the Eurozone." *CEPR Policy Insight* 51 (October): 1–15. http://www.cepr.org/sites/default/files/policy_insights/PolicyInsight51.pdf.

Bundgaard, Ulrik, and Karsten Vrangbæk. 2007. "Reform by coincidence? Explaining the policy process of structural reform in Denmark." *Scandinavian Political Studies* 30 (4): 491–520.

Burda, Michael. 2013. "The European debt crisis: How did we get into this mess? How can we get out of it?" SFB 649 Discussion Paper No. 2013-019. http://www.econstor.eu/bitstream/10419/79629/1/745234356.pdf.

Buti, Marco, Daniele Franco, and Hedwig Ongena. 1998. "Fiscal Discipline and Flexibility in EMU: The Implementation of the Stability and Growth Pact." *Oxford Review of Economic Policy* 14 (3): 81–97.

Buti, Marco, and Gabriele Giudice. 2002. "Maastricht's fiscal rules at ten: An assessment." *Journal of Common Market Studies* 40 (5): 823–848.

Caldentey, Esteban Pérez, and Matias Vernengo. 2012. "The euro imbalances and financial deregulation: A post-Keynesian interpretation of the European debt crisis." Levy Economics Institute of Bard College Working Paper No. 702. Annandale-On-Hudson, New York.

Calmfors, Lars. 2001. "Unemployment, labor market reform, and monetary union." *Journal of Labor Economics* 19 (2): 265–289.

Calmfors, Lars, Alison Booth, Michael Burda, Daniele Checchi, Robin Naylor, and Jelle Visser. 2001. "The Future of Collective Bargaining in Europe." In *The Role of Unions in the Twenty-First Century*, edited by Tito Boeri, 1–134. Oxford. Oxford University Press.

Calmfors, Lars, and John Driffill. 1988. "Bargaining Structure, Corporatism, and Macroeconomic Performance." *Economic Policy* 6 (April): 14–61.

Cameron, David. 1984. "Social Democracy, Corporatism, Labour Quiescence, and the Representation of Economic Interest in Advanced Capitalist Society." In *Order and Conflict in Contemporary Capitalism*, edited by John Goldthorpe, 143–178. Oxford: Clarendon Press.

Christopoulou, Rebekka, and Vassilis Monastiriotis. 2014a. "The Greek Public Sector Wage Premium before the Crisis: Size, Selection and Relative Valuation of Characteristics." *British Journal of Industrial Relations* 52 (3): 579–602.

——. 2014b. "The public-private duality in wage reforms and adjustment during the Greek crisis." Hellenic Foundation for European Foreign Policy Working Paper. Athens, Greece.

Crouch, Colin. 1990. "Trade Unions in the Exposed Sector: Their Influence on Neo-corporatist Behaviour." In *Labour Relations and Economic Performance*, edited by Renato Brunetta and Carlo Dell'Aringa, 68–91. London: Macmillan Press.

———. 1993. *Industrial Relations and European State Traditions*. New York: Oxford University Press.

———. 1999. "Adapting the European Model: The Role of Employers' Associations." In *The Role of Employer Associations and Labour Unions in EMU*, edited by Gerhard Huemer, Michael Mesch, and Franz Traxlers, 27–52. Aldershot: Ashgate Press.

———. 2000. *After the Euro: Shaping Institutions for Governance in the Wake of European Monetary Union*. Oxford: Oxford University Press.

Cukierman, Alex. 1992. *Central Bank Strategy, Credibility, and Independence*. Cambridge, MA. Massachusetts Institute of Technology Press.

Cukierman, Alex, and Francesco Lippi. 1999. "Central bank independence, centralization of wage bargaining, inflation, and unemployment: theory and some evidence." *European Economic Review* 43: 1395–1434.

———. 2001. "Labour Markets and Monetary Union: A Strategic Analysis." *Economic Journal* 111: 541–565.

Culpepper, Pepper, and Aidan Regan. 2014. "Why don't governments need trade unions anymore? The death of social pacts in Ireland and Italy." *Socio-Economic Review* 12 (4): 723–745.

Damgaard, Erik. 1989. "Crisis politics in Denmark: 1974–1987." In *The Politics of Economic Crisis*, edited by Erik Damgaard, Peter Gerlich, and Jeremy Richardson. 70–88. Aldershot: Avebury.

D'Amore, Antonio. 2011. "La retribuzione 'variabile' nell'impiego pubblico." Paper presented at AIDLASS Bari, 11–12 November.

Danmarks Nationalbank. 2003. "Monetary Policy in Denmark." http://www.nationalbanken.dk/C1256BE9004F6416/side/Monetary_Policy_in_Denmark/$file/pen_pol_saml.pdf.

———. 2007. "Danish Government Borrowing and Debt." http://www.nationalbanken.dk/c1256be9004f6416/side/danish_government_borrowing_and_debt_2007_publikation/$file/SLOG_UK_2007_web.pdf.

Danthine, Jean-Pierre, and Jennifer Hunt. 1994. "Wage Bargaining Structure, Employment, and Economic Integration." *Economic Journal* 104: 528–541.

De Grauwe, Paul. 1999. "Risks of a Roofless Euroland," *Time Magazine*, 11 January.

———. 2014. *Economics of Monetary Union*, 10th ed. Oxford: Oxford University Press.

De Gregorio, Jose, Alberto Giovannini, and Holger Wolf. 1994. "International Evidence on Tradables and Non-Tradables Inflation." *European Economic Review* 38 (6): 1225–1244.

Dell'Aringa, Carlo, Claudio Lucifora, and Federica Origo. 2005. "Public Sector Pay and Regional Competitiveness: A First Look at Regional Public-Private Wage Differentials in Italy." IZA DP No. 1828.

Dellepiane, Sebastian, and Niamh Hardiman. 2010. "The European context of Ireland's economic crisis." *Economic and Social Review* 41 (4): 471–498.

Der Spiegel. 2013. "EU Social Affairs Commissioner: 'Wages in Germany Must Increase,'" 29 April. http://www.spiegel.de/international/europe/eu-social-affairs-commissioner-wages-in-germany-must-increase-a-897120.html.

Diaz Sanchez, J. L., and Aristomene Varoudakis. 2013. "Growth and Competitiveness as Factors of Eurozone External Imbalances." World Bank Policy Research Working Paper 6732. Washington, DC: World Bank Group.

Dolado, Juan, Carlos García–Serrano, and Juan F. Jimeno. 2002. "Drawing Lessons from the Boom of Temporary Jobs in Spain." *Economic Journal* 112 (480): F270–F295.

Dornbusch, Rudiger. 1976. "Expectations and Exchange Rate Dynamics." *Journal of Political Economy* 84: 1161–1176.

Druant, Martine, Silvia Fabiani, Gabor Kezdi, Ana Lamo, Fernando Martins, and Roberto Sabbatini. 2009. "How are firms' wages and prices linked? Survey evidence in Europe." European Central Bank Working Paper No. 1084. Frankfurt am Main.

Dunleavy, Patrick. 1985. "Bureaucrats, budgets, and the growth of the state." *British Journal of Political Science* 15: 299–328.

Dunleavy, Patrick, Helen Margetts, Simon Bastow, and Jane Tinkler. 2005. "New Public Management Is Dead: Long Live Digital-Era Governance." *Journal of Public Administration Research and Theory* 16: 467–494.

Dunsire, Andrew, and Christopher Hood. 1989. *Cutback Management in Public Bureaucracies.* Cambridge: Cambridge University Press.

Ebbinghaus, Bernhard, and Anke Hassel. 2000. "Striking deals: concertation in the reform of European welfare states." *Journal of European Public Policy* 7 (1): 44–62.

Eichengreen, Barry. 1993. "Labor markets and European monetary unification." In *Policy Issues in the Operation of Currency Unions*, edited by Paul Masson and Mark Taylor, 130–162. Cambridge: Cambridge University Press.

Eichengreen, Barry, and Charles Wyplosz. 1998. "The Stability and Growth Pact: More than a Minor Nuisance." *Economic Policy* (April): 67–104.

Eichhorst, Werner, Michael Kendzia, and Barbara Vandeweghe. 2011. "Cross-border Collective Bargaining and Transnational Social Dialogue." IZA Research Report No. 38. July. http://www.iza.org/en/webcontent/publications/reports/report_pdfs/iza_report_38.pdf.

Enderlein, Henrik. 2006. "Adjusting to EMU: The impact of supranational monetary policy on domestic fiscal and wage setting institutions." *European Union Politics* 7 (1): 113–140.

Estevão, Marcello. 2005. "Product Market Regulation and the Benefits of Wage Moderation." International Monetary Fund Working Paper WP/09191. Washington, DC: IMF.

EU KLEMS Database. 2010. Groningen Growth and Development Centre. Last updated November 2009. Accessed December 2009–April 2010. http://www.euklems.net.

Eurofound. 2009a. "Coordination of collective bargaining." http://www.eurofound.europa.eu/areas/industrialrelations/dictionary/definitions/coordinationofcollectivebargaining.htm.

——. 2009b. "Doorn group." http://www.eurofound.europa.eu/areas/industrialrelations/dictionary/definitions/doorngroup.htm.

European Commission. 2009. "Commission assesses stability and convergence programs of Bulgarian, the Czech Republic, Denmark, Germany, Estonia, Hungary, the Netherlands, Poland, Sweden, Finland, and the United Kingdom." Press release, 18 February. http://europa.eu/rapid/pressReleasesAction.do?reference=IP/09/273.

——. 2013. "'Two-pack' enters into force, completing budgetary surveillance cycle and further improving economic governance for the euro area." Memo, Brussels, 27 May. http://europa.eu/rapid/press-release_MEMO-13-457_en.htm.

——. 2014. "Macroeconomic Imbalances, Germany." *European Economy.* Occasional Papers 174, March. http://ec.europa.eu/economy_finance/publications/occasional_paper/2014/pdf/ocp174_en.pdf.

European Commission, Directorate General for Economic and Financial Affairs (EU ECFIN). 2013a. Labor Market Reform Database (LABREF). http://ec.europa.eu/economy_finance/db_indicators/labref/index_en.htm.

——. 2013b. "Six-pack? Two-pack? Fiscal compact? A short guide to the new EU fiscal governance." http://ec.europa.eu/economy_finance/articles/governance/2012-03-14_six_pack_en.htm.

——. 2013c. "'Fiscal compact' enters into force on 1 January 2013." 1 January. http://www.consilium.europa.eu/homepage/showfocus?focusName=fiscal-compact-enters-into-force-on-1-january-2013.

——. 2014. *Annual macroeconomic database (AMECO)*. Accessed January 2011–July 2014. http://ec.europa.eu/economy_finance/ameco/user/serie/SelectSerie.cfm.

Eurostat Statistical Database. 2014. Current Account Data. Accessed February–July 2014. http://epp.eurostat.ec.europa.eu/portal/page/portal/statistics/search_database.

Fajertag, Giuseppe, and Pochet, Philippe. 2000. "A New Era for Social Pacts." In *Social Pacts in Europe: New Dynamics*, edited by Philippe Pochet and Giuseppe Fajertag, 9–40. Brussels: European Trade Union Institute.

Featherstone, Kevin. 2011. "The Greek Soverign Debt Crisis and EMU: A Failing State in a Skewed Regime." *Journal of Common Market Studies* 49 (2): 193–217.

Fischer, Stanley. 1987. "International Economic Policy Coordination." National Bureau of Economic Research Working Paper No. 2344. New York: NBER.

Franzese, Rob. 2001. "Institutional and Sectoral Interactions in Monetary Policy and Wage-Price Bargaining." In *Varieties of Capitalism: The Institutional Foundation of Comparative Advantage*, edited by Peter Hall and David Soskice, 104–144. Cambridge: Cambridge University Press.

Fulton, Lionel. 2013a. "Worker Representation in Europe: Trade Unions, Italy." European Trade Union Institute. http://www.worker-participation.eu/National-Industrial-Relations/Countries/Italy/Trade-Unions.

——. 2013b. "Worker Representation in Europe: Trade Unions, Germany." European Trade Union Institute. http://www.worker-participation.eu/National-Industrial-Relations/Countries/Germany/Trade-Unions.

Garcia-Perez, Ignacio, and Juan Jimeno. 2007. "Public Sector Wage Gaps in Spanish Regions." *The Manchester School* 75 (4): 501–531.

Garrett, Geoffrey, and Christopher Way. 1999. "Public Sector Unions, Corporatism, and Macroeconomic Performance." *Comparative Political Studies* 32 (4): 411–434.

Gaulier, Guillaume, Daria Taglioni, and Vincent Vicard. 2012. "Tradable Sectors in the Eurozone Periphery Countries Did Not Underperform in the 2000s," VoxEU.org, 19 July. http://voxeu.org/article/tradable-sectors-eurozone-periphery.

Genberg, Hans. 2004. "Monetary Policy Strategies after EU Enlargement." Paper prepared for the Conference on Challenges for Central Banks in an Enlarged EMU, Vienna, 20–21 February, http://www2.wu-wien.ac.at/ecsa/emu/papgenberg.pdf.

Giavazzi, Francesco, and Luigi Spaventa. 2011. "Why the current account matters in a monetary union." In *The Euro Area and the Financial Crisis*, edited by Miroslav Beblavý, David Cobham, and L'udovít Ódor, 199–221. Cambridge: Cambridge University Press.

Gibson, Heather, Stephen Hall, and George Tavlas. 2012. "The Greek Financial Crisis: Growing Imbalances and Sovereign Spreads." *Journal of International Money and Finance* 31: 498–516.

Giordano, Raffaela, Domenico Depalo, Manuel Coutinho Pereira, Bruno Eugène, Evangelia Papapetrou, Javier J. Perez, Lukas Reiss, and Mojca Roter. 2011. "The Public Sector Pay Gap in a Selection of Euro Area Countries." European Central Bank Working Paper Series No. 1406. Frankfurt am Main.

Giugni, Gino. 1992. "La Privatizzazione del rapporto di lavoro nel settore pubblico." *Lavoro Informazione* 11: 5–8.

Greiling, Dorothea. 2005. "Performance measurement in the public sector: the German experience." *International Journal of Productivity and Performance Management* 54 (7): 551–567.

Grilli, Vittorio, Donato Masciandaro, and Guido Tabellini. 1991. "Political and Monetary Institutions and Public Financial Policies in the Industrialized Countries." *Economic Policy* 13: 42–92.

Gros, Daniel. 2012. "Macroeconomic Imbalances in the Euro Area: Symptom or Cause of the Crisis." *CEPS Policy Brief*. No. 266 (April).

Grumbrell-McCormick, Rebecca, and Richard Hyman. 2013. *Trade unions in Western Europe: Hard times, hard choices.* Oxford: Oxford University Press.

Gunnigle, Patrick, and David McGuire. 2001. "Why Ireland? A qualitative review of the factors influencing the location of U.S. multinationals in Ireland with particular reference to the impact of labour issues." *Economic and Social Review* 32 (1): 43–67.

Hall, Peter. 1994. "Central Bank Independence and Coordinated Wage Bargaining: The Interaction in Germany and Europe." *German Politics and Society* 31: 1–23.

———. 2012. "The Economics and Politics of the Euro Crisis." *German Politics* 21 (4): 355–371.

———. 2014. "Varieties of Capitalism and the Euro Crisis." *West European Politics* 37 (6): 1223–1243.

Hall, Peter, and David Soskice. 2001. "An introduction to the Varieties of Capitalism." In *Varieties of Capitalism: The Institutional Foundations of Comparative Advantage*, edited by Peter Hall and David Soskice. 1–68. Oxford: Oxford University Press.

Hallerberg, Mark. 2002. "Introduction: Fiscal Policy in the European Union." *European Union Politics* 3 (2): 139–150.

Hamann, Kerstin. 2012. *The Politics of Industrial Relations: Labor Unions in Spain.* New York: Routledge.

Hamann, Kerstin, and Miguel Martinez Lucio. 2003. "Strategies of union revitalization in Spain: Negotiating change and fragmentation." *European Journal of Industrial Relations* 9 (1): 61–78.

Hancké, Bob. 2002. *Large firms and institutional change: Industrial renewal and economic restructuring in France.* Oxford: Oxford University Press.

Hancké, Bob, and Martin Rhodes. 2005. "EMU and Labour Market Institutions in Europe: The Rise and Fall of National Social Pacts." *Work and Occupations* 19 (1): 149–160.

Hancké, Bob, and David Soskice. 2003. "Wage Setting and Inflation Targets in EMU." *Oxford Review of Economic Policy* 19 (1): 196–228.

Hardiman, Niamh. 2002. "From conflict to co-ordination: Economic governance and political innovation in Ireland." *West European Politics* 25 (4): 1–24.

———. 2003. "Politics and markets in the Irish 'Celtic Tiger' experience: Choice, chance, or coincidence?" University College Dublin. Institute for the Study of Social Change Discussion Paper 2003-11.

———. 2010. "Bringing domestic institutions back into an understanding of Ireland's economic crisis." *Irish Studies in International Affairs* 21: 71–87.

Hassel, Anke. 2003. "The Politics of Social Pacts." *British Journal of Industrial Relations* 41 (4): 707–726.

Heckman, James J. 2000. "Flexibility, Job Creation, and Globalization: The Case of Italy." In *Third Millennium Colloquia Organised by the Instituto di Studi Economici et per l'Occupazione, Venice, Italy.* 2–3 December.

Hellwig, Martin. 2009. "Systemic Risk in the Financial Sector: An Analysis of the Subprime-Mortgage Financial Crisis." *De Economist* 157 (2): 129–207.

Hemerijck, Anton. 2003. "A Paradoxical Miracle: The Politics of Coalition Government and Social Concertation in Dutch Welfare Reform." In *Kozertierung, Verhandlungsdemokratie und Reformpolitik im Wohlfahrtsstaat*, edited by Sven Jochem and Nico Siegeleds, 232–270. Opladen, Germany: Springer-Verlag.

Hemerijck, Anton, and Mark Vail. 2006. "The forgotten center: state activism and corporatist adjustment in Holland and Germany." In *The State after Statism*, edited by Jonah Levy, 57–92. Cambridge, MA: Harvard University Press.

Hemerijck, Anton, Marc Van der Meer, and Jelle Visser. 2000. "Innovation through Coordination: Two Decades of Social Pacts in the Netherlands." In *Social Pacts in Europe: New Dynamics*, edited by Philippe Pochet and Giuseppe Fajertag. Brussels: European Trade Union Institute.

Herman, Lior. 2009. "Assessing International Trade in Healthcare Services." European Center for International Political Economy Working Paper No. 03/2009. http://www.ecipe.org/media/publication_pdfs/assessing-international-trade-in-healthcare-services.pdf.

Hochreiter, Eduard, and Georg Winckler. 1995. "The Advantages of Tying Austria's Hands: The Success of the Hard Currency Strategy." *European Journal of Political Economy*, 11: 83–111.

Hodson, Dermot. 2011. *Governing the Euro Area in Good Times and Bad*. Oxford: Oxford University Press.

Holinski, Nils, Clemens Kool, and Joan Muysken. 2012. "Persistent Macroeconomic Imbalances in the Euro Area: Causes and Consequences." *Federal Reserve Bank of St. Louis Review*, 1–20.

Holm-Hadulla, Fédéric, Kishore Kamath, Ana Lamo, Javier J. Pérez, and Ludger Schuknecht. 2010. "Public wages in the euro area: Towards securing stability and competitiveness." European Central Bank Occasional Paper 112. Frankfurt am Main.

Hood, Christopher. 1991. "A Public Management for all Seasons?" *Public Administration* 69: 3–19.

——. 1995. "The 'New Public Management' in the 1980s: Variations on a theme." *Accounting, Organizations and Society* 20 (2–3), 93–109.

International Monetary Fund. 2008a. *Direction of Trade Statistics Annual Yearbook*. Washington, DC: IMF.

——. 2008b. "Concluding Statement of the 2008 IMF Mission to Denmark," 2 October. http://www.imf.org/external/np/ms/2008/100208.htm.

Iversen, Torben. 1996. "Power, Flexibility, and the Breakdown of Centralized Wage Bargaining: The Cases of Denmark and Sweden in Comparative Perspective." *Comparative Politics* 28: 399–436.

——. 1998. "Wage Bargaining, Central Bank Independence, and the Real Effects of Money." *International Organization* 52 (3): 469–504.

——. 1999a. *Contested Economic Institutions: The Politics of Macroeconomics and Wage Bargaining in Advanced Democracies*. Cambridge: Cambridge University Press.

——. 1999b. "The Political Economy of Inflation: Bargaining Structure or Central Bank Independence?" *Public Choice* 99: 237–258.

Jaumotte, Florence. 2011. "The Spanish labor market in a cross-country perspective." International Monetary Fund Working Paper WP/11/11. Washington, DC: IMF.

Johnston, Alison. 2011. "European Monetary Union and Institutional Change: The Perverse Effects of Supranational Macroeconomic Regimes on Wage Inflation." PhD thesis. London: London School of Economics.

——. 2012. "European Economic and Monetary Union's Perverse Effects on Sectoral Wage Inflation: Negative Feedback Effects from Institutional Change?" *European Union Politics* 13 (3): 345–366.

Johnston, Alison, and Bob Hancké. 2009. "Wage inflation and labour unions in EMU." *Journal of European Public Policy* 16 (4): 601–622.

Johnston, Alison, Bob Hancké, and Suman Pant. 2014. "Comparative Institutional Advantage in Europe's Sovereign Debt Crisis." *Comparative Political Studies* 47 (13): 1771–1800.

Jones, Claire. 2014. "Bundesbank shifts stance and backs unions' push for big pay rises." *Financial Times*, 21 July. http://www.ft.com/cms/s/0/656ff1f6-10ec-11e4-94f3 -00144feabdc0.html#axzz39p20OJv1.

Jones, Erik. 2003a. "Liberalized capital markets, state autonomy, and European monetary union." *European Journal of Political Research* 42 (2): 197–222.

——. 2003b. "Idiosyncrasy and Integration: Suggestions from Comparative Political Economy." *Journal of European Public Policy* 10 (1): 140–158.

——. 2014. "Competitiveness and the European Financial Crisis." Conference paper presented at the 21st Conference of Europeanists, Washington, DC, 14–16 March.

——. 2015. "Forgotten Financial Union." In *The Future of the Euro*. Edited by Matthias Matthijs and Mark Blyth, 44–69. Oxford, Oxford University Press.

Kahn, Lawrence. 1998. "Collective Bargaining and the Interindustry Wage Structure: International Evidence." *Economica* 65 (4): 507–534.

Katzenstein, Peter. 1984. *Corporatism and Change: Austria, Switzerland, and the Politics of Industry*. Ithaca, NY: Cornell University Press.

——. 1985. *Small States in World Markets: Industrial Policy in Europe*. Ithaca, NY: Cornell University Press.

Keller, Berndt. 2011. "After the end of stability: recent trends in the public sector of Germany." *International Journal of Human Resource Management* 22 (11): 2331–2348.

Kelly, John. 2003. "The Irish Pound: From Origins to EMU." Irish Central Bank *Quarterly Bulletin* (Spring 2003): 89–115. http://www.centralbank.ie/publications/Documents /2003%20Spring%20-%20Signed%20Article%20-%20The%20Irish%20 Pound%20-%20From%20Origins%20to%20EMU.pdf.

Kenworthy, Lane. 2003. "Quantitative Indicators of Corporatism." *International Journal of Sociology*, 33 (3): 10–44.

Kittel, Bernhard. 2000. "Trade Union Bargaining Horizons in Comparative Perspective: The Effects of Encompassing Organization, Unemployment, and the Monetary Regime on Wage Pushfulness." *European Journal of Industrial Relations* 6 (2): 181–202.

Kittel, Bernhard, and Hannes Winner. 2005. "How Reliable Is Pooled Analysis in Political Economy? The Globalization–Welfare State Nexus Revisited." *European Journal of Political Research* 44: 269–293.

Kouretas, Georgios, and Prodromos Vlamis. 2010. "The Greek crisis: Causes and implications." *Panoeconomicus* 57 (4): 391–404.

Kreps, David, and Robert Wilson. 1982. "Reputation and Imperfect Information." *Journal of Economic Theory* 27: 253–279.

Kundani, Hans. 2014. "Even Germany's intellectual elite is falling out of love with the EU." *The World Today* 70 (2). http://www.chathamhouse.org/publications/twt /archive/view/198567.

Kuo, Alexander. 2012. "Origins of Repressive Employer Coordination: A Simple Model." Paper presented at 2012 Council of European Studies Conference, Boston, MA.

Lamo, Ana, Javier Pérez, and Ludger Schuknecht. 2008. "Public and private sector wages: Co-movement and causality." European Central Bank Working Paper 963, November. Frankfurt am Main.

Lane, Philip. 2012. "The European Sovereign Debt Crisis." *Journal of Economic Prespectives* 26 (3): 49–68.

Levy, Jonas. 1999. "Vice into Virtue? Progressive Politics and Welfare Reform in Continental Europe." *Politics & Society* 27 (2): 239–273.

Lind, Jens. 2000. "Recent Issues on the Social Pact in Denmark." In *Social Pacts in Europe: New Dynamics*, edited by Philippe Pochet and Giuseppe Fajertag, 135–160. Brussels: European Trade Union Institute.

López, Isidro, and Emmanuel Rodríguez. 2011. "The Spanish Model." *New Left Review* 69 (3): 5–29.

Majone, Giandomenico. 1994. "The rise of the regulatory state in Europe." *West European Politics* 17 (3): 77–101.

Manow, Philip. 2000. "Wage coordination and the welfare state: Germany and Japan compared." Max-Planck-Institut für Gesellschaftsforschung Working Paper No. 00/7. http://www.econstor.eu/bitstream/10419/44294/1/644381922.pdf.

Mares, Isabela. 2003. *Taxation, Wage Bargaining, and Unemployment*. Cambridge: Cambridge University Press.

Marginson, Paul, and Franz Traxler. 2005. "After enlargement: Preconditions and prospects for bargaining coordination." *Transfer: European Review of Labour and Research* 11 (3): 423–438.

Marks, Gary. 1986. "Neocorporatism and Incomes Policy in Western Europe and North America." *Comparative Politics* 18: 253–277.

Martens, John, and Kevin Costelloe. 2011. "Belgium's Credit Rating Lowered to AA by S&P on Bank Rescues, Politics." *Bloomberg*, 25 November. http://www.bloomberg.com/news/2011-11-25/belgium-s-credit-rating-cut-to-aa-by-s-p-outlook-negative.html.

Martin, Cathy Jo, and Dwaine Swank. 2004. "Does the Organization of Capital Matter? Employers and Active Labor Market Policy at the National and Firm Levels." *American Political Science Review* 98 (4): 593–611.

——. 2008. "The political origins of coordinated capitalism: Business organizations, party systems, and state structure in the age of innocence." *American Political Science Review* 102 (2): 181–198.

Martin, Ron. 2011. "The local geographies of the financial crisis: from the housing bubble to economic recession and beyond." *Journal of Economic Geography* 11 (4): 587–618.

Matlack, Carol. 2014. "Is Finland a Victim of the Austerity Medicine It Prescribed for Europe?" *Bloomberg Businessweek*, 23 January. http://www.businessweek.com/articles/2014-01-23/is-finland-a-victim-of-the-austerity-medicine-it-prescribed-for-europe.

Matthijs, Matthias. 2014. "Mediterranean blues: the crisis in Southern Europe." *Journal of Democracy* 25 (1): 101–115.

McNamara, Kathleen. 1998. *The Currency of Ideas: Monetary Politics in the European Union*. Ithaca, NY: Cornell University Press.

——. 2005. "European Monetary Union." In *Policy-Making in the European Union*, edited by Helen Wallace, William Wallace, and Mark Pollack, 141–160. Oxford: Oxford University Press.

Mishel, Lawrence. 1986. "The Structural Determinants of Union Bargaining Power." *Industrial and Labor Relations Review* 40 (1): 90–104.

Mishkin, Frederic. 2011. "Over the Cliff: From the Subprime to the Global Financial Crisis." *Journal of Economic Perspectives* 25 (1): 49–70.

Molina, Oscar. 2014. "Self-regulation and the state in industrial relations in Southern Europe: Back to the future?" *European Journal of Industrial Relations* 20 (1): 21–36.

Molina Romo, Oscar. 2005. "Political exchange and bargaining reform in Italy and Spain." *European Journal of Industrial Relations* 11 (1): 7–26.

Müller, Andrea, and Werner Schmidt. 2013. "Performance-related Pay and Labour Relations in German Municipalities." Paper prepared for 10th European Conference of the International Labour and Employment Relations Association, 20–22 June.

http://ilera-europe2013.eu/uploads/paper/attachment/108/Mueller_Schmidt
_Performance_related_pay.pdf.

Nickell, Stephen. 1997. "Unemployment and Labor Market Rigidities: Europe versus North America." *Journal of Economic Perspectives* 11 (3): 55–74.

Obstfeld, Maurice, and Kenneth Rogoff. 2009. "Global Imbalances and the Financial Crisis: Products of Common Causes." Paper prepared for the Federal Reserve Bank of San Francisco Asia Economic Policy Conference, Santa Barbara, CA, 18–20 October. http://www.parisschoolofeconomics.eu/IMG/pdf/BdF-PSE-IMF_paper _OBSTFELD-ROGOFF.pdf.

OECD (Organization for Economic Cooperation and Development). 1994. *The OECD Jobs Study: Facts, Analysis, Strategies.* Paris: OECD.

———. 2007. "Governance of Decentralised Pay Setting in Selected OECD Countries." OECD Working Papers on Public Governance 2007/3. Paris: OECD.

———. 2010. "Annual Labor Force Statistics." Paris: OECD

———. 2012. "Housing Price Indices." http://www.google.com/url?sa=t&rct=j&q=&esrc=s &frm=1&source=web&cd=3&ved=0CDoQFjAC&url=http%3A%2F%2Fwww .econ.queensu.ca%2Ffiles%2Fother%2FHouse_Price_indices%2520(OECD).xls &ei=R2JyU8zhFtL4oATr5YDoBg&usg=AFQjCNH3kLXRE9dAPIlrqiL4X5kbnwq 7Q&sig2=d11pmjtXW0iiwSuk0957_A&bvm=bv.66330100,d.cGU.

———. 2013. "Main Economic Indicators." http://stats.oecd.org/mei/.

Osborne, Martin, and Ariel Rubinstein. 1994. *A Course in Game Theory.* Cambridge, MA: Massachusetts Institute of Technology Press.

Pagoulatos, George. 2000. "Economic Adjustment and Financial Reform: Greece's Europeanization and the Emergence of a Stabilization State." *South European Society and Politics* 5 (2): 191–216.

Palier, Bruno, and Kathleen Thelen. 2010. "Institutionalizing Dualism: Complementarities and Change in France and Germany." *Politics & Society* 38 (1): 119–148.

Pérez, Javier, and Antonio Jesús Sánchez Fuentes. 2011. "Is there a signaling role for public wages? Evidence for the euro area based on macro data." *Empirical Economics* 41 (2): 421–445.

Pérez, Sofia. 2000. "From Decentralization to Reorganization: Explaining the Return to National Bargaining in Italy and Spain." *Comparative Politics* 32 (4): 437–458.

Petrakis, Maria. 2013. "Greeks Bearing Brunt of Merkel-Led Austerity, Blame Own Leaders." *Bloomberg*, 20 September. http://www.bloomberg.com/news/2013-09-20/greeks -bearing-brunt-of-merkel-led-austerity-blame-own-leaders.html.

Petry, Johannes. 2013. "From PIIGS and the drive towards austerity: The discursive construction of the Eurozone crisis and its impact on European welfare states." Paper presented at the DVPW, ÖGPW, SVPW Joint Conference "Drei-Länder-Tagung: Politik der Vielfalt," 19–21September, University of Innsbruck, Austria. https:// www.academia.edu/4679420/From_PIIGS_and_the_drive_towards_austerity._The _discursive_construction_of_the_Eurozone_crisis_and_its_impact_on_European _welfare_states.

Pichelmann, Karl. 2001. "Monitoring Wage Developments in EMU." *Empirica* 28: 353–373.

Plasman, Robert, Michael Rusinek, and François Rycx. 2007. "Wages and the bargaining regime under multi-level bargaining: Belgium, Denmark, and Spain." *European Journal of Industrial Relations* 13 (2): 161–180.

Plümper, Thomas, Vera Troeger, and Philip Manow. 2005. "Panel data analysis in comparative politics: Linking method to theory." *European Journal of Political Research* 44 (2): 327–354.

Pochet, Philippe. 2004. "Belgium: monetary integration and precarious federalism." In *Euros and Europeans: Monetary Integration and the European Model of Society*, edited by Andrew Martin and George Ross, 201–225. Cambridge: Cambridge University Press.

Polillo, Simone, and Mauro Guillén. 2005. "Globalization Pressures and the State: The Global Spread of Central Bank Independence." *American Journal of Sociology* 110 (6):1764–1802.

Pontusson, Jonas, David Rueda, and Christopher Way. 2002. "Comparative Political Economy of Wage Distribution." *British Journal of Political Science* 32: 281–308.

Puhani, Patrick. 2001. "Labour Mobility: An Adjustment Mechanism in Euroland? Empirical Evidence for Western Germany, France and Italy." *German Economic Review* 2 (2): 127–140.

Regan, Aidan. 2012. "The Political Economy of Social Pacts in the EMU: Irish Liberal Market Corporatism in Crisis." *New Political Economy* 17 (4): 465–491.

———. 2014. "What Explains Ireland's Fragile Recovery from the Crisis? The Politics of Comparative Institutional Advantage." *CESifo Forum* 15 (2): 26–31.

Regini, Marino. 1997. "Still Engaging in Corporatism? Recent Italian Experiences in Comparative Perspective." *European Journal of Industrial Relations* 3: 259–278.

———. 2000. "Between Deregulation and Social Pacts: The Responses of European Economies to Globalization." *Politics & Society* 28 (1): 5–33.

Rhodes, Martin. 1998. "Globalization, Labour Markets, and Welfare States: A Future of Competitive Corporatism?" In *The Future of European Welfare: A New Social Contract?*, edited by Martin Rhodes and Yves Meny, 178–203. London: Palgrave Macmillian.

———. 2001. "The Political Economy of Social Pacts: Competitive Corporatism and European Welfare Reform." In *The New Politics of the Welfare State*, edited by Paul Pierson, 165–194. Oxford: Oxford University Press.

Rodrik, Dani. 1998. "Why do more open economies have bigger governments?" *Journal of Political Economy* 106 (5): 997–1032.

Royo, Sebastián. 2006. "Beyond confrontation: The resurgence of social bargaining in Spain in the 1990s." *Comparative Political Studies* 39 (8): 969–995.

Samuelson, Paul. 1964. "Theoretical notes on trade problems." *Review of Economics and Statistics* 46 (2): 145–154.

Sapir, André. 2006. "Globalization and the Reform of European Social Models." *Journal of Common Market Studies* 44 (2): 369–390.

Scharpf, Fritz. 1991. *Crisis and Choice in European Social Democracy.* Ithaca, NY: Cornell University Press.

Scharpf, Fritz, and Vivian Schmidt, eds. 2000. *Welfare and Work in the Open Economy, Volume 2: Diverse Responses to Common Challenges.* Oxford: Oxford University Press.

Scheuer, Steen. 1998. "Denmark: A Less Regulated Model." In *Changing Industrial Relations in Europe*, edited by Anthony Ferner and Richard Hymans. Oxford: Blackwell Publishing.

Schnabel, Claus, and Joachim Wagner. 2007. "Union density and determinants of union membership in 18 EU countries: evidence from micro data, 2002/03." *Industrial Relations Journal* 38 (1): 5–32.

Shambaugh, Jay, Ricardo Reis, and Hélène Rey. 2012. "The Euro's Three Crises." *Brookings Papers on Economic Activity* (Spring): 157–231.

Sibert, Anne, and Alan Sutherland. 2000. "Monetary Union and Labor Market Reform." *Journal of International Economics* 51 (August): 421–436.

Siebert, Horst. 1997. "Labor Market Rigidities: At the Root of Unemployment in Europe." *Journal of Economic Perspectives* 11 (3): 37–54.

Simoni, Marco. 2007. "The Renegotiated Alliance between the Left and Organized Labour in Western Europe." PhD thesis. London: London School of Economics.

Soltwedel, Rüdiger, Dirk Dohse, and Christiane Krieger-Boden. 1999. "EMU Challenges European Labor Markets." International Monetary Fund Working Paper 99/131. Washington, DC: IMF.

Soskice, David. 1990. "Wage Determination: The Changing Role of Institutions in Advanced Industrialized Countries." *Oxford Review of Economic Policy* 6 (4): 36–61.

Stephens, John, and Michael Wallerstein. 1991. "Industrial Concentration, Country Size, and Trade Union Membership." *American Political Science Review* 85 (3): 941–953.

Stiglitz, Joseph E., Jean-Paul Fitoussi, Peter Bofinger, Gøsta Esping-Andersen, James K. Galbraith, and Ilene Grabel. 2014. "A Call for Policy Change in Europe." *Challenge*, 57 (4): 5–17.

Stockhammer, Engelbert. 2011. "Peripheral Europe's debt and German wages: the role of wage policy in the Euro area." *International Journal of Public Policy* 7: 83–96.

Stokke, Torgeir Aarvaag. 2008. "The Anatomy of Two-tier Bargaining Models." *European Journal of Industrial Relations* 14 (1): 7–24.

Streeck, Wolfgang. 2014. *Buying Time: The Delayed Crisis of Democratic Capitalism.* London: Verso Books.

Swank, Dwaine. 2006. "Electoral, Legislative, and Government Strength of Political Parties by Ideological Group in Capitalist Democracies, 1950–2006: A Dataset." http://www.marquette.edu/polisci/documents/part19502006.xls.

Swenson, Peter, and Jonas Pontusson. 1996. "Labour Markets, Production Strategies, and Wage Bargaining Institutions: The Swedish Employer Offensive in Comparative Perspective." *Comparative Political Studies* 29 (2): 223–250.

Tavlas, George, and Theodoros Papaspyrou. n.d. "Monetary Policy in Greece on the Road to EMU." Technical Report, Bank of Greece. http://www.bankofalbania.org/web/pub/tavlas_papaspyrou_255_1.pdf.

Thelen, Kathleen. 1993. "West European Labour in Transition: Sweden and Germany Compared." *World Politics* 46 (1): 23–49.

Thelen, Kathleen, and Ikuo Kume. 2006. "Coordination as a Political Problem in Coordinated Market Economies." *Governance* 19 (1): 11–42.

Thomas, Andrea, and Ulrike Dauer. 2014. "German Minimum Wage Plan Gains Backing from Business," *Wall Street Journal*, 28 March. http://online.wsj.com/news/articles/SB10001424052702304026304579452843363960958.

Thornqvist, Christer. 1999. "The Decentralization of Industrial Relations: The Swedish Case in Comparative Perspective." *European Journal of Industrial Relations* 5 (1): 71–87.

Timmer, Marcel, Ton van Moergastel, Edwin Stuivenwold, Gerard Ypma, Mary O'Mahony, and Mari Kangasniemi. 2007. "EU KLEMS Growth and Productivity Accounts: Methodology." http://www.euklems.net/data/EUKLEMS_Growth_and_Productivity_Accounts_Part_I_Methodology.pdf.

Traxler, Franz. 1995a. "Farewell to Labour Market Associations? Organized versus Disorganized Decentralization as a Map for Industrial Relation." In *Organized Industrial Relation in Europe: What Future?*, edited by Colin Crouch and Franz Traxler. Aldershot: Avebury.

———. 2000. "Employers and employer organisations in Europe: membership strength, density, and representativeness." *Industrial Relations Journal* 31 (4): 308–316.

Traxler, Franz, Sabine Blaschke, and Bernhard Kittel. 2001. *National Labour Relations in Internationalized Markets: A Comparative Study of Institutions, Change, and Performance.* Oxford: Oxford University Press.

Traxler, Franz, and Bernd Brandl. 2010. "Collective Bargaining, Macroeconomic Performance, and the Sectoral Composition of Trade Unions." *Industrial Relations* 49 (1): 91–115.

Traxler, Franz, and Bernhard Kittel. 2000. "The Bargaining System and Performance: A Comparison of 18 OECD Countries." *Comparative Political Studies* 33 (9): 1154–1190.

Ungerer, Horst, Jouko Hauvonen, Augusto Lopez-Claros, and Thomas Mayer. 1990. "*The European Monetary System: Developments and Perspectives*" International Monetary Fund Occasional Paper 73. Washington, DC: IMF.

U.S. Department of the Treasury, Office of International Affairs. 2013. "Report to Congress on International Economic and Exchange Rate Policies." http://www.treasury.gov/resource-center/international/exchange-rate-policies/Documents/2013-10-30_FULL%20FX%20REPORT_FINAL.pdf.

Van der Meer, Marc, Jelle Visser, and Ton Wilthagen. 2005. "Adaptive and Reflexive Governance: The Limits of Organized Decentralization." *European Journal of Industrial Relations* 11 (3): 347–365.

Van Oorschot, Wim, and Peter Abrahamson. 2003. "The Dutch and Danish Miracles Revisited: A Critical Discussion of Activation Policies in Two Small Welfare States." *Social Policy and Administration* 37 (3): 288–304.

Visser, Jelle. 1991. "Trends in trade union membership." In *OECD Employment Outlook*.97–134. Paris: OECD.

——. 1998a. "Two Cheers for Corporatism, One for the Market: Industrial Relations, Wage Moderation, and Job Growth in the Netherlands." *British Journal of Industrial Relations* 36 (2): 269–292.

——. 1998b. "The Netherlands: The Return of Responsive Corporatism." In *Changing Industrial Relations in Europe*, edited by Anthony Ferner and Richard Hyman. Oxford: Blackwell Publishing.

——. 2000. "The Netherlands." In *Trade Unions in Western Europe Since 1945*, edited by Bernhard Ebbinghaus and Jelle Visser. London: Macmillan.

——. 2002. "Unions, Wage Bargaining, and Coordination in European Labour Markets: The Past Twenty Years and the Near Future." In *Wage Policy in the Eurozone*, edited by Philippe Pochet, 39–77. Brussels: PIE-Peter Lang.

——. 2011. AIAS ICTWSS Database. University of Amsterdam, Amsterdam Institute for Advanced Labour Studies. http://www.uva-aias.net/208.

Von Hagen, Jürgen. 2002. "More Growth for Stability: Reflections on Fiscal Policy in Euroland." EMU Monitor Background Papers, ZEI, University of Bonn.

——. 2003. "Fiscal Discipline and Growth in Euroland: Experiences with the Stability and Growth Pact." ZEI Working Paper No. B 06-2003. http://www.zei.uni-bonn.de/dateien/working-papaer/B03-06.pdf.

Von Hagen, Jürgen, Andrew Hughes Hallett, and Rolf Strauch. 2001. "Budgetary Consolidation in EMU." European Economy Economic Paper No. 148.

Von Hagen, Jürgen, and Guntram Wolff. 2006. "What do deficits tell us about debt? Empirical evidence on creative accounting with fiscal rules in the EU." *Journal of Banking and Finance* 30: 3259–3279.

Wallerstein, Michael. 1989. "Union organization in advanced industrial democracies." *American Political Science Review* 83: 481–501.

——. 1990. "Centralized Bargaining and Wage Restraint." *American Journal of Political Science* 34 (4): 982–1004.

——. 1999. "Wage Setting Institutions and Pay Inequality in Advanced Industrial Societies." *American Journal of Political Science* 43 (3): 649–680.

Walsh, James. 1999. "Political bases of macroeconomic adjustment: evidence from Italy." *Journal of European Public Policy* 6 (1): 66–84.

———. 2000. *Monetary Integration and Domestic Politics: Britain, France, and Italy*. Boulder, CO: Lynne Rienner Publishers.

Weber, Axel. 1991. "Reputation and Credibility in the European Monetary System." *Economic Policy* 6 (12): 57–102.

Weeks, John. 2011. "Those Lazy PIGS: Deciphering the Euro Blame Game." *Social Europe Journal* (12 July). http://www.social-europe.eu/2011/12/those-lazy-pigs-deciphering-the-euro-blame-game/.

Wihlborg, Clas, Thomas Willett, and Nan Zhang. 2010. "The Euro Debt Crisis: It Isn't Just Fiscal." *World Economics* 11 (4): 51–77.

Wyplosz, Charles. 2013. "Eurozone Crisis: It's about Demand, not Competitiveness." Unpublished manuscript, Mimeo, Graduate Institute, Geneva and CEPR. http://www.tcd.ie/Economics/assets/pdf/Not_competitiveness.pdf.

Young, Brigitte, and Willi Semmler. 2011. "The European Sovereign Debt Crisis: Is Germany to Blame?" *German Politics and Society* 29 (1): 1–24.

Index

Abva-Kabo, 77, 79, 90–91, 97–99, 101, 132

Agency for the Representation of Public Administrations in Collective Bargaining (ARAN), 129

Ahern, Bertie, 158, 160

Amtrådsforeningen (ARF), 104

Andor, László, 180

Association of Danish State Employees (StK), 103

Association of Local Government Employees (KTO), 104–7

austerity, 13, 21, 36–38, 41, 87–90

Austria: austerity packages in, 41; credible commitment to hard currency policy, 35; entry into ERM, 170; pattern bargaining systems in, 49; sheltered sector wage growth suppression in, 46

Aznar, José, 151, 154, 198n11

Balassa/Samuelson effect, 55

Balkenende, Jan-Peter, 100, 101

banking union, 175

bargaining fragmentation: and EMU's favoritism towards low-inflation labor markets, 49–50, 51; in Germany, 121; in Spain, 140, 143–44, 146, 152–56

bargaining institutions: delivering wage moderation, 110; in EMU's core economies, 6, 48–49; in EMU's peripheral economies, 6, 49–51; and overcoming collective action problems, 166–67; in rigid public sector, 118–19; and sectoral politics, 48–52

Beamte, 125–27

Belgium: credible commitment to hard currency policy, 35; credit rating of, 14; current account surpluses of, 17; entry into ERM, 170; public sector pay austerity, 36–37, 41; state-imposed coordination regime in, 49

Bentolila, Samuel, 19

Bernanke, Ben, 15

blue-collar workers, 125, 195n38

bonus-pay, 85, 87–88, 126

British pound, 192n15

Calmfors-Driffill hypothesis, 119, 197n5

central bank independence (CBI), 34, 58–60

central banks: effects of national, on wage growth, 54–57; and hard and soft currency regimes, 169; monetary threats of, 58–62, 67–68; and promotion of real exchange rate convergence, 5, 172; removal of national-level, non-accommodating, 26, 43–44. *See also* inflation-averse central banks

centralized wage bargaining, 64, 67

centralized wage-setting, 125–27, 128, 166

Christian Democratic Appeal (of the Netherlands, CDA), 85, 91, 100

civil servants: bargaining rights of, 111, 112; in Dutch public sector, 92–93, 131–32; in German public sector, 125–27; in Spanish public sector, 153–54; wage push problems and Italian, 116

CO II (State Public Servants' Trade Union), 103

CO-Industri, 95–96

collective bargaining: coordination of cross-border, 176–77; in public sector, 118–22, 128–29; sequential games of, 29–33

competitiveness hypothesis, 11–12, 14–25

Confederación Sindical de Comisiones Obreras (CCOO), 139, 142, 154, 198n10

Confederation of Danish Employers (DA), 80, 88–89, 106

Confindustria, 116

Conservative Party (Denmark), 88

construction sector: in Spain and Ireland, 151–52; wage growth in Spanish, 140, 155

core economies. *See* northern economies

Cukierman, Alex, legal central bank independence index of, 58, 60

current account balances: and cause of euro crisis, 20; and competitiveness hypothesis, 15–17; current, for EMU11, 168*fig.*; current, for Germany, Italy, and Netherlands, 114*fig.*; worsening, in periphery, 11

Danish Central Bank, 84, 94

Danish Confederation of Trade Unions (LO), 80–90

Danish General Workers Union (SiD), 89, 194n20

217

Danish Nurses Association (DSR), 94–95, 102, 103, 104, 107

Danish Union of Teachers (DLF), 102–3, 104

Dansk Industri (DI), 95–96

decentralization: and collective bargaining in public sector, 121; and combating unemployment, 164; in Denmark, 89; in Denmark and Netherlands, 80; of Dutch public sector, 134; of German public sector, 125; institutional change through, 110–11; of Irish wage-setting, 148; in Italy, 128–31; in public sector, 111; in Spain, 140, 153

Denmark: corporatism inside and outside of monetary union, 78–80; credible commitment to hard currency policy, 35; fiscal constraints preserving wage moderation in, 90–96, 108; gap in annual wage growth in, 45; low-inflation performance of, 162; Ny Løn system, 95, 102, 103, 105; response to state-imposed austerity, 87–90; spending cuts in public sector pay, 36

Deutscher Beamtenbund (DBB), 114, 118, 125–26, 197n4

Deutscher Gewerkschaftsbund (DGB), 114, 118, 125–26, 144, 197n4

Dick, Peer-Michael, 179

disaggregation, as theme of OECD public sector reform, 123

domestic demand booms, 20–21, 138, 165

Doorn Declaration, 177

Doorn group, 176–77

Dutch National Confederation of Christian Trade Unions (CNV), 92, 100, 101

Dutch Public and Health Sector Workers' Union (CFO), 97

Dutch Trade Union Federation (FNV), 86, 90, 92, 98–99, 100, 101

Employers' Association of German Länder (TdL), 125

employment reform, and wage inflation in public sector, 122–24

EU KLEMS Growth and Productivity Accounts Database, 184

Eurobonds, 175

European Central Bank (ECB), 5, 24, 43, 60, 172

European Commission: austerity measures of, 175; introduces Fiscal Compact and "two pack," 173–74; and negotiating symmetrical adjustment from northern member-states, 179–80; and three percent Maastricht deficit criterion, 42

European debt crisis: origins of, 12–21; solutions for, 173–79

European Economic and Monetary Union (EMU): coexistence of diverse capitalist systems in, 168–69; conditionality and new constraints on sheltered sector, 39–42; Denmark and public sector pay outside of, 102–8; design flaws of, 13–14; Dutch entry into, 92–93, 96, 97, 98; and economic crisis, 2–4; favoritism towards low-inflation labor markets, 46–52; fissures of, 163; German, Italian, and Dutch wage performance under, 112–18, 135–36; inflation and wage growth convergence before, 7–12; influence on member-states' inflation performance, 165; low-inflation bias of, 5, 165–66, 169–73; macroeconomic governance vacuum of, 43–46; monetary threat on sectoral wage differences, 67–69; national corporatist institutions and wage suppression under, 69–76; re-emergence of sheltered sector dominance in wage setting under, 151–61; solutions for current crisis, 173–79; Spanish and Irish wage moderation under, 138–39; sustainability of, 179–81

European Exchange Rate Mechanism (ERM), 34–39, 144–45, 170, 192nn14,15

European Financial Stability Facility (EFSF), 163, 173

European Metalworkers' Federation (EMF), 177

European Monetary System (EMS): Danish commitment to, 87–89; Dutch commitment to, 85–87; Exchange Rate Mechanism of, 18, 34–39, 59, 70, 84, 144; inflation-averse central banks under, 9–10, 34–36; sectoral wage developments during, 8; Spanish and Irish commitments to, 146–50; wage moderation during, 23–24

European Trade Union Confederation (ETUC), 176

European Union (EU), economic calamities faced by, 1–2, 163–64

Excessive Deficit Procedure (EDP), 174

Excessive Imbalance Procedure (EIP), 174

Exchange Rate Mechanism, 18, 34–39, 59, 70, 84, 144

export competitiveness, 70–71

export-favoring corporatist institutions, 48–49, 52t, 65t

export sector dominated peak bargaining, 50

exposed sectors: assumptions and theoretical foundations regarding, 27–34; and inflation and wage growth convergence, 7–11; and meaning of wage moderation, 183–85; sheltered sector wage suppression and wage developments in, 55–56; wage moderation in, 23–25, 47–49

extra EU exports, as proportion of total exports, 178*fig.*

Fine Gael/Labour government, 143, 148–49
Finland: deterioration of monetary non-accommodation in, 40; fiscal tightening in, 13
Fiscal Compact, 173–74
fiscal hypothesis, 11–14, 137
FitzGerald, Garret, 148–49
France: credible commitment to hard currency policy, 35; entry into ERM, 170; Juppé Plan, 41; state-imposed coordination regime in, 49

General Confederation of Portuguese Workers (CGTP), 50
Geraghty, Des, 158
Germany: austerity packages in, 41; Basic Statute of the Civil Service (1998), 153, 154; centralized wage setting in public sector, 125–27; Civil Service Law Reform (1997), 126–27; collective bargaining in public sector, 120–21, 122; current account balances, 114*fig.*; current account surpluses, 17; entry into ERM, 170; export share growth under pre-crisis EMU period, 71; and fiscal surveillance, 174–75; "general framework" collective agreement (TVöD), 127; pattern bargaining in, 48–49, 126–27; and promotion of wage growth and pay increases, 180–81; public deficit levels, 14; resistance to liberalization of pay and employment conditions, 112; sheltered sector of, 192n21; sheltered sector wage growth suppression in, 46; wage performance under EMU, 112–18; wage restraint on public sector employees, 111
"global finance" hypothesis, 20
global financial crisis (2008): effect of, on EU and EMU, 1–2; origins of, 2–4
González, Filipe, 141–42
Greece: bailout plan for, 163; candidacy for EMU, 41–42; and global financial crisis, 12; institutional disarray of, 167–68; sectoral bargaining in, 50

hard currency policy: adoption of, 35–38; of Denmark, 77, 84, 94, 102; of Netherlands, 84, 85–87, 108; of Spain and Ireland, 144–45, 146
hard currency regimes, 169–70

IG Metall, 49, 115, 181
Industries' Union (IB), 86
inflation: causes and consequences of, 22; central bank non-accommodation toward, 58–60, 61*t*; before EMU, 7–12; and exchange rate movements, 170–72; implications of sectoral cleavages for aggregate, 28–29; and real exchange rate under flexible system, 47; sheltered sector wage settlements' influence on, 43; and wage moderation, 16, 22–25. *See also* low-inflation bias of EMU
inflation-averse central banks: adoption of, 5, 23, 32; effect of, 165; Exchange Rate Mechanism and, 34, 35; perception of sheltered employers and adoption of, 32–33; promote real exchange rate convergence, 172; rise of, 9–10
Intel Ireland, 160
International Monetary Fund, 2, 108, 160, 163, 175
Ireland: commitment to EMS, 146–50; credible commitment to hard currency policy, 35; current account surpluses of, 17; economic and institutional diversity of, 141–45; export share growth under pre-crisis EMU period, 71; exposure to European debt crisis, 137–40; following entry into EMU, 151, 162; nominal wage increases by sector, 157*fig.*; nominal wage restraint by sector, 157*fig.*; nonstate-led wage pacts coordination regimes in, 50; nonstate-led wage pacts in, 51; Partnership 2000 national wage agreement, 158; Programme for Competitiveness and Work (1994–1996), 150; Programme for Economic and Social Progress (1991–1993), 150; Programme for National Recovery agreement (1987), 56, 139, 149–50; Programme for Participation and Fairness (PPF), 159; public deficit levels, 14; Public Service Benchmarking Body, 159–60, 161; real estate and construction in, 151–52; reorientation toward export-driven model, 200n2; Sustaining Progress (2003–2005), 160; wage inflation in sheltered sector, 156–61
Irish Business and Economic Confederation (IBEC), 143
Irish Congress of Trade Unions (ICTU), 143, 149, 150, 158, 160
Irish Municipal, Public and Civil Trade Union (IMPACT), 159
Italy: abolishes *scala mobile*, 41, 56, 115, 155; account deficits and surpluses, 200n3; Agency for the Representation of Public

Italy *(continued)*
  Administrations in Collective Bargaining
    (ARAN), 129; Bassanini reform, 129–30;
    Brunetta reform (2008), 130; Ciampi
    Protocol, 41; collective bargaining in public
    sector, 120; current account balances, 114*fig.*;
    decentralized wage push in, 128–31; entry
    into ERM, 170; following entry into EMU,
    162; horizontal career, 110; incentive
    payments and flexible wage bargaining in
    public sector, 112; institutional disarray of,
    167–68; *legge quadro* reform (1983), 128;
    public sector wage policies of, 131; public
    sector wages in, 36; vertical career, 129–30;
    wage performance under EMU, 112–18

Jensen, Hans, 95
Jørgensen, Anker, 87
Juppé Plan, 41

Katainen, Jyrki, 13
Kok, Wim, 98
Kommunernes Landsforening (KL), 104, 105
Kreisky, Bruno, 38
Kruckow, Connie, 107
Krugman, Paul, 15

Lagarde, Christine, 15
Local Government Employers' Association (of
    Germany, VKA), 125
Løkke Rasmussen, Lars, 106–8
low-inflation bias of EMU, 5, 46–52, 165–66,
    169–73
Lubbers, Ruud, 85, 86, 92, 132–33

Maastricht conditionality: conceptualization of,
    60–62; effects of, on wage growth, 54–57
Maastricht criteria: and conservation of wage
    moderation in Denmark and Netherlands,
    90–93; Danish adherence to, 84; and
    Denmark's institutionalization of fiscal
    constraints, 96; and Italy's restrained wage
    growth, 113, 116; new constraints on
    sheltered sector, 39–42; removal of, 26, 27;
    Stability and Growth Pact compared to,
    44–45
Maastricht period, 8–9, 23–24
Maastricht Treaty, 39
Macroeconomic Imbalance Procedure (MiP),
    180
manufacturing sector: annual wage growth
    by bargaining regime, 65*t*; central bank
    non-accommodation and wage growth in,

66–67; collective bargaining in Spanish,
    147–48; influence of wage growth on export
    performance, 73; monetary union's
    association with wage growth in, 76; use to
    conceptualize exposed sector, 184; wage
    differentials between Italian public sector and,
    120; wage growth in Germany, Netherlands,
    and Italy, 116, 117*fig.*; wages in Netherlands
    and Denmark, 83*fig.*
McCreevy, Charlie, 160
Merkel, Angela, 13
Mitterrand, François, 38, 192n14
mixed-market economies, institutional disarray
    of, 167–69
monetary union(s): associated with wage growth
    differentials between sheltered and manufac-
    turing sector, 76; Denmark and consequences
    of opting-out of, 102–8; effects of, on sheltered
    sector wage suppression, 62–69; institutional
    constraints removed by, 26; and reactive
    governance, 97–101; success of rigid labor
    markets under, 164–65. *See also* European
    Economic and Monetary Union (EMU)
multinational corporation (MNC) sector, 139,
    141, 149–50

Netherlands: corporatism inside and outside of
    monetary union, 78–80; credible commit-
    ment to hard currency policy, 35; current
    account balances, 114*fig.*; entry into ERM,
    170; Experimentation Protocol, 133; fiscal
    constraints preserving wage moderation in,
    90–96, 108; incentive payments and flexible
    wage bargaining in public sector, 112; "New
    Course" accord, 92; public sector wage
    inflation in, 117; sheltered wage inflation in
    Denmark and, 80–84; Social Economic
    Council (SER), 91, 92; spending cuts in public
    sector pay, 36; state-led wage pacts in, 49;
    Wage Formation Act (1987), 100; wage pacts
    and public sector wage drift, 131–35; wage
    performance under EMU, 112–18; wage
    setting under hard currency commitment,
    85–87; Wassenaar Agreement, 80, 84, 85–87
New Public Management, 111, 122
nominal exchange rate: inflation differentials
    and imbalances in, 170–72; as proxy for
    central bank non-accommodation toward
    inflation, 59; real exchange rate and, 47;
    removed by EMU, 168
nominal interest rate(s): provided by EMU, 13;
    of Spain and Ireland, 144–45
nominal unit labor cost, 21–22, 166–67, 183

nonexport-favoring wage corporatist institutions, 49–51
nonstate-led wage pacts coordination regimes, 50–51
nontradables sector. *See* sheltered sectors
northern economies: call for harsh austerity measures, 13; competitive divergence between southern economies and, 21–22, 26; divergences in current accounts of southern economies and, 16–17; export-favoring corporatist institutions used by, 110; export performance and trade balances, 18–21; fiscal deficits of, 173; imbalances between southern economies and, 6–7; wage moderation in, 6, 8–11

pattern bargaining systems, 48–49, 64, 112, 115, 120, 127
peak bargaining coordination systems, 49–50, 64
Pedersen, Thor, 103
People's Party (Spanish, PP), 147, 151, 198n11
People's Party for Freedom and Democracy (for the Netherlands, VVD), 85, 196n64
performance pay, 126–27, 134
peripheral economies. *See* southern economies
Portugal: entry into ERM, 170; institutional disarray of, 167–68
privatization: Dutch, 132, 133; Italian, 130; Spanish, 141–42, 153–54
public sector: bargaining fragmentation in Spanish, 153; centralized wage setting in German, 125–27; collective bargaining in, 118–22; competition in, 28; decentralization in, 111; decentralized wage push in Italy, 128–31; disciplinary policies under EMS, 36, 37–38t; Dutch national wage pacts and wage drift in, 131–35; employment reform and wage inflation, 122–24; pay gap in Irish, 156; pay outside EMU, 102–8; wage adjustments in, 36–37; wage growth in Irish, 156–58; wage inflation in Dutch, 117; wage suppression in German, 117–18

quasi-public employment, in Dutch public sector, 131–33

Rasmussen, Anders Fogh, 103, 105–6
Rasmussen, Poul, 84, 94, 95, 96, 102
real estate: booms, 105, 138; sector, in Spain and Ireland, 151–52
real exchange rate (RER) competitiveness, 6, 16, 22, 27, 139, 145

real exchange rate (RER) convergence, 5, 10, 172
real exchange rate(s) (RER): and competitive decline of periphery, 47–48; inflation differentials and imbalances in, 170–72; political dynamics within EMU member-states', 169
real exchange rate shocks, 72, 75
real unit labor costs, 17–19, 21–22, 87, 145
recentralization: in Danish municipal sector, 104; in Italian collective bargaining, 113; of Spanish collective-bargaining system, 152–56
Remkes, Johan, 101
Rinnooy Kan, Alexander, 91

scala mobile, 41, 56, 115, 155
Schäuble, Wolfgang, 181
Schlüter, Poul, 88, 89
sectoral bargaining politics, 48–52
Services Industrial Professional and Technical Union (SIPTU), 158, 159
"shadow" pact, 147
sheltered sectors: annual wage growth by bargaining regime, 65t; assumptions and theoretical foundations regarding, 27–34; central bank non-accommodation and wage growth in, 66–67; competitiveness of southern, 19–20; export competitiveness and wage suppression, 70–71; German, 192n21; influence of wage growth on export performance, 73–76; influence of wage revision clauses on Spanish, 155; as low productivity sectors, 192n4; and meaning of wage moderation, 183–85; national central banks and Maastricht conditionality's effect on wage growth in, 55–56; peak bargaining coordination systems and, 50; wage growth in, 23–25, 38–39, 66
"six pack," 173, 174
Social Democrats (Denmark), 84, 87, 88, 94, 95
soft currency regimes, 169, 170
southern economies: competitive divergence between northern economies and, 21–22, 26; divergences in current accounts of northern economies and, 16–17; export performance and trade balances, 18–21; fiscal deficits of, 173; nominal exchange rate movements in, 170–72; and origins of global financial crisis, 2–3; wage and inflation adjustment in, 164–65; and wage moderation under monetary union, 27
sovereign employer model, 122–24, 126

Spain: bargaining fragmentation in, 152–56; commitment to EMS, 146–50; Economic and Social Council (CES), 143, 144; entry into ERM, 170; exposure to European debt crisis, 137–40; Interconfederal Agreement on Bargaining Coverage Gaps (AICV), 144; Interconfederal Agreement on Collective Bargaining (AINC), 144; Land Act (1998), 151; nominal wage increases, by sector, in relation to pay targets, 140*fig.*; nominal wage restraint by sector, 157*fig.*; passes Workers' Statute, 198n6; public deficit levels, 14, 137; real estate and construction in, 151–52; Royal Decree 8/2010, 199n26; wage performance of, 19; wage revision clauses, demanded by Spanish unions, 155; Workers' Statute (1980), 198m6, 198n6

Spanish Socialist Workers' Party (PSOE), 141, 143–44, 146–47, 151, 155, 198nn6,9, 198nn6,9,11

Stability and Growth Pact (SGP), 13–14, 43, 44–45, 173

state-imposed coordination regimes, 48, 49, 64

state-led wage pacts, 48, 49, 50, 64, 77, 78, 79

State Public Servants' Trade Union (CO II), 103

supranational wage-setting, 176–79

Terpstra, Doekle, 100

Thatcher, Margaret, 38

three percent Maastricht deficit criterion, 40–41, 42

tradables sectors. *See* exposed sectors

trade imbalances, between northern and southern economies, 3–4

trade shocks, 72, 75

Treaty on the Functioning of the European Union (TFEU), 174

Trichet, Jean-Claude, 13

"two pack," 173–74

uncoordinated bargaining regimes, 50, 51

unemployment: decentralization and, 164; in Denmark and Netherlands, 81; in Germany and Italy, 113–14; in Spain and Ireland, 137

unilateral privilege, in sovereign employer model, 123, 124

Unión General de Trabajadores (UGT), 139, 142, 154, 198nn9,10

United Kingdom: above-productivity wage increases in, 51; exchange rate depreciation in, 148; gap in annual wage growth in, 45;

preference for labor market deregulation in, 121; private consumption in, 151

United States: above-productivity wage increases in, 51; gap in annual wage growth in, 45; preference for labor market deregulation in, 121

van Agt, Dries, 85

ver.di, 125, 126, 181

wage-bargaining centralization, 64, 67, 73

wage coordination: nonexport-favoring systems, 49–50; supranational, 176–78

wage drift: Dutch national wage pacts as solution to public sector, 131–35; Italian, 130; Spanish, 138, 140

wage growth: convergence before EMU, 7–12; coordination of, 176; in EMU's sheltered sectors, 66; in German, Italian, and Dutch sheltered sector and manufacturing, 116, 117*fig.*; and inflation adjustment, 169–70; influence of wage indexation clauses on Spanish, 154–55; in Irish public sector, 156–58; in Italian public sector, 120; monetary union's association with differentials between sheltered and manufacturing sector, 76; national central banks and Maastricht conditionality's effect on, 54–57; suppression of German sheltered sector, 111

wage indexation: abandoned by EMU candidate countries, 40; in Belgium and Netherlands in 1980s, 36. See also *scala mobile*

wage inflation: in Denmark and Netherlands' sheltered sectors, 80–84; and employment reform in public sector, 122–24; in Irish sheltered sector, 156–61; peak bargaining coordination systems and, 50; in southern economies, 6–7, 47

wage moderation: bargaining institutions delivering, 110; by bargaining regime and country, 52*t*; bargaining regimes, 49–52; consequences of Irish, 149; in Denmark and Netherlands, 79, 81, 108; as determinant of national inflation, 16; and Dutch entry into monetary union and reactive governance, 99, 101; EMU's institutional regime and deliverance of, 43, 45; export-oriented actor organizing, in Spain and Ireland, 151; exposed and sheltered sectors and meaning of, 183–85; in exposed sectors, 23–25, 47–49; fiscal and competitiveness hypotheses on, 11–21; fiscal constraints conserving, in

Denmark and Netherlands, 90–96, 97; and German and Italian bargaining institutions, 114–15; low national inflation through, 7; under monetary union, 26–27; in nontradable sectors of core economies, 6; produced by northern economies, 3; role in driving competitive divergence between North and South, 21–22, 26; in sheltered sectors, 23–25, 38–39; of Spain and Ireland under EMU, 138–39; and transition to low-inflation regime, 33; UGT and CCOO's commitment to, 154

wage-setting: centralized, 125–27, 128, 166; and crisis management, 176–79
wage-setting institutions, 5–6, 27, 69, 164, 176
wages in efficiency units (WEU), 183–84
wage suppression: in German public sector, 117–18; monetary union's effects on sheltered sector, 62–69; and national corporatist institutions under EMU, 69–76
white-collar workers, 125, 195n38

Zalm, Gerrit, 79, 81, 99, 100